The Merleau-Ponty Dictionary

BLOOMSBURY PHILOSOPHY DICTIONARIES

The *Bloomsbury Philosophy Dictionaries* offer clear and accessible guides to the work of some of the more challenging thinkers in the history of philosophy. A–Z entries provide clear definitions of key terminology, synopses of key works, and details of each thinker's major themes, ideas and philosophical influences. The *Dictionaries* are the ideal resource for anyone reading or studying these key philosophers.

Titles available in the series:
The Derrida Dictionary, Simon Morgan Wortham
The Gadamer Dictionary, Chris Lawn and Niall Keane
The Hegel Dictionary, Glenn Alexander Magee
The Heidegger Dictionary, Daniel O. Dahlstrom
The Husserl Dictionary, Dermot Moran and Joseph Cohen
The Marx Dictionary, Ian Fraser and Lawrence Wilde
The Sartre Dictionary, Gary Cox

Forthcoming in the series:
The Deleuze and Guattari Dictionary, Eugene B. Young with Gary Genosko and Janell Watson
The Kant Dictionary, Lucas Thorpe
The Nietzsche Dictionary, Douglas Burnham
The Wittgenstein Dictionary, Edmund Dain

BLOOMSBURY PHILOSOPHY DICTIONARIES

The Merleau-Ponty Dictionary

DONALD A. LANDES

BLOOMSBURY
LONDON • NEW DELHI • NEW YORK • SYDNEY

Bloomsbury Academic
An imprint of Bloomsbury Publishing Plc

50 Bedford Square 175 Fifth Avenue
London New York
WC1B 3DP NY 10010
UK USA

www.bloomsbury.com

First published 2013

© Donald A. Landes, 2013

All rights reserved. No part of this publication may be reproduced or transmitted in any form or by any means, electronic or mechanical, including photocopying, recording, or any information storage or retrieval system, without prior permission in writing from the publishers.

Donald A. Landes has asserted his right under the Copyright, Designs and Patents Act, 1988, to be identified as Author of this work.

No responsibility for loss caused to any individual or organization acting on or refraining from action as a result of the material in this publication can be accepted by Bloomsbury Academic or the author.

British Library Cataloguing-in-Publication Data
A catalogue record for this book is available from the British Library.

ISBN: HB: 978-1-4411-2195-0
PB: 978-1-4411-7635-6
ePub: 978-1-4411-5892-5
ePDF: 978-1-4411-5200-8

Library of Congress Cataloging-in-Publication Data
A catalog record for this book is available from the Library of Congress.

Typeset by Fakenham Prepress Solutions, Fakenham, Norfolk NR21 8NN

CONTENTS

*Abbreviations of primary works by Merleau-Ponty
  cited in this dictionary* vii
Introduction xi
Acknowledgments xv

Chronology: Merleau-Ponty's life and works 1

A–Z dictionary 9

Suggested books and edited volumes in English 251
Notes 255
Index 257

ABBREVIATIONS OF PRIMARY WORKS BY MERLEAU-PONTY CITED IN THIS DICTIONARY

AD   *Adventures of the Dialectic*, trans. Joseph Bien (Evanston: Northwestern University Press, 1973).

CPP   *Child Psychology and Pedagogy: The Sorbonne Lectures (1949–52)*, trans. Talia Welsh (Evanston: Northwestern University Press, 2010).

HLP   *Husserl at the Limits of Phenomenology*, ed. Leonard Lawlor with Bettina Bergo, trans. Leonard Lawlor (Evanston: Northwestern University Press, 2000).

HT   *Humanism and Terror*, trans. John O'Neill (New Brunswick, NJ: Transaction Publishers, 2000).

IP   *Institution and Passivity: Course Notes from the Collège de France (1954–1955)*, trans. Leonard Lawlor and Heath Massey (Evanston: Northwestern University Press, 2010).

IPP   *In Praise of Philosophy and Other Essays*, trans. James M. Edie and John Wild (Evanston: Northwestern University Press, 1970).

MPAR   *The Merleau-Ponty Aesthetics Reader*, ed. Galen A. Johnson, trans. ed. Michael B. Smith (Evanston: Northwestern University Press, 1996).

N   *Nature: Course Notes from the Collège de France*, trans. Robert Vallier (Evanston: Northwestern University Press, 2003).

NC   *Notes de cours (1959–1961)*, ed. Stéphanie Ménasé (Paris: Gallimard, 1996).

P   *Parcours: 1935–1951*, ed. Jacques Prunair (Lagrasse, France: Éditions Verdier, 1997).

PHP   *Phenomenology of Perception*, trans. Donald A. Landes (New York: Routledge, 2012).

PNP   "Philosophy and Non-Philosophy Since Hegel," trans. Hugh J. Silverman, in *Philosophy and Non-Philosophy Since Merleau-Ponty*, ed. Hugh J. Silverman, 9–83 (Evanston: Northwestern University Press, 1988).

PRP   *The Primacy of Perception*, ed. James M. Edie (Evanston: Northwestern University Press, 1964).

PSY   "Phenomenology and Psychoanalysis: Preface to Hesnard's *L'Œuvre de Freud*," trans. Alden L. Fisher, in *Merleau-Ponty and Psychology*, ed. Keith Hoeller, 67–72 (Atlantic Highlands, NJ: Humanities Press, 1993).

PW   *The Prose of the World*, trans. John O'Neill (Evanston: Northwestern University Press, 1973).

S   *Signs*, trans. Richard C. McCleary (Evanston: Northwestern University Press, 1964).

SB   *The Structure of Behavior*, trans. Alden L. Fisher (Pittsburgh: Duquesne University Press, 1963).

SNS   *Sense and Non-Sense*, trans. Hubert L. Dreyfus and Patricia A. Dreyfus (Evanston: Northwestern University Press, 1964).

TD   *Texts and Dialogues: On Philosophy, Politics, and Culture*, ed. Hugh J. Silverman and James Barry, Jr. (Amherst, NY: Humanity Books, 1992).

UBS *The Incarnate Subject: Malebranche, Biran, and Bergson on the Union of the Body and Soul*, trans. Paul B. Milan (Amherst, NY: Humanity Books, 2001).

VI *The Visible and the Invisible*, trans. Alphonso Lingis (Evanston: Northwestern University Press, 1968).

WP *The World of Perception*, trans. Oliver Davis (New York: Routledge, 2002).

INTRODUCTION

Maurice Merleau-Ponty

On 3 May 1961 the history of philosophy lost a voice that was at the height of its philosophical expression, leaving behind an incredible body of published work alongside the mere traces of an emerging reflection that was to have simultaneously reshaped the form and the content of philosophy itself. Maurice Merleau-Ponty (1908–61) was a rare thinker, capable of drawing together various traditions and diverse approaches into a unique manner of questioning that remained responsible to its past and to its objects of study while creatively forging new directions through an unmistakable style. Drawing from existentialism and phenomenology, certainly, but also from empirical psychology, Gestalt psychology, neurology, psychoanalysis, Marxism, structuralism, sociology, political philosophy, the philosophy of history, and advances in literature and painting, Merleau-Ponty's approach took up not simply a set of solutions from these sources in order to create a mere philosophical hodgepodge, but rather incorporated what he understood to be their promise into a unified patchwork in the direction of a genuine philosophical interrogation. On the surface, then, Merleau-Ponty is perhaps an ideal candidate for a philosophical dictionary that would identify all of these sources and influences, and provide a record of all of his solutions.

Yet Merleau-Ponty himself resisted two dangers in approaching the history of philosophy. He suggests that a constant vigilance is required to avoid either a subjective reading, in which the reader projects his or her own questions and answers across the text, or an objective reading, in which the reader seeks to restore the exact thought of the philosopher in question. For Merleau-Ponty, the danger of an objective reading is in its assumption that "the thought" of any philosopher is a "system of neatly defined concepts, of arguments responding to perennial problems, and of conclusions which permanently solve the problems" (*HLP*, 5). Reading a philosopher is an art. It requires a confrontation or an encounter such that one gears into the open sense or the unthought directions of his or her thought, taking it up into one's own thought, which necessarily introduces something of oneself into the reading, without succumbing to the opposite danger of a subjective reading. For such a thinker, if a dictionary is to be written it must provide not the abstract network of solid definitions and synopses, but the tools for a responsible and creative reading. Indeed, as he writes of what one might call the open trajectory of sense or of history: "each creation alters, clarifies, deepens, confirms, exalts, re-creates, or creates by anticipation all the others" (*MPAR*, 149). With nearly 300 interconnecting entries in this presentation of "Merleau-Ponty, A–Z," an extensive account of his life and works, and an index which provides guidance for concepts and topics woven throughout the individual entries, *The Merleau-Ponty Dictionary* aims not to be the final word on "the" meaning of Merleau-Ponty's thought, but rather a companion for an open and responsible practice of reading, a practice in the style of Merleau-Ponty.

Merleau-Ponty certainly earned his reputation as the philosopher of the body, and the important emphasis on his return to lived experience is worth noting at the outset. In his earliest studies, he pursued the notion of behavior precisely because it is "not a thing, but neither is it an idea" (*SB*, 127). This statement is significant in what it denies, for it captures his persistent attempt to dissolve the schism between realism and idealism, or empiricism and intellectualism. For empiricism, the universe is to be explained through mechanistic causality, and the body is taken to be one object among others; for intellectualism, the universe must be explained through reason, and the body is to be understood according to its idea or transcendental organization under the dominion of a mind. For Merleau-Ponty, each of these philosophical positions—pure exteriority versus pure interiority—entails a pernicious *pensée de survol*, a thinking "from above" that mistakenly assures the philosopher a God's-eye view upon that which is to be explained.

Across all of his work, from behavior and perception to aesthetics, politics, and ontology, Merleau-Ponty insists on resisting the fictions and errors of the *pensée de survol*, and much of his early work unmasks the necessary (and often shared) errors of these traditions in order to sketch out a new approach. In his first book, *The Structure of Behavior* (1938/1942), Merleau-Ponty establishes, against empiricism, that behavior can be seen to emerge within nature through the appearance of a perceptual consciousness that is more than a sum of the mechanistic parts, and yet less than the Ego of classical intellectualism. In his magnum opus, *Phenomenology of Perception* (1945), Merleau-Ponty establishes, against intellectualism, the fundamental and inextricable ambiguity of our lived and embodied experience, our being-in-the-world. This approach reoriented philosophy and established the need to adopt an existential analysis and an expressive philosophy that might begin to understand this ambiguous body that is "always something other than what it is: always sexuality at the same time as freedom, always rooted in nature at the very moment it is transformed by culture" (*PhP*, 205). The notions of contingency and ambiguity are further explored in the late 1940s in terms of aesthetics, politics, and history.

Nevertheless, the attempt at developing a manner of expressing the non-thetic or lived experience discovered in *Phenomenology of Perception* led Merleau-Ponty to pursue a philosophy of expression and a philosophical account of "truth" in the early 1950s. Primarily through a deepening account of language and expression, now in concert with a study of speech in light of structuralism, Merleau-Ponty developed a notion of embodied expression that was to offer the beginnings of an answer to the question of truth given the rejection of *survol*, and thus a truth born within history and language rather than one discovered by a pure mind. The investigation into expression led Merleau-Ponty to begin to forge an entirely new form of philosophical reflection that he named, simply, interrogation. This was to be a form of expression insofar as it remained forever committed to openness as a manner of gearing into the trajectory of sense, toward a truth and toward an impossible task of expressing Being itself. As he argues throughout *The Visible and the Invisible* (1964), Merleau-Ponty's unfinished and posthumously published book on philosophical method and ontology, the dominant philosophical approaches of reflection, dialectic, and intuition all falter insofar as they freeze their openness to wild Being—our pre-thetic and embodied experience as the body that sees and is seen, touches and is touched. The final and tantalizing ontology presented by Merleau-Ponty is precisely a corporeal or bodily ontology. It is the attempt to express wild Being with the constant recognition of the inherent failure of this attempt. When one hand touches the other hand touching, and the touched hand then attempts to touch in return, this reversibility nevertheless eclipses at the threshold of coincidence. That is, there is always a gap [*écart*] that establishes the spacing or folding between one hand and the other, and this spacing is where Being itself and other reversibilities (others, language, history) can appear. Moreover, this reveals how, as a body, I am both an openness to the world and actively exploring it, and an object in the world and of its very substance. There is, then, a flesh of the world that as yet has no name in any philosophy, but that is given voice in the absent ontology of Merleau-Ponty.

In this brief abstract, one can see the richness of Merleau-Ponty's finished books and his unfinished texts, and this richness has made Merleau-Ponty an important figure for many different areas of contemporary thought. His work influences a wide variety of research both in "analytical" and "continental" philosophy, as well as in disciplines across the humanities, social sciences, the arts, and beyond. Indeed, Merleau-Pontian Philosophy has now become what he himself would have called a "classic," "an immense field of sedimented history and thought where one goes to practice and to learn to think" (*MPAR*, 12).

ACKNOWLEDGMENTS

In writing this dictionary, I had the luxury of embarking again upon a reading of Merleau-Ponty's entire corpus, and this approach is reflected in the direct contact with the texts that the reader will find throughout these entries. For this luxury, I gratefully acknowledge the support of a Social Sciences and Humanities Research Council of Canada Postdoctoral Fellowship, held with the institutional support of McGill University, Montréal, Canada. And yet, as a member of the community working on and influenced by Merleau-Ponty's thought, I must also acknowledge, as a whole, precisely that "immense field of sedimented history and thought" on the work on Merleau-Ponty alluded to at the end of the Introduction above. This field, which engages with Merleau-Ponty as a living thinker and as a "classic" to be taken up and taken farther, has shaped my own reading in innumerable ways. The suggestions for further readings might thus be seen as a modest first attempt to acknowledge this debt, for which I would have to add not only additional works in English, but also innumerable studies in French, for that acknowledgment to be complete.

Chronology: Merleau-Ponty's life and works[1]

14 March 1908	Jean Jacques Maurice Merleau-Ponty is born in Rochefort-sur-Mer, France, to Bernard Jean Merleau-Ponty (1869–1913) and Julie Jeanne Marie Louse Barthé (1876–1953). The Merleau-Ponty family moves to Paris the following year.
1913	Merleau-Ponty's father dies.
1923–6	Having finished his secondary schooling and discovered a vocation in philosophy, Merleau-Ponty enters the famous *Lycée Louis-le-Grand* in order to prepare for the entrance exam for the *École normale supérieure* (*ENS*). He is said to have secretly attended lectures by famous philosopher **Alain** at the neighboring *Lycée Henri-IV*.
1926–30	Having been allowed to sit the entrance exams a year before being officially eligible, Merleau-Ponty succeeds in gaining entrance to the *ENS* and begins studying philosophy with, among others, Léon **Brunschvicg** both at the *ENS* and at the University of Paris (Sorbonne). While at the *ENS*, he becomes acquainted with several future French intellectuals, notably Jean-Paul **Sartre** and Simone de **Beauvoir**.

1929	Merleau-Ponty receives his degree (*Diplôme d'études supérieures*) on the basis of a (now-lost) thesis, "*La Notion de multiple intelligible chez Plotin*" ("Plotinus's Notion of the Intelligible Many"), directed by Émile **Bréhier**. Merleau-Ponty attends Edmund **Husserl**'s "*Paris Lectures*." These lectures form the basis for Husserl's text *Cartesian Meditations*, which was published in French shortly thereafter and which contributes to Merleau-Ponty's early understanding of Husserl.
1930	Merleau-Ponty places second in the "*agrégation*" in philosophy, the highly competitive exam qualifying candidates for teaching at the *lycée* level.
1930–1	Obligatory military service.
1931–3	Merleau-Ponty is a philosophy teacher at *Lycée Félix Faure* in Beauvais, outside of Paris. During this time, his appreciation for phenomenology (through the writings of Eugen **Fink** and Husserl) deepens, thanks in part to his advancing study of German.
1933–4	Merleau-Ponty receives a leave from teaching and a research bursary for the project **"The Nature of Perception,"** which focuses on phenomenology and **Gestalt psychology**. Beginning in 1933, Merleau-Ponty regularly attends Alexandre **Kojève**'s influential lectures on **Hegel**'s philosophy.
1934–5	Merleau-Ponty is given a permanent professorship in a *lycée* in Chartres.
1935	**"Christianity and *Ressentiment*,"** Merleau-Ponty's first article, appears in *La Vie intellectuelle*.
1935–9	Merleau-Ponty is named "*Agrégé-répétiteur*" in philosophy at the *ENS*.

1936	"Being and Having," Merleau-Ponty's second article, appears, also in *La Vie intellectuelle*. He also publishes a review of **Sartre**'s *Imagination*. Merleau-Ponty's contribution is acknowledged in Aron **Gurwitsch**'s article "Some Aspects and Developments in Gestalt Psychology."
1938	Merleau-Ponty completes his minor thesis, "Consciousness and Behavior," which was later published as *The Structure of Behavior* in 1942. Participates alongside **Brunschvicg** on a panel at the *Société française de philosophie*, discussing declining performance on the *agrégation* in philosophy.
1939	Merleau-Ponty reads some key articles in a memorial issue of *Revue internationale de philosophie* dedicated to Husserl, including an article by Eugen **Fink** and Husserl's own late fragment, "**The Origin of Geometry**." In March, Merleau-Ponty is the first non-Louvain researcher to visit the newly established **Husserl Archives at Louvain**.
1939–40	During the Second World War, Merleau-Ponty is mobilized in August 1939 as a lieutenant in the 5th Infantry Regiment, and was evacuated to a military hospital in June 1940 prior to demobilization. He received the *Croix de guerre*, a medal for acts of heroism.
1940	Merleau-Ponty returns to teaching, now at *Lycée Carnot* in Paris, where among his students he meets **Claude Lefort (1924–2010)**, who would become a lifelong friend, Merleau-Ponty's posthumous editor, and an important political philosopher. In late 1940, Merleau-Ponty marries Suzanne Berthe Jolibois (1914–2010) (**Madame Merleau-Ponty**). Marianne Merleau-Ponty, Merleau-Ponty's only child, is born in June 1941.

1941	Along with **Sartre** and **Beauvoir,** Merleau-Ponty develops a short-lived underground journal (*Socialism and Liberty*).
1942	Merleau-Ponty's minor thesis "Consciousness and Behavior" is published as ***The Structure of Behavior.***
1944	Merleau-Ponty accepts a teaching post for advanced students at *Lycée Condorcet*, preparing them for the entrance exams for the "grandes écoles" (such as the *ENS*).
1945	In July, Merleau-Ponty defends his principle or major doctoral thesis, ***Phenomenology of Perception***, which is published immediately thereafter. His supervisor was **Émile Bréhier**. Along with **Sartre, Beauvoir,** and others, Merleau-Ponty founds a new journal, *Les Temps modernes*. The first edition appears in October and includes Merleau-Ponty's first explicitly political reflection, **"The War Has Taken Place."** This year also saw the publication of his first essay specifically on painting—**"Cézanne's Doubt"**—in *Fontaine*.
1945–8	Merleau-Ponty becomes a university professor at the Université de Lyon and commutes regularly between Paris and Lyon.
1946	Merleau-Ponty defends the major conclusions of *Phenomenology of Perception* at a meeting of the *Société française de philosophie*. The transcript is published under the title ***The Primacy of Perception.***
1947	Publication of ***Humanism and Terror.***
1947–8	Little is known of Merleau-Ponty's earlier courses in Lyon, but in this year he begins teaching both in Lyon and at the *ENS* in Paris, offering a preparatory course on materials for the 1948 ***agrégation***, reportedly attended

by Michel Foucault. Student notes have been published as *The Incarnate Subject: Malebranche, Biran, and Bergson on the Union of the Soul and Body.*

1948 Publication of *Sense and Non-Sense.*

1948–9 Merleau-Ponty is granted leave to travel to Mexico, where he gives a lecture entitled "Others" [*Autrui*].

1949–51 Merleau-Ponty becomes Professor of Child Psychology and Pedagogy at the Université de Paris, Sorbonne. The lecture notes from this period are published as *Child Psychology and Pedagogy: The Sorbonne Lectures (1949–52).* Also during this time, Merleau-Ponty is working on *The Prose of the World*, which would soon be abandoned or left to the side. This manuscript was published posthumously.

1950 Merleau-Ponty becomes co-director (with **Sartre**) of Gallimard's series *La Bibliothèque de Philosophie*, with the explicit task of promoting phenomenology.

1952 After three years at the Sorbonne, Merleau-Ponty is elected to the coveted and prestigious Chair of Philosophy at the **Collège de France**.

1953 Merleau-Ponty gives the Inaugural Lecture for his tenure at the *Collège de France*, **"In Praise of Philosophy."** Merleau-Ponty and **Sartre's** friendship and professional relationships suffers a major rupture, and Merleau-Ponty resigns from *Les Temps modernes*. In December of this year, Merleau-Ponty's beloved mother died. At the *Collège*, Merleau-Ponty gives two courses: "Research on the Literary Use of Language" and "The Sensible World and the World of Expression."

1953–4	Merleau-Ponty begins publishing his political commentary in *L'Express*. At the *Collège*, he teaches "Materials for a Theory of History" and "The Problem of Speech"
1954–5	*Adventures of the Dialectic* is published. At the *Collège*, Merleau-Ponty teaches "The Problem of Passivity: Sleep, Unconsciousness, Memory" and "'Institution' in Personal and Public History."
1955–6	*Les Philosophes célèbres*, edited with introductions by Merleau-Ponty, is published. At the *Collège*, Merleau-Ponty teaches "Dialectical Philosophy" and "Texts and Commentaries on Dialectic."
1956–7	At the *Collège*, Merleau-Ponty teaches: "The Concept of Nature," the first part of a course that will extend over three years.
1957–8	At the *Collège*, Merleau-Ponty teaches "The Concept of Nature: Animality, The Human Body, and the Passage to Culture."
1958–9	At the *Collège*, Merleau-Ponty teaches a course without a specific title on the "sense of the ontology of nature" and on "philosophy today."
1959–60	*Signs* is published. At the *Collège*, Merleau-Ponty teaches "Husserl at the Limits of Phenomenology" and "Nature and *Logos*, the Human Body."
1960–1	"Eye and Mind" is first published. At the *Collège de France*, Merleau-Ponty teaches "Cartesian Ontology and Today's Ontology" and "Philosophy and Non-Philosophy since Hegel."
3 May 1961	Merleau-Ponty dies at home of a heart attack while reading in his study at 10 boulevard Saint Michel, where he had lived with Suzanne since

	1951. He was reportedly studying **Descartes'** *Dioptrique* in preparation for his course the next day.
1964	*The Visible and The Invisible* is published posthumously.
1968	*Themes from the Lectures* and *The Incarnate Subject: Malebranche, Biran, and Bergson on the Union of Soul and Body* are published posthumously.
1969	Posthumous publication of *The Prose of the World*.

A–Z dictionary

A priori versus *a posteriori*; necessity versus contingency

The Latin term *a priori* describes propositions or facts whose truth can be known "prior to experience," as opposed to *a posteriori* knowledge, or knowledge "from experience." The terms are particularly important in Kant's critique of metaphysics traditionally understood as the realm of speculative *a priori* reasoning. Merleau-Ponty's phenomenological descriptions require "a new definition of the *a priori*" (229). As he writes: "Human existence will lead us to revisit our usual notions of necessity [*a priori*] and of contingency [*a posteriori*], because human existence is the change of contingency into necessity through the act of taking up" (*PhP*, 174). The new concept appears in Merleau-Ponty's reflection upon necessity and contingency in animal **behavior**. An animal's world is structured according to a *lived* necessity through something like an *a priori* of a species. Or again, to learn a particular gesture involves adopting a certain "sensory-motor *a priori*" that restructures the organism's **field** of possible actions (*SB*, 100). Finally, a subject capable of language or "symbolic behavior" again introduces new *a priori* structures (121). Merleau-Ponty concludes that lived **consciousness** resists "the celebrated distinction between *a priori* form and empirical content" (171). In ***Phenomenology of Perception***, Merleau-Ponty argues that learning to see color is a "change in the structure of consciousness, the institution of a new dimension of experience, and the deployment of an *a priori*" (*PhP*, 32). Learning a new habit or gesture thus involves taking up contingency in order to change it into necessity, and this is an *existential* rather than an intellectual act. Culture and history also represent a certain structure of possible action, and a present-day ruler takes up a "necessary" role (e.g. the "*a priori* of the threatened prince") insofar as he or she responds to "typical" situations with typical responses, just as an animal's responses are typical of the species *a priori*. The point, however, is that the "historical *a priori*" is not a "destiny," "it is only consistent for a given phase and provided that the equilibrium of *forces* allows the same *forms* to remain" (90). Thus, For Merleau-Ponty, if experience is the fundamental "beginning of knowledge," then "there is no longer any means of distinguishing a level of *a priori* truths and a level of factual ones" (229). **Existential analysis** reveals that the *a priori* is paradoxically the *contingent necessity* of experience.

Abstract movement versus concrete movement

A "concrete" movement is a gesture that responds to an actual situation, such as using a familiar tool. By contrast, an "abstract" movement is one that takes place "outside" of actual lived experience, such as being asked to perform some imaginary action, such as a military salute. This is a distinction important in **Gelb** and **Goldstein**'s studies both of **Schneider**'s morbid **motricity** and in cases where patients are able to grasp (*Greifen*) but not point (*Zeigen*). In general, patients unable to perform "abstract" movements must pass through an explicit intellectual act or conscious decision in order to approximate normal **behavior**, which reveals to Merleau-Ponty that normal behavior has no need for this extra interpretative step (*PhP*, Part One, Chapter Three).

Action

Merleau-Ponty offers a nuanced phenomenological theory of human action, even if he initially expresses some reservations regarding this term (*SB*, 162). In *The Structure of Behavior*, he argues that action must be understood as *between* a passive structure of stimulus-response and an active expression of a pure decision, or between determinism and freedom. Human action, then, is never a representation of a goal translated into some bodily mechanisms, but is rather a "directed melody," an *expression* (167–73). The notion of action is again important in *Phenomenology of Perception*, particularly in the description of spatiality, where actions (actual or possible) are not something that happens *in* space, but rather something that generates lived spatiality itself through **motor intentionality** (*PhP*, 105). We experience our bodies as a certain power for an action or for a world (111). The final chapter argues for understanding action as governed by a **situated freedom**, which foreshadows his political discussions of **historical responsibility**.

Activity versus passivity

Phenomenological description reveals that human phenomena are paradoxically both *active* and *passive*. For instance, **behavior** must be understood as somehow *between* a passive mechanical process and an active decision. Perception too must be somehow *between* a passive reception of sensations and an active thought *about* experience. Or consider higher-level human actions, whether it be the simple phenomenon of falling asleep (which is neither a mere event nor an active decision) or a political action (where the consequence is that no one is every purely innocent and no one is every purely guilty). The intertwining between passivity and activity becomes increasing important in Merleau-Ponty's work, and a key component of his ontology. See *The Collège de France Lectures* from 1954–5.

Advent

In **"Indirect Language and the Voices of Silence"** Merleau-Ponty introduces the notion of advent to characterize the logic of **history** and of **painting**. He argues that the unity of a trajectory of *sense* can be neither the unity of external relations of juxtaposition, nor a unity imposed from the outside (such as the unity imposed on art by the museum), nor again the unity resulting from a pre-existing Reason or Spirit, determined in advance. Rather, the trajectory is unified through the fact that each gesture is an **expression**, and thus takes up the past by introducing a **coherent deformation** toward an open and unpredictable future. This is the logic of "advent," which is "a promise of events" to come (*MPAR*, 106).

Adventures of the Dialectic (1955) [AD]

By 1955, Merleau-Ponty's break with **Sartre** and with other proponents of the Communist Party was definitive, and his last major contribution to political philosophy also definitively breaks with his earlier **wait-and-see-Marxism**. As an alternative, he sketches a **new liberalism** (*AD*, 225). Nevertheless, even this new approach seems a natural sequel to his evolving **Marxist humanism**, a political attitude that resisted both Communist politics and the idealist mystifications of liberalism. Although Sartre never responded to the Merleau-Ponty's criticisms, **Beauvoir** did so in **"Merleau-Ponty and Pseudo-Sartreanism,"** and several other Communist thinkers also published rebuttals in *Mésaventures de l'anti-Marxisme: Les malheurs de M. Merleau-Ponty* (1956).

Preface

For Merleau-Ponty, a political *pensée de survol* is impossible, and political philosophy must begin from within the "crucible of events." There are, according to **Alain**, two forms of political reflection: a "politics of reason" and a "politics of understanding." The first is an **intellectualism** that seeks, beyond empirical history, a universal history written in advance; the second is an **empiricism** where each event is an isolated moment, and history but a sum of these events (4). As he does in other domains, Merleau-Ponty seeks a middle ground or third way. Politics, he argues, "is an action in the process of self-invention" (4). That is, politics is a process of *expression*, and thus the most important structure in Marxism is not the "end of history" in the proletariat, but the recognition that "universal history is not to be contemplated but to be made" (5).

The political philosopher, just like the political actor, is in the process of expression and does not have access to its content in advance. This suggests a Marxist notion of **historical responsibility**, yet the failures of empirical Marxism are not accidental; rather, they show the tensions that lead the dialectic into its necessary adventures. By examining political experience "on the ground of political philosophy," this book proceeds in the hopes of offering "something else" (7; 6).

Chapter One: The Crisis of Understanding

The *Adventures* begins with **Weber**'s attempt to describe a form of liberalism *accomplished* through struggle in **history**, rather than as the pre-existence of high-flying ideals. For Merleau-Ponty, the value in Weber liberalism is that it recognizes that "history is the natural seat of violence" and that its outcome is not pre-ordained (9). Nevertheless, Weber maintains a form of dualism between understanding and action in which contradictions would be somehow clarified. And yet, history is a "strange object" in which we find the lived contradictions of subject and object, freedom and determinism, past and present. Weber believes that, by tracing an historical formation (such as the work-ethic) back to its origins and forward to its consequences, he is able to discern the "basic structure of the facts" as if he has revealed, behind appearances, a truth in itself of history and the "anonymous intention" of the dialectic itself (13–14). Yet in Weber, Merleau-Ponty detects an existential respect for reciprocal causality, which leads to the claim that "History has a meaning [*sens*], but there is no pure development of ideas. Its meaning arises in contact with contingency" (16).

Although Weber resists these existential intuitions and his advances fall short of Marxism, his work does suggest a "new" form of liberalism, a "militant liberalism" that recognizes the inadequacies of dogmatic politics. For Weber, the highest ideals are not discerned in the facts, they are accomplished within history, and thus "all politics is violence—even, in its own fashion, democratic politics" (26). Weber thus decries any propaganda that would justify repression "in the name of freedom" (26–7), and this suggests a genuine commitment to **historical responsibility** and to "mature man" who "is aware of a responsibility for the consequences of his conduct and really feels such responsibility." Thus, history must not be studied from the perspective of Spirit, but as an analysis of "political man" (28).

Chapter Two: "Western" Marxism

Whereas Weber ultimately remained committed to a political *pensée de survol* in terms of the ideal categories of his analysis, Lukács attempted to develop an absolute from within the relative. For Lukács, materialism is broader than economic determinism, and is rather a set of complex relations. As such, "alienation" is not a determinism, but rather a stage setting for an historical struggle, and his Marxism focuses all of its energies on achieving a "synthesis" of dialectical opposites. Much of this chapter focuses on how Lukács establishes a contingency of history and the role of the proletariat as a force in this conception (43–53). But perhaps most importantly, it is here that Marxist humanism must return to the fore. For Merleau-Ponty, humans are united through the form of expressive action in the contingency of history, but no "content" or synthesis is guaranteed by this open essence. Bringing out a genuine expression remains forever a task to be accomplished, and the final synthesis is always to come.

Chapter Three: Pravda

As the center of Communism shifted to Russia, the "vanguard" of the proletariat—the Party—appeared to respond to all of those duties that a Revolution cannot respond to. In practice, this Russian Marxist-Leninism replaced the engine of a powerful and self-conscious proletarian power, and the emphasis shifted from a philosophy of synthesis to a "Marxism of antithesis" (7). In short, Lenin sought to return Marxism to a materialism in order to "establish the dialectic solidly in things" (60). And yet a naive and "pre-Hegelian" theory of knowledge "places the knowing subject outside of the fabric of history" and returns the dialectic (by fiat) to a "massive positivity" that had been surpassed (60). Ultimately, neither Leninism's positivism nor Lukács own later attempts to reconcile Revolutionary optimism with the "permanent

Revolution" succeed in removing the conflict between the dialectic and realism. Invoking his discussion of the **Moscow Trials** in *Humanism and Terror*, Merleau-Ponty claims to have shown that their "principle" was to be found in the "revolutionary idea of **historical responsibility**," but that strangely the regime presented them as if standard "criminal" trials—a Revolution that no longer wants to be revolutionary or, worse, "an established regime that [merely] mimics the revolution" (72). Communist philosophy is an inauthentic expression, "a thought in the shadow of which something else is being done," a refusal to accept the task of the future in the contingency of the present (72).

Chapter Four: The Dialectic in Action

In Trotsky, the dialectic attempts a new adventure, a shift from knowledge to praxis. Trotsky resists any simple understanding of historical reason, since the future is that which we take up on the horizons of our action, not as "a divinity which guides history from the outside" (77). There is an "immanent" logic in history that eliminates "false solutions," and rejects the claims of Party. In this discussion, one can detect **Lefort**'s influence on Merleau-Ponty (79–94). And yet, Trotsky's implicit response to the question of *what happens* when the Party no longer expresses the dialectic is made explicit by Merleau-Ponty at the beginning of the next chapter: "the course of things would perhaps call into question the Marxist thesis of the proletariat as ruling class and of socialism as heir to capitalism" (95).

Chapter Five: Sartre and Ultrabolshevism

This long and complex chapter focuses on **Sartre**'s Marxism as presented in the controversial *The Communists and Peace* that was implicated in Merleau-Ponty's departure from **Les Temps modernes**. Merleau-Ponty begins by praising Sartre's attempt to "analyze communist practice directly, without the mediation of ideology," since ideology can be an inertia in the dialectic (96). And yet, although Sartre begins with the aim of agreeing with Communists on "precise and limited subjects," he ultimately offers what might indeed be "all one can say in favor of communist politics when one is on the left but is not a communist" (*AD*, 97n. 3). As such, if Sartre's enterprise fails, then so too does the left's Communist adventure, paving the way for something new.

Sartre's study of communist politics begins not from their philosophy, but from his own, which is arguably the precise opposite. Neither history nor the dialectic is allowed any productive force, and history is only rendered intelligible through individual decisions, echoing the "extreme subjectivism" of Sartre's **existentialism** (97). Sartre attempts a critique of communist *reasons* alongside an apologetics for communist *practice* in its historical expressions. Yet inverting communism and investing it in the free decision of the pure subject removes it from history. This is Sartre's *ultrabolshevism*: a communism that "no longer justifies itself by truth, the philosophy of history, and the dialectic, but by their negation" (100). Sartre's communism fails because it renounces the dialectic in favor of an absolute creation that is free of the weight of history.

This chapter explores Sartre's account of empirical politics (101–14) and Sartre's inability to account for **ambiguity** in historical facts (114–31). For Merleau-Ponty, the political action to which we are called "is, like everything we live, something in the process of becoming an expression, a movement which calls for a continuation, a past in the process of giving itself a future" (127). A third section compares Marxist concepts with the use to which they are put in Sartre's re-visioning (133–53). The fourth section deals with Sartre's moral conclusions insofar as they are related to "historical judgment" (155), and to his conception of the social in relation to expression and action (153–64). In short, Merleau-Ponty here attributes to Sartre a neo-Cartesian adoption of the *cogito*, and this is what ultimately separates Sartre from Marxism. If the subject of history is a pure nothingness, a **consciousness** without thickness or opacity, then history is simply a "series of instantaneous views," and these are necessarily views taken by a consciousness whose essence is to posit closed meanings that it knows completely and without remainder. Yet, for Merleau-Ponty, what is at stake are "open, incomplete meanings" which could not be the objects of thought for a pure consciousness, and this is precisely the situation both at the level of the perceived *and* at the level of thought. Sartre's pure consciousness fails to understand the philosophical consequences of the primacy of perception and of the study of lived experience. My life and the dialectic both unfold through the "thickness of a field of existence," which is to say that meaning appears in "the landscape of praxis" (199). And the relation to the other is not, then, one of utter negation, since the encounter is not between two absolute "for-them-selves"; two lived experiences can and do overlap, merge (for a time), and move apart, since there is no logical issue with their sharing a single lived world.

Between Merleau-Ponty and Sartre, then, there is a divergent metaphysics. For Sartre, there are but "things" and "men"; for Merleau-Ponty, there is an "interworld, which we call history, symbolism, truth-to-be made" (200). In this **intersubjectivity**, human action is subject to the paradoxical reality of **historical responsibility**: "if one thus renounces 'pure action,' which is a myth (and a myth of the spectator consciousness), perhaps it is then that one has the best chance of changing the world" (200–1).

Epilogue

Ultimately the dialectic only exists in the lived and intersubjective world where reversals, paradoxes, and contradictions can be sustained. As a process with a *sense*, the dialectic must pass through certain "adventures" or "errors"; as *expression*, the dialectic and history move obliquely. Each adventure establishes illusions because each attempts to establish fixed absolutes ("the proletariat," "History," or the pure subject). Each attempts, then, to establish a "**bad dialectic**" in which movement is frozen or institutionalized. A politics of expression would resist any regime that attempts to freeze the possibilities for expression. This suggests to Merleau-Ponty a **new liberalism**, a structure designed to encourage historical expression and humanism in political action. Refusing to abandon the powerful insights of Marxist critique, the non-communist left alone seems capable of a genuine dialectical politics, a liberalism that recognizes and engages the reality of the class struggle and the ways that economic structures are existential **dimensions** of human being. Such a new liberalism would require something of a parliamentary system, with extensive protections against parliamentary manipulations and maneuvering. It would be, in short, the institution of open communication and expression, offering both socialism and freedom with the constraints of intersubjectivity.

Adversity

This notion is invoked at the end of the essay "**Man and Adversity**" (**1951**). Merleau-Ponty argues that contemporary work in **psychoanalysis**, **structuralism**, and **history** points toward an embracing of contingency through the recognition that one must give up the rigid division between body and mind, or facts and values. Human phenomena cannot be accounted for through *causal* explanation or through the workings of *reason* and the **constituting consciousness**. Rather, the source of our errors and evils must be found in our expressive gestures. Two forms of adversity, however, threaten **expression**. First, expression can only move forward by taking up the sedimented past and introducing a **coherent deformation** into the field of meaning or of history. This anonymous adversity weighs upon our expressions. Second, our expressions themselves bring a pretense to universality, and our fear of contingency tempts us to embrace the "universal" categories of classical philosophy, political fascism, or dogmatic religion. This "menace of adversity" tempts us to freeze history and rationalize contingency, but this renders impossible an expressive **humanism**.

Affectivity

Although Merleau-Ponty criticizes the notion of affectivity introduced by intellectualist psychology (*PhP*, 95), the concept becomes important in his **existential analysis** of sexuality. Our affectivity is not a property of the body; it is a **dimension** of experience. As such, it haunts every human act, and yet no single act can be reduced to a purely affective source.

Agrégation

Highly competitive national qualifying exam for teachers in *lycée*, or secondary education in France. Preparation for the *agrégation* in fact begins in *lycée*, and the majority of successful candidates during Merleau-Ponty's time came from just two Parisian *lycées*,

Louis-le-Grand and *Henri-IV*; Merleau-Ponty attended *Louis-le-Grand*. After *lycée*, students continue preparing, with most successful candidates enrolling in the *"grandes écoles,"* which are highly selective and specialized post-secondary institutions. Merleau-Ponty attended the **École normale supérieure (ENS)** of Paris, which is particularly renown for preparing students for the *agrégation* in the humanities, including philosophy. Merleau-Ponty sat the *agrégation* in philosophy in 1930, and placed second. Merleau-Ponty also served in the late 1930s as *Agrégé-répétiteur*, tutoring or assisting students at the *ENS* to prepare for the exam. In 1938, Merleau-Ponty participated on a panel discussion (alongside **Brunschvicg**) at the *Société française de philosophie* concerning the declining performance of students on the *agrégation*. In his intervention, Merleau-Ponty took a position against the structure and content of the exams, suggesting that the questions fail to excite the students' interests in concrete philosophical issues and in figures such as Marx, Nietzsche, and "even Husserl" (*P*, 58).

Alain (Émile-Auguste Chartier, 1868–1951)

French philosopher who taught at *Lycée Henri-IV* in Paris, where he exerted a significant influence on many young thinkers of Merleau-Ponty's generation. Merleau-Ponty himself, who attended the neighboring *Lycée Louis-le-Grand*, is said to have clandestinely frequented Alain's lectures. Alain is often associated with his teacher, Jules **Lagneau**, and a classical style of philosophical reflection known as **reflective analysis**. Alain's two forms of political reflection, "reason" (intellectualist) vs. "understanding" (empiricist), shape the Preface of *Adventures of the Dialectic*.

Alexia

Condition, sometimes referred to as "word blindness" or visual **aphasia**, which is an inability to recognize words or to read. (*PhP*, 201)

Allochiria

Condition in which a patient suffering from cerebral lesions experiences sensations from one side of the body on the symmetrically opposite side. (*PhP*, 100–1)

Alter Ego

Latin term meaning, literally, "other myself." This paradoxical formulation is used by Merleau-Ponty as a shorthand for the problem of **others** and of **intersubjectivity**. The transcendental philosopher explains away the problem of the other by assuming each **consciousness** is essentially identical to each other because of a transcendental rational *Ego* that they must share (*PhP*, lxxv). For **phenomenology**, the paradoxical *experience* of others is only possible "if the Ego and the Alter Ego are defined by their situation and are not set free from all inherence; that is, only if philosophy is not completed with the return to myself" (lxxvi).

Ambiguity

Throughout *Phenomenology of Perception*, Merleau-Ponty characterizes lived experience and human phenomena as *ambiguous*. For instance, the **phantom limb** reveals that our normal experience is irreducibly *both* physical and psychical. Phenomenology discovers the **phenomenal field** as the zone that can "tolerate ambiguity" (11), such as the ambiguity between **touching/touched** (98). Indeed, ambiguities proliferate throughout the **dimensions** of our embodied experience and are to be the source of our new understanding of human nature as **being-in-the-world** (87). Thus, ambiguity is not an inconvenient aspect of lived experience that is to be transcended or dissolved in philosophical thought: "ambiguity is essential to human existence, and everything that we live or think always has several senses" (172). There is, then, "a genius for ambiguity that might well serve to define man," and everything human is at once ambiguously natural and cultural (195).

This understanding of ambiguity continues to shape Merleau-Ponty's writings. In 1952, he asserts that the distinguishing characteristic of the philosopher is the simultaneous "taste for evidence" and the "feeling for ambiguity" (*IPP*, 4). Given its source in the experience of the **reversibility** of **touching/touched**, Merleau-Ponty's evolving thought and ontology of **flesh** and **chiasm** begin with and further this rich notion of ambiguity.

Ambivalence

A notion that Merleau-Ponty first discusses in his lectures on *Child Psychology and Pedagogy* in relation to Melanie Klein. Ambivalence is when a subject maintains two distinct images of an object or being that are not yet recognized to be the same. This is contrasted with **ambiguity**, which is when the two images are preserved even when the identity of their object is recognized. The concept is used in a different sense in *The Visible and the Invisible*, where Merleau-Ponty names a **dialectical structure** "ambivalent" when it solidifies into a pure identity of opposites (*VI*, 93).

Amovable forms of behavior

The second level of **behavior** discussed in *The Structure of Behavior*, consisting of behaviors that respond to the meaning signified by the situational content, rather than that content's explicit meaning. This allows for "means–end" behavior in animals (*SB*, 105–20).

An sit versus *quid sit*

These Latin terms are drawn from an Aristotelian distinction between questions of existence (*an sit*) and questions of **essence** (*quid sit*): "is it?" versus "what is it?" Merleau-Ponty makes use of this distinction in *The Visible and the Invisible* in order to mark the progress of philosophy from Cartesian radical doubt to the study of "what the world and truth and being are" (*VI*, 107).

Anarthria

Condition in which patients have lost the motor ability for speech, rendering articulate speech impossible (see *PhP*, 180).

Anonymity/anonymous

Merleau-Ponty discusses the notion of anonymity alongside that of **generality** and of **field** in *Phenomenology of Perception*. When describing perception through phenomenological reflection, it becomes clear that perception is somewhere *between* a passive event and an active or intellectual accomplishment. Thus, it is not the accomplishment of my personal ego or "I," but rather takes place anonymously but also from a certain perspective and never in full possession of its object.

Anosognosia

Condition in which a patient is unaware or in denial of his or her paralysis, a condition parallel to **phantom limb syndrome** (*PhP*, 79ff.). For Merleau-Ponty, the condition is an expression of the **ambiguity** of **being-in-the-world,** since the anosognosic patient "puts his paralyzed arm out of play in order not to have to sense its degeneration, but this is to say that he has a preconscious knowledge of it" (83).

Aphasia

Condition in which a patient is unable to perform linguistic activities, often associated with brain damage to particular regions of the brain. Discussed at length in Part One, Chapter Six of *Phenomenology of Perception*, where Merleau-Ponty argues that

Schneider had lost neither the physical ability to speak nor the intellectual significations, but rather the manner of using the words. Thus, **Gelb** and **Goldstein**'s analyses suggest an **existential analysis** or theory of aphasia (196).

Aphonia

The loss of the ability to speak, often in association with psychological trauma. In Part One, Chapter Five of *Phenomenology of Perception*, Merleau-Ponty suggests an **existential analysis** of a case of aphonia. Like one who must tacitly know a memory in order to repress it, the young woman refuses the region of her life that is painful, namely *coexistence*. This is not a "chosen" refusal, but rather the taking up of an existential situation in which the field of linguistic "possibilities collapses," and the recovery must be worked out below the level of **thetic** consciousness (*PhP*, 164–7).

Apraxia

Condition in which a patient is unable to perform a gesture upon command despite understanding the request and being physically capable of the movement. Merleau-Ponty offers an **existential analysis** of apraxia, suggesting that since knowledge is intact, it must be a disturbance of **motor intentionality**, which reveals that "objects or space can be present to our knowledge without being present to our body" (*PhP*, 140).

Aristotle's illusion

On your right hand, cross your middle finger over your index finger, then touch their point of intersection with the tip of a pencil. Many people experience a "double" sensation, as if they are being touched by two pencils rather than one—a tactile equivalent of crossing one's eyes. For Merleau-Ponty, this does not reveal that the tactile image is made up of isolated tactile images added together by **judgment**. Rather, he argues that because the illusion appears when the fingers are unable to perform a unified gesture, the *unity* or synthesis of an object must be the result of the *unity* of **one's own body**. There is just one pencil for normal perception because there is just one touching organ, my hand (*PhP*, 211–12).

Association

In Chapter Two of the Introduction to *Phenomenology of Perception*, Merleau-Ponty considers whether introducing the notion of association to explain perceptual experience might insulate classical approaches from the critique of the **constancy hypothesis**. Might an associative force be supposed to do the work of organizing punctual sensations? Yet if **consciousness** is, according to the empiricist, defined as sensation, then all of its clarity and evidence will have to come from this most basic level. Such a structure will only ever allow for *external* relations between parts, and never the *internal* unity of the **field** structure. Grasping a figure is not simply associating related sensations; it is the grasping of a *sense*, which is in fact "the condition of association" (*PhP*, 17).

Attention

In Chapter Three of the Introduction to *Phenomenology of Perception*, Merleau-Ponty considers whether it is possible to save classical theories of perception from the critique of the **constancy hypothesis** by introducing the concept of *attention*. For **empiricism**, attention creates nothing; it is simply a power for illuminating what already exists. For **intellectualism**, attention becomes a universal power of structuring, since perception must already contain "the intelligible structure that attention draws out" (*PhP*, 29). And yet, empiricism cannot find an internal connection between an object and the act of attention, whereas intellectualism cannot find any contingency in the relation. By contrast, Merleau-Ponty suggests that attention involves a "transformation of the mental field, a new way for consciousness to be present toward its objects" (31). The act of attention restructures the experience of the field itself and "is the active constitution of a new object that develops and thematizes what was until then only offered as an indeterminate **horizon**" (33).

"Attention to life" (Bergson)

In *Matter and Memory*, **Bergson** discusses how psychological life can be lived at different levels depending upon its degree of "attention to life." Insofar as it turns toward action and toward real situations, our attention to life adjusts us to the external world or the present, insofar as it turns away from life, our attention leads us into the imaginary (and paradigmatically into memory). How might this concept relate to the phenomenological notion of **being-in-the-world**? For Merleau-Ponty, they are not interchangeable, because Bergson preserves the distinction between sensation and movement, or between the objective body and consciousness (*PhP*, 514n. 23). By contrast, Merleau-Ponty's account of reflex movement does not require that the objective processes of the body be "observed by consciousness" (81).

Bad ambiguity versus good ambiguity

In "An Unpublished Text" (1952), Merleau-Ponty suggested that the success of *Phenomenology of Perception* was limited because there is only a "bad ambiguity" to be found in the study of perception, since it resulted only in a mixture of oppositions. Yet the study of **expression** promised a "good ambiguity" that would draw opposites together into a single whole, thereby offering a metaphysics and the principle of an **ethics** to be pursued in his future projects (*PrP*, 11).

Bad dialectic versus good dialectic (or hyper-dialectic)

First introduced in *The Collège de France Lectures* (from 1955–6) and in *Adventures of the Dialectic* (1955), Merleau-Ponty offers a critique of dialectical thinking that fails to think *according to* the **dialectic**, and thereby ends up freezing the movement into a set of absolutely opposite concepts or negative relations. This becomes central to his critique of **Sartre** in *The Visible and the Invisible*, where he defines bad dialectic as "that which, against its own principles, imposes an external law and framework upon the content and restores for its own uses the pre-dialectical thought" (*VI*, 94). This is compared to an open dialectic that resists all final synthesis—a good or "**hyper-dialectic**"—pursued through a genuinely expressive form of philosophical **interrogation**.

"The Battle over Existentialism" (1945) [*SNS*]

This essay addresses the controversies and various interpretations of **Sartre**'s *Being and Nothingness* (1943). Merleau-Ponty offers a lively defense against both left and right attacks upon **existentialism**, and suggests that the critics are perhaps horrified by the consequences of this line of thought, but unable to disprove it according to its content (*SNS*, 71). For Merleau-Ponty, **existentialism** is the embracing of **ambiguity**, such as that between freedom and determinism (72). Nevertheless, Sartre's thinking may indeed remain dialectical, and thus fail to reach the genuine paradoxical structure of lived experience, foreshadowing Merleau-Ponty's later criticisms (72). The essay also considers alternative Christian and Marxist versions of existentialism. For Merleau-Ponty, existentialism requires nothing less than a new concept of **consciousness** (82).

De Beauvoir, Simone (1908–86)

French philosopher and author, a key figure in both **existentialism** and feminism. Beauvoir is often discussed in relation to **Sartre**, her long-time intellectual and romantic partner, and described herself as the "midwife" of Sartre's existential ethics. Nevertheless, her own contribution is an extremely important body of work, including her book *The Ethics of Ambiguity* (1948), likely partially inspired by Merleau-Ponty's use of **ambiguity** in ***Phenomenology of Perception***.

Beauvoir and Merleau-Ponty met at the *ENS* in 1927, and she describes Merleau-Ponty as "a young man, frank, simple, so gay and so serious!"[2] Her positive feelings sour, however, when she is deeply disappointed in Merleau-Ponty's abandonment of a courtship of her childhood friend Elizabeth Mabille ("Zaza") upon pressure from Mabille's overbearing and deeply religious mother.[3] In 1940 Beauvoir was involved with Sartre and Merleau-Ponty in the formation of the short-lived group "**Socialism and Liberty**," and in 1945 she also worked on the founding of *Les Temps modernes*. At this time, Merleau-Ponty seems particularly struck by Beauvoir's abilities as a writer, citing her novel *She Came to Stay* (1943) in his thesis (*PhP*, 555n. 25) and publishing a review, "**Metaphysics and the Novel**" **(1945)**. For her part, Beauvoir published one of the first reviews of ***Phenomenology of Perception***, recognizing it as "not only a remarkable specialist work but a book that is of interest to the whole of man and to every man; the human condition is at stake in this book."[4]

Nevertheless, the break with Sartre was also a break with Beauvoir, and indeed it was she who responded to Merleau-Ponty's critique of Sartre in ***Adventures of the Dialectic*** **(1955)** with her article "**Merleau-Ponty and Pseudo-Sartreanism**," accusing Merleau-Ponty of attacking nothing but a straw man of Sartre.

Behavior

For Merleau-Ponty, behavior "*is not a thing, but neither is it an idea*" (*SB*, 127). As such, it offers a neutral concept with regard to the debate between **empiricism** and **intellectualism**, and reveals the necessity of adopting a phenomenological perspective capable of describing our **pre-thetic consciousness** and lived experience.

Behaviorism

Classically understood through the works of B. F. Skinner and Ivan Pavlov, behaviorism assumes it possible to explain **behavior** through a mechanistic description of externally related events in the animal's body and environment. Merleau-Ponty critiques this theory and its conception of behavior *as* reflex in the first two chapters of *The Structure of Behavior*.

"Being and Having" (1936) [*TD*]

Merleau-Ponty's second article, published in 1936, was a review of **Gabriel Marcel**'s *Being and Having* (1925). Merleau-Ponty introduces an early formulation of his account of embodiment, his critique of Cartesian philosophy, and his understanding of the distinction between **problems versus mysteries**.

Being and Nothingness (1943)[5]

Sartre's magnum opus, which established him as the central figure of **existentialism**. Merleau-Ponty responded critically to Sartre's arguments in several places, including *PhP*, Part Three and VI, Chapter Two.

Being-in-itself/being-for-itself

Appearing in various formulations and in various contexts across Merleau-Ponty's work, the classical distinction between the "in itself" (the world or universe as it exists indifferent to human knowledge or perception) and the "for itself" (the transparent and reflective existence of **consciousness**) structures much of his research. He often identifies the "in itself" with **empiricism**, and the "for itself" with **intellectualism**, and the attempt to synthesize or sustain the two as related opposites with **bad dialectic**. Whether through a philosophy of **ambiguity** or **interrogation**, Merleau-Ponty is constantly attempting to *think* the intertwining of the terms that classical philosophy would prefer to hold distinct. The return to our lived experience as **being-in-the-world** suggests that ontology must be pursued on this side of such extreme categories, as, for example, between the visible and the invisible.

Being-in-the-world [*être au monde*]

The term being-in-the-world is adopted from **Heidegger**'s use of the term in *Being and Time* (1927). Although Merleau-Ponty first adopts the notion when he is less familiar with Heidegger's work, he nonetheless acutely corrects the French translation of the term from *dans le monde* to *au monde*, since the latter is a more rich formulation that resists misunderstanding this as a relation between a container and a contained object. The notion of "being-in-the-world" is an existential one that characterizes the fundamental **ambiguity** of all human experience and phenomena (*PhP*, lxxviii). Our "being-in-the-world" is not a relation between an **objective body** and a consciousness; rather, it is a "pre-objective perspective" that undermines the very distinctions between first person and third person perspectives, and thus represents a genuine intertwining between consciousness and nature (81). It is, in short, the "junction of the 'psychical' and the 'physiological'" accomplished in the ambiguity of **one's own body** (82). The early formulations of "being-in-the-world" foreshadow the ontology of **reversibility**, since this perspective is precisely the place from within Being that I am open to Being, that I am both open toward the world and also *of* the world (*VI*, 134–45).

Bergson, Henri (1859–1941)

French philosopher and writer. Merleau-Ponty's early relation to Bergson is ambivalent. Following his own generation's tendency to dismiss Bergson's philosophy as overly intellectualist, he criticizes Bergson's account of **intuition** (*PhP*, 58–63) and of "**attention to life**" (81, 514n. 23). On the other hand, Merleau-Ponty also pursues a critique of Bergson's realism in relation to the ontology of images in *Matter and Memory* by which consciousness is a structure "cut out" of a larger reality that pre-exists it (*UBS*,

89ff.). By the early 1950s, Merleau-Ponty had come to appreciate a certain **ambiguity** in Bergson's thought, identifying an important philosophy of **expression** in his early writings (*IPP*, 29–33), and a later positive reading of early Bergson in **"Bergson in the Making" (1959)**. Bergson's theory of intuition reappears in Merleau-Ponty's last work alongside the phenomenological intuition of **essences**, where Merleau-Ponty criticizes the attempt to discover a coincidence between fact and essence in immediate experience (*VI*, 122–3).

"Bergson in the Making" (1959) [S]

Bergson's philosophy attempted to establish a middle ground, and was thereby attacked from both sides, yet this did not deter the public and his followers from their reverence for the great thinker. Nevertheless, Merleau-Ponty detects two distinct "Bergsonisms": one that is alive and at work, *in the making*, in the early books, and one that is merely "external" as a generalized philosophy and the source of spiritualism in the later books. This second Bergsonism distorts Bergson, but one should not allow the end of the journey to stamp out the value of the journey that, for that matter, Bergson himself "never renounced" (*S*, 183). Bergson sought not philosophical products, but a genuine contact with things; a true homage to Bergson thus involves showing where he makes this contact, where his life as a philosopher is most alive, and how his trajectory can take us further.

Bergson was, in the strong sense, a *philosopher*. From an insight into the experience of duration as a continual birth that nonetheless remains the same *thanks to* its changing nature, Bergson unfolds an entire ontology. Since I could never perceive time from outside of time, I must *be* time, duration, and thus "absolute knowledge is not a detachment; it is inherence." I am not an "I think," I am a being whose "self-cohesion is also a tearing away from self" (184). Duration is not something I observe, it is what I *am*; any access to Being must be found through time. In *Matter and Memory*, Bergson approaches this intuition in a surprising way by seeking to understand the relation between soul and body, and finds himself again led back to duration, but now in a different light.

The present becomes identified with the body, the past with the mind, and their difference in nature is overcome in their passing into each other through experience. Intuition moves beyond self-coinciding with the inner experience of duration, and leads to the "limits" of experience, "pure perception" without any mind and "pure memory" without any body. This relation is in a being that opens to the present or to space insofar as it "aims at a future and makes use of a past" (185). Thus, perception is a condition of a meaningful world, and the presence of others is established "when incarnate subjects mutually perceive one another—that is, when their perceptual fields cut across and envelop one another and they each see one another in the process of perceiving the same world" (186). Such an intuition is, for Merleau-Ponty, a deep recognition that the universal of philosophy must rest on the "mystery of perception," and perceptual life is associated with the unity of a gesture. These fundamental insights are as far from a return to a pure "inner" landscape as Merleau-Ponty's own **phenomenology**.

Yet Bergson himself fails to sustain this contact with lived experience. For instance, he fails to follow **Péguy**, who shows how events emerge through an intertwining, a duration, in a trajectory that is always "different and the same" in its movement toward a fulfillment that is never predictable and yet never merely the result of juxtaposed events (187). Or again, in Bergson's *Two Sources* Merleau-Ponty senses that the earlier "relations of implication" have been subtly re-articulated as categories "of a clear delimitation" (188). The salve for the vertigo of nothingness is no longer a fusion with "creative evolution," but rather an attainment of a "semi-divine" state; that is, becoming a mystic and not a philosopher (188–9). "It would have been nice," then, if Bergson had not converted and had remained true to the rich directions of his thought (191).

Binswanger, Ludwig (1881–1966)

Swiss psychiatrist and writer who adapted many of **Heidegger**'s insights into his psychotherapy. Merleau-Ponty was influenced by Binswanger in *Phenomenology of Perception*.

Body

Merleau-Ponty's insistence that philosophy must return to embodied and lived experience begins through his analysis of the *living body* in *The Structure of Behavior*, but becomes central in *Phenomenology of Perception*. Adopting a formulation from **Marcel**, Merleau-Ponty asserts that my body is not a mere physical object in the world, or the simple vehicle for my consciousness; rather, "I *am* my body" (*PhP*, 151). As a result, the body is a natural subject and expresses the existential **dimensions** of my being-in-the-world. The body is "always something other than what it is: always **sexuality** at the same time as freedom, always rooted in nature at the very moment it is transformed by culture; it is never self-enclosed but never transcended" (205). This description foreshadows Merleau-Ponty own philosophical development, since the body remains present in all of his further studies including art, language, politics, and history—never self-enclosed as the *cause* of these phenomena, but never transcended either. In his late phenomenologically inspired ontology, the body remains central through the functions of **reversibility** and **touching/touched**, as the *exemplar sensible* that accomplishes and clarifies the intertwining of the in-itself and the for-itself (*VI*, 135). See also **one's own body**.

Body schema (image) [*schéma corporel*]

The term "body schema" is a difficult term to situate historically and conceptually. It is meant to indicate the non-explicit awareness one has of the position, posture, and capabilities of **one's own body**. Regardless of the physical complexity of a gesture such as reaching, I do not need to first explicitly identify the starting point of my hand, elbow, and hip. As soon as I form the intention, my body gathers itself up toward the task at hand (*PhP*, 103). The body schema provides the implicit knowledge that I must have in order to complete any such task. For Merleau-Ponty, the body schema expresses not just our current position, but encompasses our lived possibilities such that it expresses our habits and our style of **being-in-the-world**. Merleau-Ponty develops the notion beginning from early neurological studies by **Head**, **Lhermitte**, and **Schilder**. The translation question between "body schema" and "body image" is delicate. Lhermitte used *"l'image de notre corps"* ("body image"). Schilder used *das Körperschema* ("body schema") in German and "body image" when he wrote in English. Merleau-Ponty writes *schéma corporel* in French, which resists any misconception of this as a notion of representation.

Bréhier, Émile (1876–1952)

French philosopher specializing in the history of philosophy. Bréhier was Merleau-Ponty's supervisor for his doctoral thesis, **Phenomenology of Perception**. Bréhier's questions to Merleau-Ponty in *Primacy of Perception* reveal his historical approach and some tension between the two thinkers (*PrP*, 27–31).

Brunschvicg, Léon (1869–1944)

Influential French philosopher of Kantian idealism at the Sorbonne, and a teacher of Merleau-Ponty's at the *ENS* between 1926 and 1930. Brunschvicg's philosophy is identified by Merleau-Ponty as one of the key sources of his generation's understanding of Kant and **Descartes**, and the general method of **intellectualism** and **reflective analysis** by which philosophy was to turn inward toward the pure and constituting structures of the mind. Despite Merleau-Ponty's personal reverence for his "extraordinary personal qualities" (*TD*, 130), much of Merleau-Ponty's critique of intellectualism can be understood as a response to Brunschvicg and the transcendental idealism he represented.

Cassirer, Ernst (1874–1945)

German philosopher of both the natural sciences and the human sciences. Merleau-Ponty was influenced by Cassirer's *The Philosophy of Symbolic Forms* and its discussion of the **Schneider case**. Despite some significant sympathy, Merleau-Ponty ultimately critiques Cassirer for remaining within the confines of **intellectualism** (*PhP*, 521–2n. 67).

Categorial attitude

Gelb and **Goldstein** draw a distinction between the "categorial attitude" and the "concrete attitude." A concrete attitude is when a person attends to the individual or particular qualities of a perceptual experience, and the categorial attitude is when a person experiences some perceptual object according to the category, **essence**, or *eidos* to which it belongs. Normal subjects move freely between the two attitudes depending upon the task at hand. Yet patients with brain lesions are often incapable of adopting a categorial attitude, thereby suggesting that they live in world much like the one described by **empiricism** in which sensuous givens are experienced only concretely and never according to the sense or essence of an event or object. In *The Structure of Behavior*, Merleau-Ponty identifies the importance of this attitude in rethinking the notion of higher-level **behavior** (*SB*, 64–7). The pathological case demonstrates that normal perception is not what is *observed* or recorded by the sense organs, but rather what is *understood* by the organism within its milieu. As such, normal behavior is not a sum of isolated pathological behaviors properly organized, but is rather *qualitatively* different (65). The concept is also important in *Phenomenology of Perception*, where Merleau-Ponty discusses it in relation to speech. When the patient is unable to adopt the categorial attitude required for a linguistic task (such as sorting colors according to a name such as "blue" or "pale"), this indicates not just a breakdown of the mental process (intellectualist interpretation), but a structural alteration in the existential configuration of their world. The colors, for instance, simply no longer appear to *go together* (*PhP*, Part One, Chapter Six).

Cézanne, Paul (1839–1906)

Post-Impressionist French painter, known for his use of color and his studies of nature. Cézanne's paintings offer Merleau-Ponty a visual example of his own understanding of **expression** and phenomenological inquiry. In *Phenomenology of Perception*, Merleau-Ponty associates the "painstaking" work of **phenomenology** with the expressive practice of Balzac, **Proust**, **Valéry**, and Cézanne (*PhP*, lxxxv), characterized as an unwavering demand to return to lived experience and the birth of meaning. Indeed, Cézanne's expressive practice becomes the focus of Merleau-Ponty's first essay on **painting**, "Cézanne's Doubt." In the preface to *Sense and Non-Sense*, Merleau-Ponty writes that Cézanne provides an example for the precarity of every attempt at expression, "like a step taken in the fog—no one can say where, if anywhere, it will lead" (*SNS*, 3).

"Cézanne's Doubt" (1945) [*SNS, MPAR*]

Merleau-Ponty's first explicit essay on **painting** develops his phenomenological thought through the concepts of **expression** and **situated freedom**. The primary focus is **Cézanne**, with a concluding section discussing Leonardo da Vinci in relation to **Freud** and **Valéry**. Merleau-Ponty is not concerned with Cézanne's place in the history of painting or with Cézanne's own explicit intentions, but rather with Cézanne's practice as the attempt to capture the pre-**thetic** experience of the world. In short, Merleau-Ponty sees Cézanne as enacting a *phenomenology in painting*.

I. A phenomenological description of Cézanne's practice opens the essay as a way of resisting two reductive interpretations of his work. On the one hand, Merleau-Ponty resists the temptation to explain the meaning of the paintings through Cézanne's personality and life, for this would fail to give the positive side of his expression. Cézanne's life is not *irrelevant* to the interpretation, but "[t]he meaning [*sens*] of his work cannot be determined from his life" (*MPAR*, 61). On the other hand, Merleau-Ponty denies that the meaning of Cézanne's work is exhausted by placing it into the movement of art history. Not only is his place in art history somewhat **ambiguous**, his practice itself challenges the very structures of classical thought that are represented in the dichotomies of art history as told from the perspective of a *pensée de survol*. His use of perspective is neither simply an objective error nor a shift to subjective experience, but the attempt to respond to the "chaos of sensation" prior to the objective world of intellectual **judgment**. Thus, Cézanne expresses a pre-reflective knowledge of lived experience in which distortions and contradictions exist without rupturing our contact with the world. As such, Cézanne's efforts constitute a fundamental challenge to objective thought by remaining committed to our lived perspective. Cézanne, much in the manner of **Gestalt psychology**, attempts to capture an "emerging order" that nevertheless is "organizing itself before our eyes" (65). This is why he must remain committed to the color rather than the line, since the color is of lived experience and the line is an intellectual construct. Each stroke is a part of a whole, and thus must contain the whole through its meaningful horizons. Of course, this reveals that "[e]xpressing what *exists* is an endless task" (65–6). Like **phenomenology**, Cézanne's paintings "suspend" the natural "habits of thought" in order to disclose the lived world beneath the categories of objective or classical thought (67).

II. Turning more directly to the paradoxical structures of expression, Merleau-Ponty is careful to emphasize that expression is not a simple "subjective" experience as opposed to **science**. Science and tradition underlie each of Cézanne's strokes, just as the rules of a game weigh upon each player's gestures without being explicitly held in mind. Expression is both passive and active, weighed upon and yet open. The painter is besieged by a feeling of wonder or strangeness and draws together her skill and her experience in order to capture this passing moment and bring it to expression, making it available for all of those with eyes to see. Art is about neither truth nor pleasure; art *is expression*, the paradoxical taking up of the past toward a future in a response to that which only exists after the expression. For Merleau-Ponty, "'conception' cannot precede 'execution.'" The artist is struck by a "vague fever," but this fever is not the *content* to be expressed: "only the completed work itself [...] will prove that there was *something* rather than *nothing* to be found there" (69).

This raises the question of the relation between expression and communication, which can no longer be the simple invoking in others of ideas that pre-exist the expression. Merleau-Ponty suggests that the material traces of my expressive activity have the power to awaken the ***sense*** of the expression for another person with a body and language similar to my own. The reader or viewer is "guided by the con-fused clarity of style," by which she intentionally gears into the expressive movement recorded in the text. The artwork, once it is spoken and heard, "will dwell undivided in several minds, with a claim on every possible mind like a perennial acquisition" (70). This is not, however, to say that each person possesses the same idea, but rather that each feels the weight of a shared cultural acquisition that solicits further expression though its *sense*. The life of the artist can be understood not as determining the expression, but as "the text which nature and history gave him [or her] to decipher" (70). There is neither a total determinism nor a total freedom; artistic expression takes up the given and responds to what it will mean in the future. In short, "freedom dawns in us without breaking our bonds with the world" (72).

III. The conclusion of the essay considers the relationship between freedom and determinism through two competing interpretations of Leonardo da Vinci. **Valéry** suggests that Leonardo is an example of a pure intellect possessed of a pure freedom, an "intellectual power" in complete mastery and freedom (72). Yet **Freud**'s study of Leonardo's "Saint Anne, the Virgin, and Child" suggests that even for Leonardo there is an enigma haunting this supposedly "transparent consciousness" (73). Although he does not endorse Freud's interpretation, Merleau-Ponty agrees that *something* of Leonardo's past is always expressed in his paintings and his practice, and that even the "pure" freedom of Leonardo's highest flights of knowledge and creation are related to the influences of his "personal history" (74). Yet this weight of the past is not, for Merleau-Ponty, a determinism. The error is to take the psychological history as a *cause* rather than a *motivation*. Leonardo's life or his works are not the necessary outcome of his past, they are responses to that past that take it up and capture its *sense* toward further expressions.

Chiasm

The term derives from the Greek letter *chi* ("*x*") and indicates an intertwining or a crossing-over relation or arrangement. This is often employed to describe a rhetorical structure or to describe the crisscrossing structures of nerves in the brain. Merleau-Ponty uses the term in his late ontology as a manner of capturing his understanding of **flesh** and the **reversibility** of **touching/touched** or of the visible and the invisible.

Child Psychology and Pedagogy: The Sorbonne Lectures (1949–52) [CPP]

It was not without some surprise that the philosopher of *Phenomenology of Perception* and the political editor of *Les Temps modernes* was offered a post at the Sorbonne as Professor of Child Psychology and Pedagogy in 1949. Even his first book, which focused extensively on psychology, only rarely discussed child psychology, and always with an eye toward the overall philosophical aims of that text. Nevertheless, the task of teaching this material helped Merleau-Ponty become conversant with a variety of new sources, perhaps most notably his newfound appreciation of **Saussure** and **structuralism**. These courses survive thanks to an established practice of publishing approved student notes from the lectures in the *Bulletin de psychologie*. After Merleau-Ponty's death, the courses were collected together and published as a single volume. Although the content is shaped by Merleau-Ponty's pedagogical duties of preparing students for exams toward their degrees in psychology, he nevertheless furthers his study of **Gestalt psychology** (now with an emphasis on child perception), **psychoanalysis**, and **structuralism**.

Consciousness and Language Acquisition (1949–50)

In the opening lines of this lecture, Merleau-Ponty asserts that "the problem of language is situated between philosophy and psychology" (3). Language is not an external accompaniment of thought, as established through **phenomenology** and **Gestalt psychology**, and thus he adopts a "phenomenological method" in order to "give an interior sense to the facts themselves" (7). Through the study of the development of language in children, he emphasizes that a relation with others is always implicit in these phenomena. Moreover, language solicits the child as a whole thanks to the child's immersion in the linguistic environment even prior to speaking. Once language appears, it proceeds in a discontinuous development, and Merleau-Ponty discusses here the work of **Piaget** on the stages of language. Shifting to the philosophical level of offering an account for this phenomenon, Merleau-Ponty suggests that both **intellectualism** and **empiricism** are insufficient. Rather, as **Gestalt psychology** would say, the child moves through successive appropriations of new structures, and these appropriations are not accomplished through an intellectual activity or a passive imitation of others. After an extended critique of Jakobson and Guillaume (14–26), Merleau-Ponty offers a phenomenological approach through the work of **Husserl** and **Scheler** on the problem of **others** (26–33).

Rejecting Piaget's manner of defining all stages negatively and as incomplete in comparison to adult consciousness, Merleau-Ponty turns to the role of pathology in understanding normal experience. Following **Minkowski**, he emphasizes that pathological experience is never *absolutely* other to normal experience, but forever upon its horizon. The same, then, would be true for childhood experience in relation to adult experience, and this holds for hallucination, **aphasia, the phantom limb,** and breakdowns in the **categorial function** of language (41–50). The course concludes with a shift to **structuralism** in linguistics, and attempts to pose the question of the origin of language. Nevertheless, linguistics treats language as an object, emphasizing structures of which speakers are wholly unaware, and this appears to institute a *pensée de survol* that Merleau-Ponty wants to avoid. Structuralism requires a phenomenological grounding that will return to the lived experience of speaking. Since "[a] language is an ideal that is sought, a reality in [potentiality], a future that never arrives" (60), **Saussure**'s approach makes possible a return to the paradoxical logic of **expression**.

The Adult's View of the Child (1949–50)

Beginning with a philosophical reflection on the relation between child psychology (as a science) and pedagogy (as a practice or ethics), Merleau-Ponty insists that "the child" does not exist first in a pure state to be discovered by science; rather, the child becomes what he or she is through his or her relation with the adult in an evolving situation "where envelopment is reciprocal"

(69). As such, child psychology, pedagogy, and morality must be pursued as mutually intertwining disciplines with different points of entry. Yet, what emerges in this course is a discussion of both psychoanalysis and historical materialism. The course introduces a distinction between a "narrow sense" of psychoanalysis (early **Freud**) in which **behavior** is *reduced* to its **unconscious** sexual content stemming from childhood, and a "broad sense" (later Freud) where "infantile prehistory" itself is not a fixed object in the unconsciousness, where the notion of unconsciousness (as a thing) becomes replaced by something like **ambivalence**, and where **sexuality** is taken much more broadly as "affective investment" (73–4). Just as Freud's broader approach offers incontestable descriptions of human attachments, **Marxism** clarifies how "economic phenomena have human significance" (77). The error is to believe that such significance amounts to a *causality*. With these two "broad" methodologies on the table, Merleau-Ponty turns to consider the concrete situation of the child in the familial milieu and contemporary society, before turning to historical and contemporary understandings of child pedagogy. The course briefly considers several notions from **Lacan**, including the "mirror stage" as well as his structural understanding of "complexes" (84ff.). The course concludes with several long expositions of "Work in Cultural Sociology" and research in "Sociometry," both preceded by bibliographical notes for the texts to be explicated.

Structure and Conflicts in Child Consciousness (1949–50)

For Merleau-Ponty, child consciousness is a genuine *structure*, and not a deficient example of adult consciousness (contra **Piaget**). Nevertheless, child consciousness is not utterly closed off from normal experience. Communication is possible across structural differences, although this will never be a transparent or complete communication. For instance, child drawings should not be viewed as poor approximations of adult drawings, but rather as different modes of expression of a different world. By the notion of "conflicts," Merleau-Ponty aims to understand consciousness not according to identifiable stages, but according to an unfolding and contested development—the child's behavior develops not simply through causal mechanisms and physicochemical properties, but "out of a **communion** with the environment" (140). Turning his attention to the "child's lived experience" of perception, Merleau-Ponty attempts to demonstrate the direct experience of a child before it is "systematized by language and thought" (141). Weighing several competing interpretations, he discusses how children's drawings relate to society and to their perceptual experience (165–76). He adopts **Wallon's** concept of "**ultra-things**," namely things that remain active in child experience even though they do not adhere to spatial or temporal laws. Merleau-Ponty ventures that despite its repression of them, even adult experience is haunted by these "ultra-things" (the sky, one's own birth, etc.) (192–3). As such, the child's world remains on the horizon of the adult world, and nurturing this understanding presents the possibility for a more genuine relation and communication.

Child Psycho-Sociology (1950–1)

In contrast to traditional approaches, **Gestalt psychology** offers a way of establishing that *development* is neither mechanistic (through accumulation) nor idealistic (as an existential leap to a pure Ego), but rather a trajectory of new structures that proceeds in a motivated way. This conception also found in "certain psychoanalysts" who recognize a reciprocal relation between libido (internal) and the parental milieu (external) (198). After a critical reading of **Piaget** (198–208), Merleau-Ponty explores how **Gestalt theory** might move from perception to intelligence (209–19). Turning to Marxism and psychoanalysis as two complementary theories of "development," Merleau-Ponty suggests they are able to understand development as an expressive taking up of the past toward an open future. Human development has "a certain order and a certain sense" (222) that moves according to a progressive *restructuring* in a non-continuous *and* non-discontinuous movement, paradigmatically represented in the trajectory of puberty (223–8). The course concludes with a focus on the relationship between psychology and sociology in child development, offering some critique of Freud's attempts in this direction. Merleau-Ponty offers a positive analysis of the collaborative approach by **Mauss** or the hybrid psycho-social studies of **Lévi-Strauss**.

The Child's Relations with Others (1950–1)[6]

This course marks an important shift away from the child's relation to nature through perception and language to the child's relation to others: "parents, brothers and sisters, other children, and even, if there is time, with his school environment, his social class, and, in general, his relation to culture" (*PrP*, 97). This is not, however, simply a shift from the "infrastructure" of child consciousness to the child's "**affectivity**." Indeed, perceptual experience and linguistic development are both profoundly influenced by the child's relations with others and his or her affective situation within the human world (100).

Merleau-Ponty introduces Melanie Klein's distinction between **ambiguity** and **ambivalence**. Ambivalence is a form of perceptual rigidity (each representation must entail a *different* object), whereas ambiguity is a form of perceptual liberalism that embraces a mature response to the fact that "[t]he entire world is ambiguous" (*CPP*, 244). This suggests an **expressive** relation between psychology, perception, and social structures. Or again, the learning of language occurs thanks to affectivity with the parents, and this involves a "lived *decentration*" more than an intellectual operation (245). Stressing the role of *preconscious* experience and the lived and embodied phenomenon of imitation, Merleau-Ponty suggests that Lacan's work is ultimately more promising than Wallon's, since Wallon seems committed to understanding development in the context of a "work of consciousness" (254).

Turning his attention to psychoanalysis (Freud, Klein, and Anna Freud), Merleau-Ponty considers whether their approach reveals some insight into the lived intertwining between the present and the past (262–300). The final section explores the important relationship between the child and the parents as a first step toward the child's relation to others, society, and culture. In fact, parents "communicate" not only their personal influence, but also the very culture in which they raise the child, and social initiation is thus "accomplished by the intermediary of parental influence" (302). As such, rather than being in an external relation, "psychological and social" factors "**encroach** upon each other" (303). The psychical and the social are in a relation of **expression** insofar as neither can be considered *causally* determined.

Human Sciences and Phenomenology (1950–2)[7]

The course begins with a reflection on Husserl's account of the "crisis" whereby the human sciences (psychology, sociology, and history) were adopting the attitude that external structures and causal relations were fully explanatory of the phenomena in questions, an attitude named **psychologism, sociologism,** and **historicism**. In practice, this commitment ultimately undermines the human sciences themselves, since the claims of the human scientist must also be reduced to external causes. Indeed, philosophy too needs some solid foundation in order to assure itself that it is not merely the effect of contingent and accidental causes. The opposite of this position, **logicism**, posits the existence of a realm of truths in themselves capable of resisting the skepticism of psychologism. Husserl's aim was to place the very possibility of **science**, the human sciences, and philosophy upon the solid foundation of the **phenomenological reduction**. Such would be a philosophy situated within time and the world, and in communication with others (*CPP*, 319–20).

Yet the relations between the human sciences and **phenomenology** remain marked by misunderstandings. For instance, Husserl rejected **Gestalt psychology** because he believed all psychologies tend to *naturalize* consciousness. And yet with his own "eidetic psychology," there is an important convergence between Husserl and the Gestaltists. The same is true with regard to linguistics. As Merleau-Ponty suggests, following Pos, although early Husserl focused on a "universal grammar," his later works return to the experience of the speaking subject, which converges with the best of **structuralism**. This convergence is made possible by Husserl's development beyond **transcendental phenomenology** toward **genetic phenomenology**. On Merleau-Ponty's reading, **Heidegger** and **Scheler** *oppose* the ontological to the ontic, whereas Husserl explores "the secret connections between these two orders" (337).

As the course notes make clear, Merleau-Ponty seeks to identify the "diffuse" influence of phenomenology in contemporary psychology such as in **Jaspers, Binswanger,** and **Minkowski** (318). Although psychology essentially abandoned any appeal to philosophy for insight or clarification, some areas of psychology had begun questioning the presuppositions behind its realist ontology, such as in **Gestalt psychology**. The conclusion is clear: contemporary psychology requires the methods and concepts of phenomenology, and vice versa. Nevertheless, the course ends without Merleau-Ponty having fulfilled the promise to "define a compatible psychology and philosophy" (337).

Methods in Child Psychology (1951-2)

The study of child psychology presents some significant difficulties. Not only is the object of study alien (since the researchers are adults), but also the very act of observation influences the object of study. Like primitive consciousness, pathological consciousness, or the "psychology of women" (373), there are structural difference between the object of research and the researcher. The key is to avoid assuming oneself as the "norm" and the other as failing to reach this norm. To the attitude of treating women as somehow not quite reaching human (masculine) ideals, Merleau-Ponty sardonically responds that women and their experience deserve "neither this excessive honor nor this debasement" (374). Between adult and child, this tendency is even more prevalent. To understand a structurally other consciousness, one must initiate a communication through shared horizons of experience (377).

This leads Merleau-Ponty to posit a general principle for child psychology: "we have to reconstitute an interpersonal dynamic rather than simply arrange various characteristics of an infantile 'nature'" (381). Children must not be observed in laboratories and outside of their lived experience, and the researcher must seek to ask questions that connect to this experience. The researcher must gear the research to the structures of the child's experience, such as when Wallon posits "**ultra things**" (384). Or again, Mead is able to establish that masculinity and femininity can only be understood through "interpersonal relations," thereby moving psychoanalysis beyond the more traditional divisions that appear in Freud. One must find open concepts that can capture the nuance and complexity of inter-human relations. Finally, the study of puberty requires a nuanced notion of "development" as a meaningful process rather than as a set of isolated stages. Taking up the work of Deutsch (398–407), Merleau-Ponty echoes his understanding of movement in psychoanalysis and Marxism, rejecting any approach that would offer either a purely psychological account or a purely corporeal account. Development, he argues, "*is neither causal nor final*" (406). Rather, it follows a paradoxically "contingent order," which nevertheless surges forth in a certain direction: "for the individual always accomplishes a decisive act of development in a particular corporeal field" (407).

The Experience of Others (1951–2)

The problem of **others** is a relatively recent question because in an absolute and consistent empiricism, the other is radically unknowable, whereas for a purely "reflexive" philosophy, pure minds are absolutely self-coincident and exist beyond the world of experience. On both accounts, the question of *the experience* of others is essentially meaningless, even if they often talk about the *knowledge* of others. For Husserl and phenomenology, "there is a problem of the other," at least once we have embraced the notion of an "incarnate mind" (434). It is only "in the world that we have the chance to have an experience of the other" (435). How, then, can we conceive of a world in which others are possible? For Merleau-Ponty, we "must think about the inherent paradoxes of this world, in particular [the paradoxes] of the other" (436).

In fact, lived perception includes more than the isolated objects perceived; the objects are "encircled by an interior and exterior **horizon**" (437). Perception is thus a lived synthesis of the thing as "a system of experiences" articulated according to my possible movements. Or again, the *sense* of the world is primary and results from the relationship of our embodied **being-in-the-world**, while signification (as an intellectual relation to a realm of meaning) comes only later. Our experience of things "helps us thereby understand how there can be a perception of the other" (437). Or consider **painting**, where the painter is not discovering the world, but *creating* it, and his or her own *openness to it*, at the same time (438). Thus, the history of art or expression must avoid two dangers: reducing the movement of **history** to the predetermined plan of a World Spirit, or reducing the history of expression to a random and chaotic progression (439). Painting moves in response to a problem that is "felt vaguely as an unresolved situation," and the *sense* of its movement involves a certain lived logic or rationality, a temporal taking up toward the future that is neither comprehended in advance nor simply chaotic (440).

Thus, the problem of the other is not different in kind from the problem of lived perception itself. Just as when we see a "cube" thanks to the rich horizons of perceptual experience, from the moment we perceive a *behavior* in the strong sense (or the trace of a behavior in the painting), we are oriented toward the other through a phenomenal "direct contact" (441). Following Diderot, Merleau-Ponty invokes the manner in which actors express through what might seem like magical relations. The *sense* of their gestures emerges neither from an explicit intellectual act, nor from some accidental juxtaposition; rather, "the expressed and the expression are reciprocal and indiscernible" and, in the case of a play, each performance is a "re-creation" (450). In developing a character, an actor begins with an intellectual understanding of the role, followed by a "concrete construction" by which the role is *performed*, much like learning a **habit**. And yet, at the second stage "everything remains to be done," since all the insights have to be taken up and reshaped into a *style* of which "only the performance counts" (452). Dramatic "magic" is no more mysterious than is the "magic" by which the body snaps into shape when acquiring a new habit—both are "existential operations." And indeed, it is precisely in the presence of another creating a role that I am struck by the presence of another person: "The perception of others is that of a freedom that takes place through a situation and, at the same time, transforms that situation" (456).

"Christianity and *Ressentiment*" (1935) [TD]

Merleau-Ponty's first published article, a review of **Scheler**'s book *Ressentiment*, offers a defense and development of Nietzsche's understanding of *ressentiment* in *Genealogy of Morals* and a discussion of how Christianity might resist Nietzsche's attributions of "slave morality." Merleau-Ponty emphasizes Scheler's notion of **intentionality** through the discussion of "oriented acts," as well as Scheler's identification of a class of intentional acts (such as sympathy or love) that cannot be described in isolation from their objects.

Classical philosophy/objective thought

These categories are used by Merleau-Ponty to refer, most generally, to pre-phenomenological philosophies involved in the debate between **empiricism** and **intellectualism**.

Claudel, Paul (1868–1955)

French literary, political, and religious figure. Claudel figures in an important way in Merleau-Ponty's work on "Temporality" (*PhP* 409, 432, 453–4), and in *The Visible and the Invisible* (*VI*, 103, 121).

Cogito

Latin for "thinking," this term is often used as shorthand for either **Descartes'** classic formulation "I think, therefore I am" and the argument that supports this statement from *Meditations*; or it is used simply to refer to the Cartesian mind or thinking thing, for the "I think." This conception of thought as ultimately self-transparent and singular is the primary source of the philosophy of **intellectualism**. For Merleau-Ponty, a return to lived experience and **being-in-the-world** necessitates a *new cogito*, and he begins to sketch this in Part Three of *Phenomenology of Perception*. He argues that Descartes' *cogito*, a spoken or articulated *cogito*, presupposes a tacit *cogito* that is situated and understood as a **project of the world**, and as always overflowing any attempt at reflection. Shifting away from this Cartesian vocabulary, Merleau-Ponty will prefer in his later works to speak of unreflected experience as **wild Being** to avoid any threat of a philosophy of consciousness undermining his phenomenologically inspired ontology.

Coherent deformation

Initially adopted from **Malraux** in the context of creative **expression**, Merleau-Ponty deploys the notion in various contexts. An expression is creative insofar as it takes up the available means of expression (the constituted language) and expresses something by introducing into the field a coherent deformation that will reshape the constituted language. This is at once the possibility for communication and what precludes any pure and transparent communication. See particularly "Indirect Language and the Voices of Silence."

Collège de France (est. 1530)

The *Collège de France* is one of the pre-eminent research institutions in France. Structured according to research chairs in various disciplines, whenever a chair becomes vacant, a new professor is appointed by the current members. The members have the power to rename the chair in order to promote the latest research directions. Members are given institutional support, and in return they must offer free and open public lectures on their current research. The institution does not grant degrees, but houses important laboratories and library collections, and runs international conferences and specialized courses.

In 1952, Merleau-Ponty became the youngest member elected to the Chair of Philosophy[8] and his "Inaugural Address" was published as *In Praise of Philosophy*. In the opening lines he offers the following characterization of the institution itself: "Since its foundation the *Collège de France* has been charged with the duty, not of giving to its hearers already-acquired truths, but the idea of free investigation" (*IPP*, 3). Between 1952 and his sudden death in 1961, Merleau-Ponty carried on just that, "free investigation." Much of what we know of his late philosophy comes from the surviving course summaries, lecture materials, and working notes from his time at the Collège.

The Collège de France Lectures (1952–61) [*IPP*]

At the *Collège de France*, Merleau-Ponty regularly offered two courses per academic year, although he merged his courses between 1956 and 1958 when lecturing on the concept of nature. One course was generally the "principle" course, focusing on ongoing research (usually his Thursday course), and the other was to offer summaries of research or commentaries on texts. From his preparation, Merleau-Ponty clearly took both of his courses very seriously. Given the nature of his death and the incomplete status of his late research, the traces of these lectures have taken on an important weight in Merleau-Ponty studies. The first source is Merleau-Ponty's own brief "summaries" composed and published upon the completion of all but the final courses. Second, Merleau-Ponty's papers contained extensive lecture notes, although many remain unpublished and untranslated. Even so, the lecture notes are fragmentary and elusive at best, as Merleau-Ponty improvised his lectures from them rather than reading a precomposed speech. Only rarely have student notes from these lectures been made available (see the lectures on nature below). Despite these difficulties, what we know of these lectures remains an invaluable insight into the directions of his late philosophy.

As a very schematic guide, the early lectures (1952–4) will be illuminating for those reading *The Prose of the World*; the middle lectures (1954–6) for those reading *Adventures of the Dialectic*; and the later lectures (1956–61) for anyone approaching the incomplete work of *The Visible and the Invisible* or the elusive ontological suggestions of "Eye and Mind."

1953

The Sensible World and the World of Expression (Thursday Course)[9] *[IPP]*

Even the title of Merleau-Ponty's first course is a tantalizing suggestion that these lectures were to draw together his earlier work on perception and his emerging work on language and **expression** toward a new philosophy. Rejecting the classical focus on the thinking subject as "as the pure power of bestowing significations and the capacity of absolute survey" or *pensée de survol*, the attempt to return to a **perceptual consciousness** is often dismissed by idealism as a naive return to naturalism (*IPP*, 71). Yet the discovery of perceptual consciousness demands a *new* philosophy, since this form of intentionality does not have any pretense to the absolute self-transparency of explicit consciousness, and the world it intends is an open **field** rather than a mere collection of sensations. When we go from the sensible world to the world of expression, one need not introduce a realm of truth and meaning, since the possibility of expression is already anticipated in the expressive embodiment of lived experience in the perceived world.

Taking movement and the perception of movement as his examples, Merleau-Ponty discussed **Bergson**'s understanding of movement, alongside **Gestalt psychology**. In fact, Merleau-Ponty argues that "perception is already expression" (74). Movement reveals a paradoxical relationship between moving and the presence of the world itself. Through an extensive return to the notion of the **body schema**, these lectures sought to demonstrate how our particular modalities of embodiment make possible the shift from implicit expression to manifest expression, from **motricity** to symbolic gestures. This made possible a discussion of **painting** as indirect expression of movement, since the perception of movement is always a paradoxical question of a force that can be read in the trace of time in space. Film, through its use of montage, would be a similar structure. Finally, Merleau-Ponty suggests that the study of language and expression will reveal a paradoxical relationship between natural expression and cultural expression.

Research on the Literary Use of Language (Monday Course) [*IPP*]

In general, theories of language focus on linguistic structures rather than that experience of speaking or writing. And yet, **constituted language** is derivative of a more originary form of language, constituting language or **expression**. By contrast, writers have not failed to note the "paradoxes that make the writer's craft an exhausting and never-ending task" (81). Invoking the famous book by **Sartre**, Merleau-Ponty suggests that the writer is naturally drawn to the philosophical question "*What is Literature?*" And yet, focusing upon the *practice* of writing rather than explicit claims *about* literature, he singles out the work of **Stendhal** and **Valéry**. For instance, Valéry discovers that in using language its access to truth is solid, whereas upon reflection this solidity is revealed as fleeting, and this forces him to give up the idea that intellectual consciousness is pure and separate from language. Or again, Stendhal's practice is itself "the story of an apprenticeship to speech" (85). Despite his early scientific aspirations for a pure language, when Stendhal gives up attempts at providing a "science of life," he suddenly finds himself "capable of improvisation, conviction, creation" (85). By writing, he learns the inability to distinguish thought and speech, life and expression, and the result is nothing less than "an entirely new art" (85).

1953-4

The Problem of Speech (Thursday Course) [*IPP*]

Merleau-Ponty suggests **Saussure**'s significance is less his identification of the relation between sign and signification and more his radical return to *speech* (87). For Merleau-Ponty, the purpose of the course was to "illustrate and extend the Saussurean conception of speech as a positive and dominating function" (88). The course focused on Jakobson and discusses the child's acquisition of language. Critiquing Jakobson's "classical" commitments, Merleau-Ponty suggests that child psychology moves forward when it adds to Jakobson's emphasis on attention and judgment an important set of affective relations to the environment and others. Yet, "[t]he relations to others, intelligence, and language cannot be set out in a linear and causal series: they belong to those crosscurrents where *someone lives*" (89). Turning to the later work of **Goldstein**, Merleau-Ponty suggests that **Gestalt psychology** of language offers significant insight into the fundamental structures of linguistic experience, an insight that remains to be raised to a philosophical status. Shifting to the writer's practice, Merleau-Ponty suggests that "**Proust**'s Platonism" is not about ideas, but rather a work of language and signs that introduces into language the **coherent deformations** that will allow this new meaning to appear. This is a paradoxical translation of an experience that only properly exists after its translation into language. Thus, the study of speech demands a careful account of the paradoxes of **expression**.

Materials for a Theory of History (Monday Course) [*IPP*]

History cannot be reduced to an unfolding of a transcendent Spirit, nor can it be viewed as a mere juxtaposition of externally related events, and both accounts mistakenly attempt to *explain* history through a causal logic. A genuine theory of history must begin, rather, from an open "**interrogation**" of the expressive processes of convergence and recuperation (96). In fact, for Merleau-Ponty there is no history at all "where the course of events is a series of episodes without unity, or where it is a struggle already decided in the heaven of ideas. History is there where there is a logic *within* contingence, a reason *within* unreason, wherever there is a historical perception" (97–8). History, then, must be practiced as a form of perception and expression. This sketch was, admits Merleau-Ponty, not systematically developed in his course, but rather implied through his reading of **Weber** and **Lukács**. From the summary, it appears these lectures contributed to or reflected Merleau-Ponty's research for *Adventures of the Dialectic* (1955).

1954-5

Institution in Personal and Public History (Thursday Course) [*IPP, IP*]

The definition of **institution** in this course suggests an important shift in Merleau-Ponty's philosophy: "In the concept of institution we are seeking a solution to the difficulties found in the philosophy of **consciousness**" (*IP*, 76). Perhaps the very notion of consciousness precludes a reciprocity between consciousness and its objects, and introduces the fatal distinction between being and nothingness, or the in-itself and the for-itself. The instituting subject can be temporally thick and non-self-transparent, and can sustain a rich relation with others. Moreover, what is "instituted" is potentially shared, and thus can be the engine for **intersubjectivity** and communication as re-creation. "Thus," writes Merleau-Ponty, "the instituted exists between others and myself, between me and myself, like a hinge, the consequence and the guarantee of our belonging to one selfsame world" (76). Depersonalizing the logic of **expression**, the institution is a **coherent deformation** of the past or the present, and an open call or field for a future of creative repetitions.

In the course, Merleau-Ponty identifies four levels of institution. The first takes place at the level of a personal and interpersonal institution (animality and affectivity). On the vital side, Merleau-Ponty considers the development of puberty (21–7), and on the affective side an analysis of **Proust** (28–40). The second level involves the institution of works or of painting and communication more generally, moving through expression toward more "public" forms of institutions. At a third level, language *institutes* the domain of knowledge and the field of culture (50–61). Merleau-Ponty argues that even in the case of knowledge (such as geometry), the institution is not a revelation of a pre-existing truth, but rather the putting to work of a process of **sedimentation** that, by taking up the past toward a future, necessarily leads to a forgetting of origins (51). The institutions are "trans-phenomenal," but not ideal objectivities outside of time and history; they are on the horizons of the phenomenal world. The fourth level is the level of historical institution, and suggests how history itself is an open trajectory with a sense. Yet in order to truly understand the movement of history as an open institution, one must pursue an analysis according to **"interrogation,"** a new form of philosophical methodology developed in Merleau-Ponty's late work. The course ends with a re-assertion of Merleau-Ponty's attempt to bring together **structuralism** and **phenomenology**. "It is," writes Merleau-Ponty, "this development of phenomenology into the metaphysics of history that we wished to pursue here" (79).

The Problem of Passivity: Sleep, Unconsciousness, Memory (Monday Course) [*IPP, IP*]

What is the relationship between **activity and passivity**? Perception seems to require a certain passivity in the perceiving subject in relation to the information coming from the world perceived of which the subject is a part. And yet, the subject is not *merely* inserted in the world, but is also open to that world and somehow sustains its *sense*. By exploring the notions of sleep, of the **unconscious** (a past that remains forever elusive), and memory (the explicit reopening of the past), Merleau-Ponty aims to develop an account of **consciousness** that is essentially neither active and sense-bestowing nor passive and receptive. Rather, consciousness is a certain "divergence" [*écart*] or "variation in an already instituted existential field, which is always behind us and whose weight [...] intervenes up into the actions by which we transform it" (*IP*, 206). Consciousness is thus a trajectory that begins at birth and represents the dialectical interplay between activity and passivity, **institution** and **sedimentation**.

The course begins with an overview of phenomenological accounts of the **body** and of the *Lebenswelt* (117–32) and a brief study of what a phenomenological "ontology" would entail (132–7). Such an ontology must resist the extreme terms of classical ontology (such as the distinction between being and nothingness), and must establish terms such as passivity and activity where passivity "does not render activity impossible" (136). Since consciousness is within the world, it is capable of both "wakefulness and sleep, consciousness and unconsciousness, memory and forgetfulness" (137). Indeed, "to sleep" is not strictly speaking an action, but the event of a withdrawing of consciousness to a "pre-personal relation to the world" (206). Or again, the act of dreaming is also *between* activity and passivity, and Freud's most important contribution is a recognition that there is a creative activity in the dream or in language that involves responding to a rich symbolism that both shapes the expression and is reshaped by it. In terms of memory, the past remains *both* immanent and transcendent, and the act of memory is both active and passive. The body, and not a representational mind, must be recognized as that rich relational structure that remains open to the past through the intentional horizons of the present (209).

1955–6

Dialectical Philosophy (Thursday Course) [*IPP*]

The goal of this course was not to define **dialectical** philosophy, but rather to allow "dialectical thought" to speak for itself in order to identify some common themes. Merleau-Ponty begins by considering dialectical thought that focuses on "contradictories," and he labels this the **bad dialectic** of absolute opposites or of negative relations. For Merleau-Ponty, negation must have a sense of transcendence, which requires a distance that precludes any coincidence. Even a relation to the self must go through the non-self, and hence must be mediated beyond presence. Second, certain dialectical philosophies make the dialectic "subjective" insofar as all that appears must be a response to someone's interrogation. Yet one cannot complete this dialectical relation with the classical concepts of subject and object. Dialectical thought must forever remain in motion as the "simultaneous development and destruction of that which preceded it" (124). The dialectical philosopher is forever starting over and "dialectical thought is an uneasy equilibrium" (125).

Texts and Commentary on the Dialectic (Monday Course) [*IPP*]

The summary of the secondary course for this year is very brief, and suggests that the sessions provided a "free commentary" on various texts that expressed dialectical thought, either explicitly or implicitly. Authors studied included Zeno, Plato (*Parmenides*, *Theaetetus*, *Sophist*), Montaigne and **Descartes** (as implicitly dialectical thinkers). The course ended with a study of the shift from Kant to **Hegel**.

1956-7

The Concept of Nature, I (Monday and Thursday) [*IPP, N*]

Combining his two courses under a single topic, Merleau-Ponty set about a project that he already sensed would last several years: the study of the concept of nature and its place in ontology—not to reduce ontology to a naive "naturalism," but rather to tease out the ontological weight of the unexamined concept of nature in philosophies of history. Thus, the shift to nature is not a break with his philosophical or political projects. In perception or in institution, the "originary relation between man and nature" should not be understood according to an external relation between the in-itself and the for-itself. Rather, all relations emerge in a primordial world that is always already there (*IPP*, 133). Yet this "primordial being" neither engenders itself (*naturans*) nor is engendered by another (*naturata*); it is this paradoxical structure of being created and also creating. As Merleau-Ponty writes, echoing Husserl's discussion of the Earth: "Nature is an enigmatic object, an object that is not an object at all; it is not really set out in front of us. It is our soil [*sol*] [...], that which carries us" (*N*, 4).

This first year of lectures attempts to draw together historical elements of this nuanced account of nature, beginning with **Descartes**' concept of nature. On the dominant Cartesian understanding, nature is the pure product (the *naturata*) of God's creative power (the *naturans*), and the parts of nature are wholly in existence and related to each other through external relations, *partes extra partes* (*IP*, 137). And yet, moving from ontology to our experience, Descartes hesitates over one's body, which resists being categorized as merely an object in the world (*N*, 15). Or again, Kant defines nature as the "sum of meaningful objects," and hence the only nature we can speak of is nature *for us*. It seems that nature is noumenal, and yet constructed according to a human conception. The *Critique of Judgment* attempts to reconnect "receptivity and spontaneity," but it fails account for the "resistance of a Nature [...], the residue that we cannot eliminate [...], the romantic idea of a savage Nature" (23, 35). Turning to the Romantic approach of Schelling (and **Bergson**), Merleau-Ponty discovers a reciprocal relation between humans and nature. "We are the parents of a Nature of which we are also the children" (43). Yet Bergson's positivism and, reciprocally, **Sartre**'s philosophy of nothingness ultimately fail to provide a space for a genuine account of nature. Turning to **Husserl**, Merleau-Ponty recognizes a tension between nature as the "pure correlate of consciousness" (*IP*, 151) versus nature in relation to the **"I can"** that requires a natural stratum in which the "body is both object and subject" (*N*, 75). Husserl's analyses reveal relations to ***quasi-objects*** such as "the Earth," since the "earth" is neither an object of perception nor alien to our perception, it must be understood as the "soil of our experience" (*N*, 77).

Turning his attention to **science**, Merleau-Ponty asserts that the philosopher's role is not to intervene in internal debates or empirical questions, but to respond to those moments when scientists must employ a language by which "they cross over into philosophy" (153). The philosopher aims, then, to make explicit the ontological commitments of the scientist's practice (cf., N, 84–7). The role of reflection on science is to provoke philosophy to new conceptions, and to clarify to science the underlying presuppositions that structure their very practice. Merleau-Ponty concludes, "[t]he perceptual field offers us the first model of Being, with which science works in order to give an articulated vision of Being" (N, 105). The first year ends with a careful reconstruction of Alfred North Whitehead's understanding of nature as "process" (N, 113–22), insofar as nature is temporal and only ever appears in manifestations which, nonetheless, do not exhaust its being. Indeed, nature and history bear striking resemblance in these descriptions.

1957–8

The Concept of Nature, II: Animality, The Human Body, Passage to Culture (Wednesday and Thursday Course) [*IPP*, *N*]

The schism between **empiricism** and **intellectualism** results in a situation in which "naturalism," "humanism," and "theism" "have lost all clear meaning in our culture, and they cease-lessly pass into one another" (N, 135). Focusing this year on the biological sciences, Merleau-Ponty returns to the question of **behavior**. Several writers seem to be moving toward an "operational" or expressive notion of behavior that is neither mechanical nor spontaneous. Yet the life sciences fail to transcend the classical concepts that undermine the richness of their account (*IPP*, 162; N, 158). Targeting the influence of cybernetics upon these sciences, Merleau-Ponty again militates against such a reductive account of language to a code (N, 163–6).

In terms of the "different levels of behavior," Merleau-Ponty critiques **Uexküll**'s account of the *Umwelt* (milieu) and the being of the "natural subject," arguing that the animal is not related to the exterior world in terms of a causal structure. The *Umwelt* is present to the animal, but not thematized as a goal or idea; it is "a theme that haunts consciousness." This reveals an inextricable intertwining between mind and body, consciousness and nature, such that we "no longer see where behavior begins and where mind ends" (*N*, 178). Merleau-Ponty sketches the need for a third way between the "ultra-mechanism or ultra-finalism" that seems to emerge from the Neo-Darwinian approaches discussed. In organisms and communities, we find "dynamic, unstable equilibria in which every rearrangement resumes already latent activities and transfigures them by decentering them" (*IPP*, 165). In short, it seems one finds an expressive process of institution, and this leads Merleau-Ponty in the direction of embryology, ontogenesis, and the "possible" as a real "ingredient of the existing world itself, as *general reality*" (166).

1958-9

The Possibility of Philosophy (or Philosophy Today, or Philosophy as Interrogation) [*IPP, NC*]

Postponing the course on nature due to a teaching reduction related to his initial writing of *The Visible and the Invisible*, Merleau-Ponty dedicated his shortened course to "the meaning [*sens*] of this inquiry [on nature] and the question of the possibility of philosophy today" (*IPP*, 167). Indeed, what becomes of classical ontology? Is this an "end" of metaphysics, or a revitalization of it? Is philosophy after Hegel genuinely a "non-philosophy," and what is philosophy today after Nietzsche, Kierkegaard, and Marx? As Merleau-Ponty writes, "we involve them in our own problems rather than solving theirs with ours" (169). Their answers are "too simple" because their problems are not our own. Nevertheless, they provide the example of a "pure **interrogation**," and thus although their non-philosophy cannot become our own metaphysics, their example serves to orient a creative taking up of our own situation of "crisis." Despite advances, modern thought in general remains mired between an "extreme naturalism" and an "extreme artificialism" that seems to allow no exchange, let alone any synthesis. In the expressive arts (literature, painting, music) and in **psychoanalysis**, one detects a way out of the crisis through a genuine openness to "the plurality of possibilities" (172).

But what is philosophy today in the face of this crisis? For Merleau-Ponty, it is phenomenology, and this course begins with Husserl's evolution from **transcendental phenomenology** to an authentic "philosophy of interrogation" (173). Husserl's research led him to the Other, to the "world, to time, to nature, to contemporary and living history" as a way of completing the aspirations of philosophy that had been blocked by philosophy's own presuppositions (173). Indeed, the experience of the **other** reveals the essential paradox by which "there is an indeclinable subjectivity, an insurmountable solipsism—and yet, for this very subjectivity, there is an intentional "transgression" or '**encroachment**'" which enables an **intersubjectivity** or **intercorporeality** (175). Classical ontology dissolves through the notion of the *Lebenswelt* (lived-world), in which there is no longer an absolute for-itself and an absolute in-itself, but rather "the inherence of a self-in-the-world and of the world-in-the-self, what Husserl calls the *Ineinander*" (176). Turning to **Heidegger**, Merleau-Ponty emphasizes that Heidegger was forever after Being-there (*Da-sein*) itself, and only privileging human existence insofar as "man *is* the interrogation of Being" (177–8). Heidegger's philosophy provides an example of the interrogation of Being, a task that remains for philosophy today. The (untranslated) course notes on Heidegger are one of the most extended discussions offered by Merleau-Ponty on Heidegger's philosophy. (*NC*)

1959–60

Husserl at the Limits of Phenomenology: Translation and commentary on texts from his late philosophy (Monday Course) [*IPP, HLP*]

This course consists, for the most part, in a detailed reading of Husserl's late fragments **"The Origin of Geometry"** and "Foundational Investigations of the Phenomenological Origin of the Spatiality of Nature: The Originary Ark, The Earth, Does Not Move," with some extended commentary on Heidegger. Beginning with a theory of *reading* the **history of philosophy**, Merleau-Ponty identifies two dangers. On the one hand, we might attempt an "objective reading" that would seek to restore or repeat the objective thought of the author. On the other hand, one might pursue a "subjective reading" that would find in an author only what the reader had put there, projecting across any text his or her own understanding of the concepts invoked and of the problems to which they respond. Merleau-Ponty proposes a form of reading that would attempt to gear into the "unthought" of the text, to take up the *sense* of the text as both meaningful and open (see **"The Philosopher and His Shadow"**).

In "The Origin of Geometry," Husserl attempts to understand how ideal objectivity or meaning can be brought into the world in history and through empirical uses of language. Are not the truths (ideal objectivities) of geometry *discovered* as having been true for all peoples and all time, regardless of their knowledge of them? Yet geometry is gradually *established* in history and remains open to further developments. Exploring Husserl's notion of the "genesis of ideality," it appears that every institution or "originary founding" now must be seen not as a closed event, but as an opening of a field that invites further acts of production. Insofar as I have a body, I can understand meaningful gestures by other bodies like mine, I can gear into the sense of their communicative intentions by entering into a field in which they are meaningful. Moreover, *writing* documents the expressive act in a more anonymous realm, a "virtual" communication, a "speaking of x to x, which is not carried by any living subject and belongs in principle to everyone" (*IPP*, 187). As a body capable of expressive gestures, I can also gear into the sedimented speech I find in the written traces and lend them my voice. These expressive acts are not translated into my ideas, but rather enter into my experience through a **coherent deformation**, insofar as I bring with me all that I know and have experienced, and thus there is never an absolute coincidence between the writer and the reader—yet there is genuine communication.

The notions of openness and horizon are radicalized in Husserl's notion of the Earth as the "ark" that does not move. The Earth is that **quasi-object** that is never itself explicitly perceived for itself, never itself "moves," and yet remains the ground of all of our perceptions of objects and the condition for all movement (and all rest). **Classical philosophy and objective thought** remain mystified by a *pensée de survol* unable to account for such aspects of our experience. Although Heidegger's presence in the course is not explicitly clarified in the summary, Merleau-Ponty notes show that he focused on Heidegger's understanding of language in relation to the famous notions of *Denken* (thinking) and *Ereignis* (event/appropriation), and how language is not an object we possess, but one that somehow possesses us—perhaps suggesting that language too is a quasi-object. After a brief study of the nature of the "abyss" of language and the convergence of Heidegger's account with Husserl, Merleau-Ponty ultimately seems to prefer Husserl's analysis as resisting any "mysticism" of languages (see *HLP*, 49–54).

Nature and Logos: The Human Body (Thursday Course) [*IPP, N*]

Returning to "nature," Merleau-Ponty reminds his audience that he is not after "the theory of knowledge of Nature" (*N*, 203), nor is his goal to offer a meta-science of nature. Rather, his goal is to understand nature in relation to general ontology, as what he calls a "leaf or layer of total being" (204). In contrast to Cartesian philosophy, Merleau-Ponty aims to find *internal* relations between us and nature, or nature as the place of intertwining of all that is horizontal and that is vertical in Being. Science is read not for its content, but for its ontological commitments (206). The topic for the course, then, is "the human body" (*N*, 208) or "the appearance in nature of man and the human body" (*IPP*, 196). The human body is that which, paradoxically, perceives nature and also inhabits nature, a genuine *Ineinander* (intertwining). The human body must be understood through "how the invisible is divergence in relation to the visible" (*N*, 208).

The notes that survive from the remaining weeks of this course are divided into eight intriguing "sketches." The first sketch explicitly identifies Merleau-Ponty's late philosophy of "flesh" and his earlier discussion of the concept of **body schema**. The human body is peculiar insofar as it both perceives and moves and insofar as it is capable of a certain **reversibility: touching/touched, seeing/**

seen, "the place of a kind of reflection and, thereby, the capacity to relate itself to something other than its own mass, to close its circuit on the visible" (209). Not only does this spacing introduce desire and libido, but also allows the human body to exist as a symbolism, as the emergence of language and thought which are made possible as the invisible of the visible, the inverse or the other side of nature—hence the title of this course, *Nature and Logos*. In the following sketches that comprise the notes, the reader will find extended readings of embryology or Neo-Darwinism, which offer important illustrations of Merleau-Ponty's reading of science. The summary of the course concludes that these analyses leave open the relation between the symbolism of the human body and its relation to ideal being and truth, and that a subsequent course will have to explore the structure of the "explicit logos of the sensible world" (*IPP*, 199).

1960–1

Cartesian Ontology and Ontology Today [NC]

Although there are no summaries of Merleau-Ponty's final two courses, his lecture notes are available. From the notes it is clear that Merleau-Ponty envisioned this course as a study of the history of philosophy in order to gain access to the philosophical questions of the present. He argues that the present is clarified in exploring how "we" are no longer Cartesians, a question that remains unasked in the dominant philosophy of **Sartre** and Camus. Again invoking his understanding of how one reads the **history of philosophy**, Merleau-Ponty suggests that one must read Descartes to see how he speaks to our questions, not to his own. The goal of this course is to seek out and articulate the implicit ontology of present-day thought, the ontology that is in the air, and to do so through its distinctive contrast with Cartesian ontology. The course begins through a survey of how present-day questions are implicit in the art and literature of contemporary society in particular; Merleau-Ponty studies the role of **Proust, Claudel,** and Simon, among others. The course also offered several lessons devoted to Cartesian ontology, and the notes that survive include even the lecture notes for a lesson on Descartes that was scheduled to be held the day after Merleau-Ponty's untimely death.

Philosophy and Non-Philosophy Since Hegel [NC, PNP]

Although the final course offered at the Collège promises in its title a study of philosophy and non-philosophy *since* Hegel, it fact it offers primarily a reading *of* Hegel (and Marx). This close study of texts from Hegel and Marx demonstrates the role of dialectical ontologies in Merleau-Ponty late and unfinished ontology.

Communion

Merleau-Ponty's use of the term "communion" occurs in the *Phenomenology of Perception* as a manner of illustrating through phenomenological description the intimate relationship between **activity and passivity**. The structure of communion is very much related to his understanding of communication, and appears in phenomena such as sleep, but also more generally in sensing, since sensation occurs when the body is capable and prepared to take up the vibrations offered to it from the outside such that the sensible itself becomes "nothing other than a certain manner of **being-in-the-world**" and "sensation is, literally, a communion" (*PhP*, 219).

"Concerning Marxism" (1946) [SNS]

A discussion of fascism through the writings of French journalist and writer Thierry Maulnier (1909–88). Maulnier floated the idea that the morally repugnant aspects of fascism could be removed in order to offer a "true" fascism with socialist principles that might save Western Europe from the worst of nationalism and capitalism. Merleau-Ponty attacks Maulnier's imaginary ideal fascism, suggesting that the attempt to put nationalism and socialism together is a mistake of levels and a sure route to horrific consequences.

Consciousness

From the opening lines of *The Structure of Behavior*, which was originally titled "Consciousness and Behavior," Merleau-Ponty makes it clear that his overall philosophical goal is to understand "the relations of consciousness and nature" (*SB*, 3). In his first book, he argues that **behavior** reveals to an **outside spectator** the emergence in the world of *perceptual* **consciousness**. Consciousness is understood as a "a network of significative intentions which are sometimes clear to themselves and sometimes, on the contrary, lived rather than known" (172, 173). In *Phenomenology of Perception*, Merleau-Ponty argues that since all consciousness is perspectival, ultimately all consciousness is *perceptual* consciousness (*PhP*, 416). He introduces a notion of **non-thetic consciousness** as a way of describing our meaningful though non-reflective lived experience. Consciousness is ultimately our presence in the world, which is the intertwining of our existential **dimensions** and expressed through our fundamentally oriented **being-in-the-world**. By the time Merleau-Ponty reaches his ontological reflections, he becomes suspicious that the notion of consciousness itself, even if nuanced in these ways, undermines his attempt to think beyond the dichotomies of classical thought. As a result, his *The Visible and the Invisible* represents an attempt to leave behind any remnants of a philosophy of consciousness (*VI*, 183; 200).

Consciousness and the Acquisition of Language (1949-50)

Originally published in English separately, this now appears in the collection of the Sorbonne lectures. See *Child Psychology and Pedagogy*.

Constancy hypothesis

Given the **unquestioned belief in the world**, **empiricism** attempts to build perception out of the objective events of the perceived world, and **intellectualism** fails to question this assumption. This results in the constancy hypothesis, namely the positing of a "point-by-point correspondence and a constant connection between the stimulus and the elementary perceptions" (*PhP*, 8). Merleau-Ponty adopts **Gestalt theory**'s critique of this assumption, and argues that rejecting it leads to an entirely new theory of "reflection and a new *cogito*" via **phenomenology** (51).

Constituted language versus constituting language

Constituted language is the systematic repository of acquired significations and their relations; constituting language is speech in the process of establishing meanings in the lived context of **expression** (*PhP*, 194). Constituted language is the material of expression, like colors in a painterly expression (409), yet the constituting language or speech takes up and reshapes this system through what Merleau-Ponty will come to call a **coherent deformation**. The alternative constituted/constituting is often repeated in other contexts as well, such as space and time. See also **speaking speech versus spoken speech**.

Constituting consciousness

A notion attributed to intellectualism and other idealist philosophies whereby a transcendental or transcendent consciousness is responsible for constituting the universe or the meaningful world. **Reflective analysis** thus works backwards from the world of experience in order to discover the structure of this consciousness. The phenomenological analysis "of **one's own body** and of perception revealed to [Merleau-Ponty] a deeper relationship to the object and a deeper signification than this idealist one" (*PhP*, 453).

Descartes, René (1596–1650)

French mathematician, scientist, and the founder of modern philosophy. Given his presence throughout Merleau-Ponty's writings, Descartes is arguably Merleau-Ponty's most consistent interlocutor. Across his writings, Merleau-Ponty identified Descartes' philosophy as the common source of **empiricism** and **intellectualism**, identifying the former with the mechanistic understanding of perception found in Descartes' *Dioptrics* and the latter with the intellectualism of his *Meditations*. In addition, Merleau-Ponty regularly cites a letter from Descartes to Princess Elizabeth in which Descartes himself sensed that the solution to the union of the soul and body, between thinking substance and extended substance, was experienced in our everyday life (e.g. *PhP*, 205).

Dialectic/dialectical reasoning

Merleau-Ponty often invokes the notion of dialectic or dialectical reasoning as an alternative to **empiricism** and **intellectualism**. Although the source of this terminology is certainly **Hegel**, his use of it is not strictly Hegelian. For instance, he describes a "dialectical relationship" between the various orders of reality (physical, vital, cultural) in *The Structure of Behavior*. He argues that the higher layer does not *transcend* the lower, but rather remains *internally* related to it and in fact reshapes it. Or again, there is a dialectical relationship within experience between the organism and the milieu, insofar as the organism's capacities shape the appearance of the milieu, and the milieu solicits the organism's capacities and contributes to reshaping them. In *Phenomenology of Perception*, Merleau-Ponty describes the relationship between the **active and passive dimensions** of our fundamentally **ambiguous** way of **being-in-the-world** as dialectical. For instance, perception itself is a dialectic between constituted and constituting time, such that time is paradoxically "self-constituting" *through us* (*PhP*, 250). The discovery of the lived body and the **phenomenal field** establishes the place where the contradictions and ambiguities of dialectical relations can be sustained (129). **Existential analysis**, then, discovers the dimensions of our experience as dialectically related, revealing that dialectic is: "the tension from one existence to another existence that negates it and without which it can nevertheless not be sustained" (170–1). Moving to Merleau-Ponty's later work, dialectic continues to unfold within the lived world wherein its reversals, contradictions, and paradoxes can be sustained, and this requires understanding dialectic *as* expression, an open movement that has a trajectory and a *sense*. Such an understanding leads Merleau-Ponty to critique any form of **bad dialectic** that would artificially freeze the movement of dialectic either by positing an end-point or by institutionalizing a rigid structure of oppositions. Ultimately, dialectical philosophy is left to the side in favor of a philosophical **interrogation** (*VI*, Chapter Two).

Dimension

In the **existential analysis** of lived experience, dimension refers to those aspects that haunt all of experience without thereby reducing experience to them. For instance, **sexuality** is a dimension of every human act, and yet no human act is purely sexual.

Double sensations

My body has the "ambiguous organization" such that my two hands (for instance) can alternate between touching and touched. Merleau-Ponty rejects this notion as an attempt to save intellectualist psychology's conception of the body (*PhP*, 95), yet the figure of **touching/touched** becomes increasingly central to his thought.

École normale supérieure (est. 1794) [*ENS*]

The *ENS* of Paris (famously located at rue d'Ulm) is one of the pre-eminent post-secondary institutions in France. As a "*grande école*," the *ENS* employs a highly selective entrance exam, contributing to the meritocracy of training the intellectual elites of France. It is particularly renown for preparing students for the *agrégation* in philosophy. Merleau-Ponty attended the *ENS* between 1926 and 1930.

Eidetic reduction

The method of **transcendental phenomenology** that involves shifting focus from the **facticity** of experience to the essential or necessary structures of that experience.

"Einstein and the Crisis of Reason" (1955) [S]

This essay illustrates the directions of modern **science** through a study of Einstein as both a "classical" realist with "wildly speculative" constructions, and **Bergson**'s attempt to offer Einstein a way out of the resulting contradictory claims by referring back to lived experience in *Duration and Simultaneity* (1922).

Ek-stase/ecstasy

Inspired by **Heidegger**'s use of this term, Merleau-Ponty adopts the etymological sense of "ecstasy" to refer to **intentionality** as "outside of self" since intentionality is always directed toward its objects out in the world. This notion is particularly important in Merleau-Ponty's discussion of **temporality**, which is accomplished between the absolute unity of **consciousness** and the absolute disintegration of the ek-stase (*PhP*, 444).

Empiricism (or mechanism)

General category of philosophical approaches (opposed to **intellectualism**) privileging causal or mechanistic explanations of the world or of human experience. For an empiricist, the world is made up of parts that exist in isolation, *partes extra partes*, and this includes the parts of perception (conceived as punctual sensations or impressions) or the parts of the body (which is understood as merely one object among all others). They conceive of the universe as a *pure exteriority*. This category thus includes both philosophical empiricists as well as scientists and any other theorists privileging causal explanations.

In his first book, *The Structure of Behavior*, Merleau-Ponty's primary aim is to demonstrate how empiricism ultimately undermines itself. In order to do this, he takes the view of the "**outside spectator**" and describes the emergence of **consciousness** (as **structure**) in the world. His critique of the position continues in *Phenomenology of Perception*, where he identifies a myriad of important phenomena that fall outside the explanatory scope of empiricism, namely, the entire human and cultural world that makes up almost our entire experience (*PhP*, 24–5), and also the phenomena of the natural world, which it falsely describes as a sum of stimuli and qualities (26). See also **empiricism versus intellectualism (Merleau-Ponty's methodology)**.

Empiricism versus intellectualism (Merleau-Ponty's methodology)

One of Merleau-Ponty's most consistent philosophical styles involves identifying the common presuppositions between two supposed opposite approaches to a philosophical problem. In the study of behavior, perception, sexuality, language, movement, history, freedom, and even interpreting the history of philosophy itself, he regularly distinguishes between an **empiricist** approach that explains the phenomena according to *causes* and external relations, and an **intellectualist** approach that explains the phenomena according to *reason* and through a **constituting consciousness**. This is the explicit methodology employed throughout *Phenomenology of Perception*, but can also be found in almost all of Merleau-Ponty writings even if the categories of empiricism and intellectualism fall away or evolve. **Phenomenology** and philosophical **interrogation** provide a new approach through the return to our ambiguous **being-in-the-world** and the structures of **reversibility**.

Encroachment [*empiétement*]

In *Phenomenology of Perception*, Merleau-Ponty's account of our relation with others is described in generally positive terms, such as communication, yet by the late 1940s he increasingly described our relation with others as an *empiétement*, a transgression or an encroachment. This is likely a result of his deepening understanding of **historical responsibility** and its implications for the violence of **freedom** and **intersubjectivity**. The term takes on a significant role in his late ontology as a manner of describing the relation between **dimensions** given the **reversibility** of the **flesh** of the world. There is an encroachment between vision and touch, for instance, which is the primary structure of **chiasm** (*VI*, 123).

Enveloping/enveloped

This seemingly paradoxical relation, captured by the German word *Ineinander*, becomes increasingly common in Merleau-Ponty's later texts and notes as a way of characterizing the relations of the **flesh**. **Reversibility** suggests that the body, as open to the world, envelops the world with its gaze, and yet, as a body *of* the world, it is simultaneously enveloped (*VI*, 268).

Essences

Husserl described the aim of the **phenomenology** as gaining access to essences through eidetic seeing or intuition (***Wesensschau***). This might lead one to consider phenomenology a naïve idealism or Platonism. And yet, the shift from existence to essence is a function of the shift of attitude, and the essence becomes the intentional object pole or ***noema*** of phenomenologically reduced **consciousness**. Rather than seeing some red, I grasp the essence "red" as an essential structure of lived experience. For Merleau-Ponty, this clarifies how the inclusion of "essence" is not meant as the goal of the investigation, but rather as a means of returning to our lived experience or **facticity**. The eidetic **reduction** is not an attempt to "reduce" the world to an idea of the world, "it is the attempt to match reflection to the unreflective life of consciousness" (*PhP*, lxxix–lxxx).

"Everywhere and Nowhere" (1956) [S]

The content of this chapter in *Signs* is drawn from the section introductions to *Les Philosophes célèbres* (**1956**), a collected volume on great thinkers edited by Merleau-Ponty. The volume was divided into major historical periods, and these introductions illustrate Merleau-Ponty's approach to the **history of philosophy** and his creative reading practice. The introductions begin characteristically by raising the philosophical difficulties in assembling such a volume, between a mere recording of isolated philosophers and an overly ideal telling of a single unified drama (in an Hegelian fashion) (*S*, 127). For Merleau-Ponty, neither empiricist history of juxtaposition nor idealist history of a single teleological story captures the lived work of philosophy (126). The history of philosophy is not a closed or predestined system, but an open and growing trajectory in which the "past transgresses and grows through the present" and the notion of a Truth orients the research but remains forever presumptive. There is not "*a* philosophy which contains all philosophies [...] philosophy's center is everywhere and its circumference nowhere" (128).

Thus, any history of philosophy is already *philosophy*. Moreover, since philosophy is *expression*, the philosopher's life or times does not *determine* his or her philosophy, yet his or her philosophy is also not a purely free activity of the mind. As expression, philosophical reflection is **motivated**; it takes up the past as a response to an open future. Philosophy is "everywhere, even in the facts," and yet it "nowhere has a private realm which shelters it from life's contagion" (130). The practice of reading the history of philosophy, then, demands that each be acutely aware of the dangers of slipping to either an objective or a subjective approach.

The subsequent sections engage with the following topics: "The Orient and Philosophy" (133–40) explores Merleau-Ponty's understanding of the place of "Eastern" thinkers in the general history of philosophy, and particularly in relation to Hegel and to Husserl. "Christianity and Philosophy" (140–6) considers how philosophy ultimately defines its nature against dogmatic beliefs in essences, the real history of Christian institutions, and the shaky relationship between rationalism and faith in Malebranche and **Descartes**. "Major Rationalism" (147–52) explores a "privileged moment" when metaphysics and natural science "believed they had discovered a common foundation" (148). "The Discovery of Subjectivity" (152–4) draws together many apparently discordant philosophies in which, nonetheless, "it is the same subject-being which is at issue" (153). This section ends with a particularly striking claim against **Heidegger** who, for Merleau-Ponty, represents a nostalgia of attempting to return to a time when our relation to Being was pure, a time before "subjectivity" (154). The final section, "Existence and Dialectic," poses Merleau-Ponty the difficult task of summarizing "our famous contemporaries," an impossible task since determining in advance what the contemporary generation will mean for future generations is something that "all the 'objectivity' in the world cannot do" (154–5). In contrast to existence and **dialectic**, Merleau-Ponty here suggests that logical positivism is nothing more than "the last and most energetic 'resistance' to the concrete philosophy" of the twentieth century (157). For Merleau-Ponty, philosophy today is the effort to establish a philosophy of expression without the belief in a universal truth.

Evidentness [*évidence*]

Merleau-Ponty draws this term from **Husserl**'s use of *Evidenz*, which characterizes the appearing of the phenomenon as that which shows itself in its obviousness. Sometimes translated as "evidence," it should be noted that this term is not meant to be a source of "proof," but rather a characteristic of the phenomenon itself, hence the idiosyncratic term in English "evidentness" (*PhP*, 495n35).

Existential analysis

Much of Merleau-Ponty's early work could be characterized as existential analysis, which captures his particular understanding of the junction between **phenomenology** and **existentialism**. Through phenomenological reflection, one is able to identify the **dimensions** of lived experience. For instance, **spatiality** and **sexuality** are dimensions insofar as *every* human experience is spatial and sexual, and yet *no* human experience is purely spatial or purely sexual.

Existentialism

Controversial approach to philosophical reflection that has origins in Nietzsche and Kierkegaard, and is associated with (among others) **Heidegger, Jaspers, Marcel, Sartre, Beauvoir,** and Merleau-Ponty. In its most famous assertion, Sartre claims that existence *precedes* essence, which is to say that human nature is not the expression of a predetermined essence, but that it is *accomplished* in the concrete actions of lived experience. This contrasts with the classical philosophical search for a more fundamental realm of truth in **essences** or in transcendental consciousness. As Merleau-Ponty writes, expressing his commitment to this position, "I am not a 'living being,' a 'man,' nor even a '**consciousness**' [...] Rather, I am the absolute source. My existence does not come from my antecedents, nor from my physical and social surroundings; it moves out toward them and sustains them" (*PhP*, lxxii). Thus, for Merleau-Ponty, existentialism (and **existential analysis**) is what makes possible an understanding of the **ambiguous** structures of our **being-in-the-world**, subject *and* object, nature *and* culture, free *and* determined. As such, existentialism for Merleau-Ponty is characterized by an openness to our situated and paradoxical experience of the world. Indeed, in **"The Philosophy of Existence,"** Merleau-Ponty distanced himself from "existentialism" in favor of the *philosophy of existence* that emphasizes situated lived experience and embodiment, perhaps lost in Sartre's approach in *Being and Nothingness*. (See *TD*, 134–9.)

Expression

The phenomenon of expression is a central concern throughout Merleau-Ponty's work. Classical philosophy assumes that thought exists in itself, and that language is the optional means by which thought might be *ex-pressed*, or translated into perceptible signs to facilitate communication. As such, language is understood as an *external accompaniment* of thought, and communication is understood as *interpretation*. Throughout his work on language and other modes of expression, Merleau-Ponty repeatedly demonstrates the insufficiency of this account by offering a phenomenological description of the paradoxical experiences and structures of expression and a new understanding of meaning as *sense*. In **Phenomenology of Perception** and other texts from his early period, Merleau-Ponty explores the paradoxes of expression in terms of speech, and offers this exploration as an analogy for other paradoxical structures (such as perception, **painting**, sexuality, or the relation between soul and body). All of the rich **dimensions** of human experience begin from the fact that "the body is a natural power of expression" (*PhP*, 187). By the early 1950s, Merleau-Ponty was further emphasizing that embodied expression itself offered a fundamental account of all of human experience. As he writes: "All perception, all action which presupposes it, and in short every human use of the body is already *primordial expression*" (*MPAR*, 104). When he approaches his final ontological position, he is forging a notion of philosophical **interrogation** that remains authentic expression as a hyper-reflection or **hyper-dialectic** that refuses to close the gap between our lived experience of **wild Being** and our expression of it. The complex structure of expression at various explicit and implicit moments in Merleau-Ponty's writings is discussed throughout this dictionary, as indicated in the Index.

"Eye and Mind" (1960) [*MPAR*]

The last philosophical essay that Merleau-Ponty published during his lifetime was a dramatic and creative ontological theory of **painting**. As he writes in these pages, "any theory of painting is a metaphysics," and the theory of painting in this short essay offers an important insight into Merleau-Ponty's own unfinished ontology through the concepts of **flesh, chiasm, reversibility,** and others, and constitutes a rethinking of his earlier approaches to the **body** and **expression**. I have included some schematic sections titles that do not occur in Merleau-Ponty's text.

[I. Science and the things themselves]

The essay begins with a comparison between painting and **science**. The scientist observes the world as if from outside or above, he or she "manipulates things and gives up living in them" (*MPAR*, 121). By focusing on abstract objects that can be known by a transcendental observer, science loses touch with the real world in which our lives unfold. Alternatively, science sometimes unfolds (as in cybernetics) as an absolute mechanism or artificialism, turning any successful technique in one region loose on others, without ever asking *why* the technique works here, but not there (122). This operational thinking is a genuine threat to humanity—since human nature is existentially created, science threatens to turn us into "human machines" by destroying the expressive **being-in-the-world** and essentially intercorporeal being that we are. This is a "nightmare from which there is no awakening" (*MPAR*, 122). The only protection is to identify and refuse the *pensée de survol* by returning to the "there is" of the concrete world as the place of our lives. A genuine philosophy must begin from the phenomenological world of *the things themselves*, and not the scientific world of *things in general*.

Art, and "especially painting," begins from precisely this "fabric of brute meaning" that is the lived world. The painter is charged with no other task that to capture the appearing of the things themselves, taking up the world through and from the visible, and this, Merleau-Ponty suggests, is the "fundamental of all painting, perhaps of all culture" (123).

[II. Expression and the body, and painting]

The section considers the relationship between the body and expression. Citing **Valéry**, Merleau-Ponty writes: "The painter 'takes his body with him'" (123). Bodies, and not minds, *paint*. As such, painting cannot be reduced to the intentions or the personal history of the painter; rather, "we must go back to the working, actual body—not the body as a chunk of space or a bundle of functions but that body which is an intertwining of vision and movement" (124). Vision itself is not passive, since my **field** is structured according to a tacit "**I can**," reflecting back to me the powers of my own body. The visible world and the world of my possible actions overlap, or intertwine in my body, which opens to the world and is yet itself *of* the visible.

The entire "enigma" of embodiment, then, must be understood through **reversibility**. My body is at once seer and seen, toucher and touched. Rather than a body united with a mind, the self of reversibility is one of "confusion, narcissism, inherence [...]—a self, then, that is caught up in things, having a front and a back, a past and a future" (124). Moreover, this reversibility produces others. Raising the description of the **intentional arc** to an ontological level, it seems the body "holds things in a circle around itself" such that the things of the body's milieu are internally related to what my body *is*, they are part of its "full definition"—the body is, then, *essentially* relational. As such, the *phenomenological* description leads to the *metaphysical* conclusion that things are an essential "prolongation" of my body, they are "incrusted in its flesh," such that my existence itself is the spacing through which my body and the world can appear (125). Neither the result of an empirical fact of our body, nor of a mind infusing the body and world with meaning, a "human body is present when, between the see-er and the visible, between touching and touched, between one eye and the other, between hand and hand a kind of crossover occurs, when the spark of the sensing/sensible is lit" (125). According to Merleau-Ponty, painting expresses this enigma of "visibility."

If reversibility establishes the spacing by which things appear, then the visibility of things must be subtended by the latent visibility of my body. That is, for color, lighting, textures, and other qualities to appear at all, they must resonate with my body, and initiate a "carnal formula of their presence" (126). This carnal formula can be *expressed* by a sketch, for instance, which is not an objective representation, but a witnessing of the object as it speaks to the powers of my body. As such, the sketch expresses not some thing in the world, but the intertwining between my body and its world, and this invites the viewer to see the world *according to* these traces of a moment of visibility. This is the essence of communication, a taking up of the gestures and traces of others in an expressive reading. The painting does not provide a representation, "it offers the *gaze* traces of vision, from the inside, in order that it may espouse them" (126).

The painter's gaze thus interrogates the world in order to discover "what it would need to be a painting" or what is required of the next stroke so that a painting underway can become itself, expressing a moment of visibility through the simple "traces of a hand" (127). This requires the deft skill of configuring the visible such that the invisible can appear. The painter's gaze is trained to unveil the tacit premises of profane vision in order to express visibility itself and this vision of this world, and in order to communicate the invisible (meaning, for instance) to those with eyes to see. And indeed, the painter's privileged access to reversibility can be seen when they report a confusion of "between who sees and who is seen, who paints and what is painted" (129). The poles of the reversible relation express an intimacy that could not be captured with the diametrically opposed categories of traditional metaphysics, such as Being and Nothingness. Even the possibility of seeing ourselves seeing in the mirror anticipates and illustrates "the metaphysical structure of our flesh" (129). Others and things are part of my world thanks to a universal magic that "converts things into spectacle, spectacle into things, myself into another, and another into myself" (130).

[III. Cartesian Painting]

In the middle section of the essay, Merleau-Ponty turns his attention to **Descartes'** theory of perception in *Dioptrics* and its relationship to painting as an example of a theory that resists the reality of lived experience in favor of the rigorous world of thought. Descartes' approach to vision here is from the perspective of a *pensée de survol,* and when he discusses light or color, he does not mean phenomenal light and color, but these elements insofar as they enter our eye and begin a causal process that produces vision. This is particularly clear in Descartes' understanding of the mirror, where he sees a flat image of colors from which he will interpret depth and the presence of an image of himself.

Leaving aside the details of Descartes' theory of vision, Merleau-Ponty focuses on his allusions to engravings so as to reveal how "every theory of painting is a metaphysics" (132). For instance, the appearance of depth must be considered an interpretation rather than something "visible, since it is reckoned from our bodies to things" (134). There is not place in Descartes' ontology for "latency and depth" (135). As a "metaphysics that gives us definitive reasons to leave off doing metaphysics," Cartesian thought believes it has mastered the "anxious trembling" we sense in the lived world, and as a result it destroys any possible balance between science and philosophy (137). In short, it rings in the victory of operational thinking that is both "fundamentally hostile to philosophy as thought-in-contact" and is the danger of the victory of **adversity** over humanism (137). Yet this victory is overstated. I am in the world, I live it from within, and this requires a new philosophy, one "which is yet to be elaborated" but that can be observed *animating* the painter "when, in Cézanne's words, he 'thinks in painting'" (139).

[IV. Painting Ontology]

The "entire history of modern painting" also has a "metaphysical significance," and this section attempts to identify the ontology at work in modern painting (139). That is, he attempts a *reading* of painting in its lived exploration of ontology in order to grasp the *sense* of this ontology through the enigmas of its *expression*.

The first is the enigma of *depth*. Painting and phenomenology both reveal that depth is not an interpretation from the content of the field or "as if" from a third person perspective. Rather, objects are *seen in place*, not according to external relations in space, but a phenomena of "envelopment" by which each thing is at once dependent *and* autonomous (140). This depth is lived and experienced because of the fundamental **reversibility** of dimensions. Or again, *color* is an enigma of painting, since color is not simply a surface property or quality. Color is a dimension that introduces "identities, differences, a texture, a materiality, a something," which cannot be reduced to a simple impression or isolated sensation. Moreover, color and depth intertwine and reshape each other; there is no "one master key of the visible" (141). These are dimensions, rather, of the **flesh** of the world, and not relations between isolated poles. The flesh relates to itself by folding back upon itself to create the spacing for the appearance of Being itself. The visible is animated from within itself, folding back upon itself in an inexhaustible richness Merleau-Ponty calls the flesh of the world, and it is this invisible richness that "the painter seeks beneath the words *depth, space,* and *color*" (142).

The ontology that emerges in painting is a certain "system of equivalences, a *Logos* of lines, of lighting, of reliefs, of masses—a nonconceptual presentation of universal Being" (142). In short, painting is the attempt to gear into the unreflected or brute Being of lived experience and of which science is but a secondary expression. In fact, in its inexhaustible nature, brute Being would invite an open proliferation of expressions, always transcending our efforts to express it yet existing nowhere other than in our gestures, words, and institutions. To demonstrate the welcoming nature of this Being, Merleau-Ponty considers the evolution from the "prosaic" outline of objects to the modern notion of line. Lines are, of course, fictions of representation, in the world lines are merely borders regions between things (143). Nevertheless, lines render visible the world, and in modern painting the line is not "rejected," but rather re-conceived as "a certain disequilibrium contrived within the indifference of the white paper; it is a certain hollow opened up within the in-itself, a certain constitutive emptiness" (144). The line becomes a dimension of the whole, generating space rather than representing shape. The same movement from representation to dimension can be seen in movement. Following Rodin, Merleau-Ponty suggests that movement is given not through the presentation of successive "instantaneous views" of an object in motion, but through "an image in which the arms, the legs, the trunk, and the head are each taken at a different instant, an image which therefore portrays the body in an attitude which it never at any instant really held" (145). Motion appears insofar as the body "bestrides" duration, rather than suffering the monotonous passing of points of time.

All of this comes down to vision. Explaining the essay's title, Merleau-Ponty suggests that the *eye* is not a mere sensory organ providing information to the *mind*; rather, painting reveals that "[t]he eye accomplishes the prodigious work of opening the soul to what is not soul—the joyous realm of things and their god, the sun" (146). Vision unveils things as *both* external to each other and yet essentially *together* in the world. Vision, then, reveals the "dehiscence" or springing forth of Being (or the invisible) accomplished by the folding back of the visible upon itself (147). And this intertwining is precisely the paradoxical logic of expression: "it is impossible to say that here nature ends and the human being or expression begins. It is, then, silent Being that comes to show forth its own meaning" (147).

[V. Intertwining and Interrogation]

The intertwining of these dimensions is such that any solution painting might find in expressing one dimension will reshape all of the others and demand further "solutions." In painting, then, "nothing is ever finally acquired and possessed for good" (148). Nevertheless, since all paintings express **wild or brute Being**, they are all moments in the general trajectory of expression. Thus, painting as a history has a *sense*, but it is one that proceeds through "detours, transgression, slow encroachments and sudden drives" (149). The sense is born within this movement itself.

Human expression and history is condemned to never fully express Being, but is one really to believe that the highest point of philosophy is the realization that "the soil beneath our feet is shifting?" Is philosophical method restricted to an interrogation of Being that never fully dominates being? Yet these questions emanate from a "spurious fantasy"—the illusion of a *pensée de survol* (149). There is a method of philosophical **interrogation** that, like painting, gears into the open trajectory of expression and history by recognizing that "each creation alters, clarifies, deepens, confirms, exalts, re-creates, or creates by anticipation all the others" (149).

Facticity

Our concrete and embodied experience as **being-in-the-world** (*PhP*, lxxxi).

"Faith and Good Faith" (1946) [*SNS*]

In the opening paragraphs of this essay, Merleau-Ponty relates the experiences of a certain "young Catholic" (in all likelihood himself) who began to recognize the failings of Catholic socialism in relation to social causes. This young Catholic, whose faith had led him naturally toward the left, was outraged by the hypocrisy of the Austrian Christian Socialist government, led by Dollfuss, who consolidated power by attacking the Viennese workers in 1936.[10] The mentors around this young Catholic refused to condemn this act, sheepishly acknowledging the state's right to its power and police force. To sustain these contradictions, there must be a pernicious **ambiguity** in the Catholic way of life, both spiritually and socially (*SNS*, 173). Between the demands to return to the "inner man" of Saint Augustine, Catholics must also embrace the Incarnation, God's *externalization* in time and space. This results in a genuine paradox and initiates the attempt to reach a place beyond this contradiction, the founding of a religion of Spirit. The farther Christianity leans to the inner man, the more it is conservative; the farther it leans toward the externalized relational God, it is socialist and revolutionary. Moreover, by never choosing, the Catholic is always free to retreat to the other side. In the first case, being faithful means being true to one's inner self, faith as "good faith" (174). Yet "faith" is about being in the world and making a commitment that, as faith, is never "completely justified"—and this is not a question for a pure inner self. Thus, faith seems to paradoxically demand "bad faith," not being "true to oneself" but rather being wholly outside of one's self. This **ambiguity** in human experience requires that each must navigate between faith and good faith, both trusting and questioning (180). Merleau-Ponty suggests that perhaps the communist intermediary of the Party between the individual and historical reality is necessary for resolving this paradox, and that the highest virtue would thus be "living actively *with* the party, not just passively obeying" (181).

Field

The concept of a "field" is developed through Merleau-Ponty's study of **Gestalt psychology** in relation to perception. For Merleau-Ponty, every perceived thing *necessarily* belongs to a field that is charged with value and *sense*, such that experience can never be wholly explained by its component parts. Moreover, anything that is experienced is also shaped by a tacit set of **horizons** (such as the anticipated other side of an object, or the weight of past experience) that provides the atmosphere of meaning and temporality. This culminates in the **phenomenal field** as the structure capable of sustaining the fundamental **ambiguities** of our lived experience.

Figure/ground structure

Merleau-Ponty often invokes the figure/ground structure, identified by **Gestalt psychology** as the foundational form of all perceptual experience. Against atomistic understandings (governed by the **constancy hypothesis**), the observation is made that the most basic perceptual given is never an isolated, punctual bit of sense data, but always some "figure" against some "background." Moreover, this "structure" is not found in the world in itself; rather, the concept is necessarily borrowed from the phenomenal or perceived world (*SB*, 92). This is not a "contingent" fact that might be overcome by some more refined look, it is "the very definition of the perceptual phenomenon" (*PhP*, 4). As such, Merleau-Ponty generalizes the insight to suggest that anything that appears at all does so "in the middle of some other thing, it always belongs to a 'field'"(4).

"The Film and the New Psychology" (1945) [*SNS*]

This essay is one of Merleau-Ponty's rare discussions of film. This essay begins with an extended discussion of **Gestalt psychology**, from which Merleau-Ponty concludes that Gestalt psychology offers a genuinely new way of understanding human beings as being in the world through a "natural bond" (*SNS*, 53). Applying Gestalt principles to the experience of film, Merleau-Ponty argues that the film (like all objects of perception) is not a sum of images or sensations, but rather a "temporal *gestalt.*" Through montage and editing, which are thus considered temporal decisions, the director has a possible genuine expressive art. As with a painter like **Cézanne**, who expresses through color and strokes, the director's *style* infuses the whole with a *sense* through the rich temporal combination of the visual and the aural, and its *sense* is not separable from its concrete expression: "the film does not mean anything but itself" (57).

Fink, Eugen (1905–75)

German phenomenologist and long-time assistant to **Husserl**. Fink's work influenced Merleau-Ponty's understanding of Husserl, and his characterization of the **phenomenological reduction** as "'wonder' before the world" is inspired by Fink (*PhP*, lxxvii). Merleau-Ponty was also one of only a few researchers with access to Fink's *Sixth Cartesian Meditation*, intended as an extension to Husserl's *Cartesian Meditations* and written in collaboration with Husserl. Merleau-Ponty met Fink during his visit to the **Husserl Archives at Louvain** in 1939.

Flesh

The shift to an ontological study of embodiment leads Merleau-Ponty away from the original structure of **ambiguity** toward a more robust account of **reversibility**. Stemming directly from the image of **touching/touched**, by which the body is both actively touching and passively touched, and the necessary spacing that eclipses any coincidence between these two aspects of my total being, he introduces the concept of *flesh*, which as yet "has no name in any philosophy" (*VI*, 147). As **touching/touched, seeing/seen**, my body is both open *to* the world and itself *of* the world, a moment or node of flesh in the flesh of the world. This implies a reversibility or a folding back that is in principle possible but that is forever eclipsed, since any accomplished *coincidence* would in fact collapse Being itself. Thus, the very experience of Being is dependent upon the "thickness of flesh between the seer and the thing" (*VI*, 135). The flesh is the name for an ontological principle or element, and through an **enveloping/enveloped** relation, it allows for the space or *écart* for Being itself to appear. Moreover, the flesh allows for innumerable reversibilities such that the invisible and ideality can be understood as the lining or depth of the visible world.

"For the Sake of Truth" (1945) [*SNS*]

This essay is an extended analysis of the two main left-wing political parties in France, primarily after 1936. Refusing to take sides, Merleau-Ponty insists on a return to an underlying **Marxist humanism**. From within the movement of lived history, one must adopt a **wait-and-see Marxism** that will reserve judgment until the path of history reveals the truth (*SNS*, 170–1). Yet in a striking final footnote presumably added in 1948 for the essay's inclusion in *Sense and Non-Sense*, Merleau-Ponty rejects his own earlier optimism in Soviet politics. He suggests that the attitude of his essay reflected the hope of "saving both socialism and liberty," and such a goal will lead him to the **new liberalism** proposed in *Adventures of the Dialectic*.

Form

Merleau-Ponty's use of the term "form" is drawn from **Gestalt psychology**, and is used more or less interchangeably with the concept of **structure**.

Freud, Sigmund (1856–1939)

German doctor, neurologist, and founder of **psychoanalysis**. Merleau-Ponty was only partially sympathetic to Freud's work, often offering criticisms particularly of Freud's early formulations. In both *The Structure of Behavior* and *Phenomenology of Perception*, Merleau-Ponty critiques Freud's reliance upon *causal* explanations, such as between instinct and consciousness, or sexuality and human experience (*SB*, 178; *PhP*, 160). Nevertheless, he quite explicitly pursued psychoanalytic insights through his own phenomenological investigations, and suggested that Freud's work opened the possibility for an **existential analysis** or phenomenological approach to **sexuality**. Freud recognized that "every human act 'has a **sense**'" (*PhP*, 160–1), and this sets up a rethinking of explanation according to the expressive and ambiguous nature of motivation rather than causality (*MPAR*, 73–4). Sexuality can be a **dimension** of experience without thereby reducing all experience to merely sexuality. In an introduction to **Hesnard**'s 1960 book on Freud, Merleau-Ponty agrees with Hesnard that Freud's work opens up the possibility for a "new" philosophy, namely, **phenomenology** (see *PSY*).

"From Mauss to Claude Lévi-Strauss" (1959) [S]

Merleau-Ponty's most explicit consideration of sociology and social anthropology. The focus is on **Lévi-Strauss**, Merleau-Ponty's friend and newly appointed colleague (in the newly named chair in Social Anthropology) at the *Collège de France*. This essay is particularly revelatory of Merleau-Ponty's reading of **structuralism**. Whereas "The Philosopher and Sociology" (1951) focuses almost exclusively on Husserl and does not name a single sociologist, this later essay is quite the opposite, tracing out the developments from within sociology and social anthropology, from Durkheim to **Mauss** to structural anthropology. Only with Lévi-Strauss's "brilliant" integration of structuralism with social anthropology is a genuine understanding of the social possible.

For Lévi-Strauss, the social is composed of intertwining systems (exchange, kinship, art, myth, etc.), which are not ideas in the minds of the society's members, but the lived structures of possibilities. Just as the speaker deploys the linguistic gesture without interpretation, the social being too lives and acts within the structures without thereby being able to "know" them. Social structures are not possessed by conscious social agents, rather social agents are possessed, so to speak, by social structures (117). Yet for Merleau-Ponty, social structures are not, so to speak, fate—they must be taken up in creative repetitions and in commerce with all other structures at work within "society" as the "structure of structures," the anthropologist must bring together "objective analysis" and genuine "lived experience," that is, it must become a phenomenological anthropology. Ultimately, "man is eccentric to himself and the social finds its center only in man," and elucidating this intertwining is precisely Merleau-Ponty's constant aim (123). The essay ends, however, with a discussion (revealing a keen interest and intimate knowledge) of Lévi-Strauss's developing work. For Merleau-Ponty, the analyses accomplished and to come show a genuine philosophical significance and bears "the marks of a great intellectual endeavor" (125).

Fundierung

German for "founding." Merleau-Ponty adopts this term from Husserl in order to discuss a paradoxical "two-way" relationship between terms that classical philosophy obscures through its categories. For instance, the relationship between reflection and the unreflected is a *Fundierung* relation insofar as each reflection emerges from and articulates the unreflected, *sustains* that unreflected and reshapes it, and yet never exhausts or absorbs the unreflected. This relation is equally to be found between time and eternity, thought and language, thought and perception, and reason and fact (*PhP*, 414). This interpretation of Husserl foreshadows Merleau-Ponty's discussions of the paradoxical logic of **expression** and his later notions of intertwining and **chiasm**.

Gelb, Adhemar (1887–1936)

Gestalt psychologist who worked primarily on visual perception. Merleau-Ponty was particularly influenced by Gelb's work on **color** constancy and his collaborative work with **Goldstein** in interpreting the **Schneider Case**.

Generality

In *Phenomenology of Perception*, Merleau-Ponty discusses generality alongside **anonymity** as a way of clarifying how perception is neither wholly passive nor wholly active. Perception is "as a modality of a general existence, already destined to a physical world, which flows through me without my being its author" (*PhP*,

224). Vision is not something "I," as a transcendental subject, accomplish through an intellectual act or decision, and yet vision is importantly intentional and oriented. Thus, it takes place in a certain **field** of generality, a certain anonymity by which it is impersonal (insofar as I do not explicitly accomplish this act) but not non-personal (since it remains perspectival). This generality is not such that we all are ultimately "one" through a transcendental principle, since this is the error of **transcendental idealism**; rather, we are all, precisely through our individuality and perspective, open upon a general Being that we share. Thus, since I am not a self-transparent **constituting consciousness**, my individual **anonymous** existence brings with it a "halo of generality," and this anonymity and generality are what make possible an "**intersubjectivity**" (474).

Genetic phenomenology

Approach to phenomenological reflection expressed in Husserl's final works as a response to the distinction between "static" constitution and "genetic" constitution. **Transcendental phenomenology** provided methods for examining the **noetic/noematic** structures of **consciousness**, yet Husserl came to recognize the need for a parallel investigation into the historical genesis of certain aspects of our experience or of cultural institutions such as language. Merleau-Ponty was greatly influenced by this later work, offering several critiques of the earlier transcendental phenomenology and attempting to bring together genetic phenomenology with the insights of either **Gestalt psychology** or **structuralism**.

Gestalt psychology/Gestalt theory

An approach to psychology that explores the structure of perception according to the notion of "*Gestalt*," which means "form" or "figure." Developed in Germany in the late nineteenth and early twentieth centuries by **Wertheimer, Köhler,** and **Koffka** (among others), Gestalt psychology offered a response to theories that attempted to reconstruct perceptual or mental experience by building it up through mechanistic or atomistic building blocks.

Its fundamental insight, that a whole is not simply the sum of its parts, implies that the immediate perception of meaning and value occurs within a *field* structured according to figure/ground. Their work initially explored visual perception and the perception of movement as offering a critique of the **constancy hypothesis**. Subsequent studies developed the implications of their principles in a much broader set of questions, from **behavior** and learning in organisms (**Goldstein**) to psychological, social, and political issues.

Merleau-Ponty was attracted to Gestalt theory from the earliest period of his philosophical development as a way of describing perception that might dissolve the schism between **empiricism** and **intellectualism** (see "The Nature of Perception"). Influenced by **Gurwitsch**, who convincingly identified the methods of Gestalt theory with the **phenomenological reduction**, Merleau-Ponty's first book focuses more on the philosophical consequences of Gestalt theory than on the study of **phenomenology** (see *The Structure of Behavior*). Gestalt psychology reveals the emergence of meaningful structures in the world that in fact dissolve the categories of classical thought, and **behavior** is just such a notion: "*not a thing, but neither is it an idea*" (*SB*, 127). "Structure" is nothing less than "the joining of an idea and an existence which are indiscernible, the contingent arrangement by which materials begin to have meaning in our presence, intelligibility in the nascent state" (206–7).

Nevertheless, Merleau-Ponty always maintained (following **Gurwitsch**) a certain critique of Gestalt psychology. For instance, he argues that Gestalt theorists (such as Koffka) ultimately retreat from the philosophical consequences of their theory in order to adopt the "realistic postulates which are those of every psychology" (*SB*, 132). By attempting to identify some "real" forms in the universe that might be used to build the higher-level forms of behavior or experience, such theorists are "no longer thinking according to 'form'" (136–7). The underlying realism of Gestalt theory must be overcome through a return to the **phenomenal field**. As Merleau-Ponty writes: "Ultimately they consider the structures of the perceived world as the simple result of certain physical and physiological processes [...]. Ultimately the real world is the physical world as science conceives it, and it engenders our **consciousness** itself" (*PrP*, 23).

Gestural theory of meaning

The theory of meaning and speech established by Merleau-Ponty in *Phenomenology of Perception*. According to Merleau-Ponty, speech is not a mere external accompaniment of thought, but rather that speech accomplishes thought and that language itself bears its **sense** in the very style of its gestures or the traces of its gestures. As such, the "sense" of the gesture is written into the gesture itself, and since speech too is a "genuine gesture," it too must contain "its own sense" (*PhP*, 189). Thus, every communication remains contingent upon an embodied taking up, and there is never a pure meaning first in the head of the speaker and then in the mind of the listener by which we might judge a complete and successful communication. Beneath any secondary use of constituted or spoken language one finds a "primordial silence" of pre-**thetic** *sense*, a silence that speech comes to break as a gesture that signifies not an idea or meaning, but an entire world.

Thus, how do we understand gestures? When we see a gesture, we do not turn inward in order to interpret its meaning through an analogy with our own experience: "The gesture does not *make me think* of anger, it is the anger itself" (190). Of course, I do not *perform* these gestures or emotions, but I catch on to their *sense*, I *understand them* in a non-thetic, non-reflective way. Communication occurs when I gear into the sense of the other's gestures. "I do not understand the other person's gestures through an act of intellectual interpretation," but rather "through my body" insofar as it "merges with the structure of the world that the gesture sketches out and that I take up for myself" (191–92). The same structure holds for linguistic gestures, allowing for a continuity that dissolves the question of the origin of language. **Behaviors** establish meanings or *sense* in the world, and speech is just a particular case of this paradoxical relation between immanence and transcendence. But language does provide a special case because it is "capable of sedimenting and of constituting an intersubjective acquisition" (196). Not simply because writing down makes the expression more transposable, but because in speech there is the idea of reaching a truth and because speech can itself be the object of speech. Nevertheless, the phenomenologist resists this direction in order to place "thought back among the phenomena of expression" (196). Ultimately, it is the very possibility of expressive gestures that makes meaningful experience of any kind possible. "Thus we must recognize as an ultimate fact this open and indefinite power of signifying—that is, of simultaneously grasping and communicating a sense—by which man transcends himself through his body and his speech toward a new behavior, toward others, or toward his own thought" (200).

Goldstein, Kurt (1878–1965)

German neurologist and psychologist, and important figure in **Gestalt psychology**. Goldstein is an important influence in Merleau-Ponty's first two books, particularly in his study (with **Gelb**) of Schneider.

Gurwitsch, Aron (1901–73)

Lithuanian-born phenomenologist influential on the young Merleau-Ponty, particularly on the link between Husserl's **phenomenological reduction** and **Gestalt psychology**'s critique of the **constancy hypothesis**. Merleau-Ponty met Gurwitsch in the mid-1930s (via **Marcel**). He began attending Gurwitsch's lectures in Paris and editing his articles for French expression.[11]

Habit

In *Phenomenology of Perception*, the analysis of habit acquisition is an important step in Merleau-Ponty's account of **one's own body**. He argues that habits are not acquired through the establishing of a specific set of physical movements, nor through an intellectual decision or grasping of a movement. Rather, the habit is a "reworking and renewal of the **body schema**" and involves catching on to the *sense* of the gesture. The body *grasps* the *sense* of the gesture as a "motor signification" (*PhP*, 144). Indeed, having a habit is precisely that which alleviates us from having to *think* about the action, and it also is what opens up the possibility for that habit to play forward into differently constructed situations that nevertheless share the same *sense*. "Habit," then, "expresses the power we have of dilating our **being in the world**, or of altering our existence through incorporating new instruments" (145). This leads to the conclusion that the body is "an expressive space" (147). Moreover, every motor habit, argues Merleau-Ponty, is simultaneously a perceptual habit insofar as perception is our body's fundamental **being-in-the-world**. Thus, the above conclusions need to be generalized to the claim that the acquisition of a perceptual habit is the acquisition of a world. Gaining a habit is to enter into a world that can speak to that power of my body (153–5).

Habitual body versus actual body

Given the nature of embodiment, as we learn **habits** our world becomes reshaped according to our possible actions and gestures. As such, the objects of the world *appear* to us as manipulable *in themselves*. Yet there are cases in which our habitual body or our motor intentionality may continue to intend a world that is no longer accessible given changes to our actual body. Our body is a lived reservoir of potential actions that may remain intact though the body's capacities have been broken. In the extreme case of **phantom limb syndrome**, the world speaks to a part of my body that I no longer possess (*PhP*, 84).

Haecceity

Deriving from the Latin root *haec* ("this"), the term *"haecceity"* indicates the properties or qualities of a thing which make it a particular thing, or which offer a thing its individuation, its *thisness*. This is often opposed or related to a thing's *quiddity*, the more general qualities or properties that make something *what* it is, its *whatness*. The term appears several times in the context of Merleau-Ponty's critique of **reflective analysis**. For an intellectualist, there is no *thisness* to consciousness, and the Ego and the **Alter Ego** are thus simply two moments of the same rational principle, and thereby identical. In short, it is **phenomenology** that allows us to see how we experience *particularity* without reducing perception to a merely passive recording of properties actually presented. The world I see has a certain "accent" or a certain "style," and this is what constitutes its *haecceity* (*PhP*, 428).

Head, Henry (1861–1940)

English neurologist and physiologist. Merleau-Ponty cites Head's thesis and other works in *Phenomenology of Perception*, and is particularly influenced by Head's use of the notion of **body schema (image)**.

Hegel, Georg Wilhelm Friedrich (1770–1831)

German philosopher and central figure in post-Kantian German Idealism. Although many important aspects of Merleau-Ponty's thought might be understood as echoing Hegelian insights, he only rarely discusses Hegel in relation to the notion of **history** and the movement of **dialectic**.

"Hegel's Existentialism" (1946) [*SNS*]

This essay, a report on a lecture by **Hyppolite**, reveals Merleau-Ponty's understanding of **Hegel** and his relation to **phenomenology** and **existentialism**. "All the great philosophical ideas of the past century," suggests Merleau-Ponty, including "Marx and Nietzsche, phenomenology, German existentialism, and **psychoanalysis**—had their beginnings in Hegel" (*SNS*, 63). The essay focuses primarily on Hyppolite's claim that Hegel was an "existentialist." Nevertheless, existentialism experiences a shift from a German preoccupation with death toward a French commitment to intentional freedom and **intersubjectivity**, and this shift is decisive for Merleau-Ponty. Speaking of death and anxiety only offers a restricted existentialism, whereas a focus on intersubjectivity, "a reason immanent in unreason, of a freedom which comes into being in the act of accepting limits," and on the **body** as the source of *sense*, leads to a more authentic existentialism (70).

Heidegger, Martin (1889–1976)

German philosopher most famous for his study of *Dasein* and **temporality** in *Being and Time* (1927). Although the young Merleau-Ponty was only loosely familiar with Heidegger's work, he nevertheless adopted several key concepts and arguments that would have been "in the air" in Paris at the time. For instance, *Phenomenology of Perception* adopts Heidegger's notions of **being-in-the-world, temporality, ek-stase,** and transcendence. By the time of his late courses of the *Collège de France* **Lectures**, Merleau-Ponty was engaging much more directly with Heidegger's writings, particularly those on language, and Heidegger's influence is arguably more pronounced in Merleau-Ponty's late essays and *The Visible and the Invisible*.

Herder, Johann Gottfried (1744–1803)

Prussian philosopher who had a wide influence in various disciplines. Merleau-Ponty only mentions Herder in passing (see: *sensorium commune*), but his influence is arguably present in Merleau-Ponty's approach to perception and language.

Hesnard, Angelo Louis (1886–1969)

French doctor, writer, and intellectual figure in the psychoanalytic community, and President of the *French Society for Psychoanalysis*. He was influenced by Merleau-Ponty's concepts of lived or pre-reflective **consciousness** and the lived body. Hesnard believed that **Freud's** work could lead quite naturally toward an embodied **phenomenology**, and invited Merleau-Ponty to write an introduction to his book on Freud. (See *PSY*; **psychoanalysis**.)

Historical responsibility

Suggesting that the categories of political morality are too narrow in relation to the complexities of concrete and lived historical experience, Merleau-Ponty adopts an existential **Marxist humanism**. This implies, he argues, two forms of *historical responsibility*. On the one hand, the categories of pure guilt or pure innocence are meaningless in the complex structures of historical reality. Our actions take up and sustain both explicit and *potential* actions, and the possibilities of violence are sustained in our culture and language by our very actions or inactions. As such, "we all played a part in the events of 1939" (*SNS*, 141). On the other hand, any "political conduct, however justified it may once have been," can be altered by the course of history itself and in fact become its opposite (*HT*, xvi). Thus, it appears we require an ethics capable or recognizing responsibility for both our intentions *and* the historically contingent consequences.

Historicism

The approach to the study of history that interprets all historical events according to external structures and causal relations. See **psychologism**.

History

Merleau-Ponty often discusses history with the intention of establishing an **existential analysis**. He argues that history cannot be understood as a mere juxtaposition of event, or as the unfolding of a pre-determined Rationality or Hegelian Spirit. Nevertheless, he insists that the contingent movement of history has a *sense*, if not a "direction." He argues that a *sense* of history emerges through us, but is not our explicit doing. The historical actor gears into the sense of history by taking up the past toward a sensed future, and this is possible through the notion of a **situated freedom**. Moreover, this structure is precisely what lays the groundwork for **historical** responsibility. This account of history is also importantly related to the concept of **expression**, notably in "Indirect Language and the Voices of Silence."

History of philosophy

In several places, Merleau-Ponty argues that the study of the history of philosophy must not be an objective reading, seeking to restore or repeat the exact thought of the philosopher in question, nor a subjective reading, which would project across the text one's own philosophical preoccupations or questions. In fact, no system of ideas is an ideal "system of neatly defined concepts, of arguments responding to perennial problems, and of conclusions which permanently solve the problems (*HLP*, 5). Rather, "[t]he history of philosophy is a confrontation, a communication" between the philosopher being studied and the philosopher seeking an understanding (*UBS*, 31). One must, then, develop a responsible practice of reading that gears into the open trajectory of thought that is neither a mere juxtaposition of positions nor a simple expression of a single *telos*.

Horizon/horizonal structure

Merleau-Ponty follows **Husserl**'s observation that when one grasps or understands an object, more is given in the experience than just the actual appearing profile of the object. The perceptual act, then, must "intend" or be tacitly oriented toward other aspects not actually given, but which are either held as previously present or anticipated such as to give sense to the presentation. When an object is viewed, then, I intend all of its other sides through the horizons of this actual appearing. For Merleau-Ponty, this is an important point of contact between **phenomenology** and **Gestalt psychology** (*PrP*, 14–16). Temporal experience also involves horizonal structures that include a **retention** of the past and a **protention** of the future of the actual present. Phenomenology, then, provides a description of a thick notion of experience that cannot be accounted for through classical concepts. The natural world is thus the "horizon of all horizons" that provides the ultimate unity of my life (*PhP*, 345).

Humanism and Terror (1947) [*HT*]

Merleau-Ponty's *Humanism and Terror* is a collection of political essays from **Les Temps modernes**, focused on **Koestler**'s novel *Darkness at Noon*, which generally offers him a pretext for developing a subtle or difficult humanism through a position he will later himself call his **"wait-and-see-Marxism"** (*AD*, 227–33).

Author's Preface

The collection begins with a preface in which Merleau-Ponty outlines his position and responds to the initial attacks on his essays. Indeed, in 1947 Merleau-Ponty was still optimistic that Communist structures might embody a genuine **Marxism**, and this preface clarifies his preference. Communism is attacked for its willingness to embrace "deception, cunning, violence, propaganda" in political practice, and the criticism draws upon the intuitive attraction of liberal ideals such as truth, law, and individual freedom. Yet, such proclaimed ideals do not necessarily reflect the real relations between citizens in these countries whose structures include violence, economic wars, suppression of unions, and colonialism. The distance between the ideals and the reality is a form of "mystification in liberalism" (*HT*, xiii). Communism, then, is perhaps more honest, refusing to mask its own violence with high-flying ideals. But the deeper point is one of Marxist analysis: The function of a political system is to establish and regulate "relations among men," and each political system ought to be judged according to its ability to "establish among men relations that are human" (*HT*, xv).

With this in hand, Merleau-Ponty examines *Darkness at Noon*, not to critique its historical accuracy, but to demonstrate its failure to reach the level of Marxist analysis, for which Bukharin's behavior cannot be reduced to the classical categories of individual ethics and objective ethics, liberalism or communism. For Merleau-Ponty, every political actor is caught in the "inevitable **ambiguity**" of historical action and becoming aware that the *sense* or meaning of any "political conduct, however justified it may once have been," can be altered by the course of history itself and in fact become its opposite (*HT*, xvi). Since even the best of intentions to further the Revolution can have counter-revolutionary consequences, Merleau-Ponty suggests a form of **historical responsibility** that encompasses both intentions *and* consequences.

Even though he is optimistic in these essays, he does admit the important complementary question to his critique of liberal mystification: "Is communism still equal to its humanist intentions?" (*HT*, xviii). In this question one can see Merleau-Ponty fundamental commitment to a **Marxist humanism**, a commitment he will not renounce even when the cracks in his optimism break open. For Merleau-Ponty in 1947, this was already a real threat, as he sensed: "It is impossible to be an anti-Communist and it is not possible to be a Communist" (*HT*, xxi). The subtlety of his position resulted in either misunderstandings or deliberate misreadings, and the remainder of this preface addresses these critics. For Merleau-Ponty, "an action can produce something else than it envisaged, but nevertheless political man assumes its consequences. Our critics want no such harsh conditions. They need a black and white line between the guilty and the innocent" (*HT*, xxxvi).

Chapter One: Koestler's Dilemmas

The first chapter examines *Darkness at Noon* in relation to its depiction of materialism, and Merleau-Ponty critiques the overly simplistic presentation of Bukharin (as Rubashov). **Koestler** presents Rubashov as confessing as a traitor because of the arid materialism of his "objective" ethics, and Merleau-Ponty concludes that there is "very little Marxism in *Darkness at Noon*" (*HT*, 4). The presented caricature of Marxism fails to capture the spirit of Marxist humanism, which requires recognizing the paradoxical and existential structures of the lived experience of political action. Yet establishing Koestler's tenuous understanding of Marxism is just the beginning of these essays. The question for Merleau-Ponty is a philosophical one: How can one develop a political thinking that sustains the paradoxical structures of political action? How can one embrace the ambiguity between the Commissar and the

Yogi without being forced to choose? For Merleau-Ponty, Marxism is "a theory of concrete subjectivity and concrete action—of subjectivity and action committed within a historical situation" (*HT*, 22).

Chapter Two: Bukharin and the Ambiguities of History

The second chapter shifts from Koestler's novel to the real events around the trial of Bukharin in 1938, which amounted to but "a few facts in a fog of shifting meanings" (*HT*, 27). Despite the pretense to a "classical" trial structure, it had the tenor of a Revolutionary trial in which events require an historical interpretation of still-open questions (*HT*, 27). Although the trial does not have the view from above it pretends, recognizing this fact would undermine its authority and make explicit the tribunal's political action in creating history rather than judging in History's name. The meanings of one's actions are open to historical contingency, and successful political action is as difficult as any form of expression. Such a proposal leads Marxist humanism to a "harsh notion of responsibility, based not on what men intended but what they find they have achieved in the light of the event" (*HT*, 42). The structure of **historical responsibility** gives a sense to the political actor who admits having performed a treasonous act while denying the label of "traitor" (*HT*, 46). Moreover, Bukharin's actual claims on the stand reveal a subtle humanism becoming aware of the existential contingency of the meaning of political action. There are no "separate" individuals, and "no one can flatter himself that his hands are clean" (*HT*, 60). For Merleau-Ponty, the insight of the novel is that objective ethics and individual ethics can exist in the same person at the same time, an ambiguity that cannot be registered in classical ethics.

Chapter Three: Trotsky's Rationalism

And yet, to what extent is History "rational"? Discussing Trotsky in relation to Bukharin, this chapter considers the lived experience of political action. Action never takes place from a position outside of history, and thus the actor must take their "bearings at every moment in a general situation which is changing, like a traveler who moves into a changing countryside continuously altered by his own advance" (*HT*, 94). From within history, Stalin, Trotsky, and Bukharin all must respond to the future they sense as probable but never certain (*HT*, 95). Like an artist, the political actor responds to an urgency or question that is only latent in the landscape and only exists after it has been addressed, and the political expression is successful when it has established an audience and a place in common history as the now seemingly natural sequel of events. Marxism, then, is like a philosophy of political **expression**.

Chapter Four: From the Proletarian to the Commissar

Through Marxist humanism, Merleau-Ponty asks whether the communist regimes of his day deserve the title of "Marxist," to be evaluated according to the actual "system of relations among men" and to nature through production (*HT*, 101). Merleau-Ponty again makes the point that violence is a reality of both communist and liberal politics, yet beyond the simple frankness of the communist relation to violence, Merleau-Ponty here introduces a second reason to prefer the communist alternative: "All we know is different kinds of violence and we ought to prefer revolutionary violence because it has a future of humanism" (*HT*, 107). But can this future justify present violence? This question, however, is based upon a classical conception of the subject as pure **consciousness**, above the throes of history and violence, and fails to address the existential reality of political experience: "We do not have a choice between purity and violence but between different kinds of violence. Inasmuch as we are incarnate beings, violence is our lot" (*HT*, 109). For Merleau-Ponty, the present and the future, the self and others *encroach upon each other*, and this intertwining reality is what gives rise to historical responsibility for our actions, since indeed, *we are our actions and our relations* (cf. *HT*, 109–10). A properly balanced theory of the proletariat would offer a natural source of humanism in its reconfiguration of the relations among humans and between humans and nature, and this would be a humanism won in history, not thought from above. This is what justifies a **wait-and-see-Marxism**: history has a *sense* if not a direction; that is, it is moving toward the power of the proletariat and the reconciliation of the contradictions inherent within capitalism, yet this resolution is guaranteed by neither History nor World Spirit.

Chapter Five: The Yogi and the Proletarian

If the Commissar (the Party) might not be wholly trusted to direct the Revolution, can a return to individualism guarantee a humanist future? Given that a universal class revolution was not sparked and that the survival of the Revolution had to be guaranteed by the Commissar, it appears that classical Marxism might be nothing more than a utopia. Yet for Merleau-Ponty, Marxism remains not simply one philosophy of history among others, one form of humanism among others; rather, is it "*the* philosophy of history" and "*it cannot be surpassed*" as a mode of humanistic "critique" since it recognizes our coexistence as the engine of history and demands a *material* analysis of relations (153). The existential structure of lived experience demands that we consider all **dimensions** at once, not reduce history to merely economic causality. Even if Marxism was wrong in its revolutionary predictions, "it still makes us understand that humanity is humanity only in name as long as most of mankind lives by selling itself, while some are masters and others slaves" (155). According to Merleau-Ponty, Koestler's error arises insofar as he misinterprets Commissar politics for Marxism and thereby inclines toward the Yogi of individual revelation. His fear comes from a personal distrust of materialism, or an inability to imagine an ethics in which no one is purely innocent and no one absolutely guilty. Koestler had, in short, "had enough of ambiguities," "enough of problems," such as to spark a desire for "absolute values and clear ideas" (*HT*, 167). Yet the solution to one's personal psychological situation ought not to be offered up as "a solution for the problems of our times" (*HT*, 167). Such a solution can only genuinely be found in embracing the ambiguous structure of lived experience and historical responsibility.

Conclusion

After offering some broad rules to help encourage a return of Marxist humanism despite super-power politics, the book concludes with an exhortation to embrace the link between existential thought and Marxist humanism by seeking "harmony with ourselves and others [...] not only in *a priori* reflection and solitary thought but through the experience of concrete situations and in a living dialogue with others" (*HT*, 187). Such a marriage of **existentialism** and Marxism reveals that "[t]*he human world is an open or unfinished system and the same radical contingency which threatens it with discord also rescues it from the inevitability of disorder and prevents us from despairing of it*" (*HT*, 188).

Husserl, Edmund (1859–1938)

German philosopher and founder of **phenomenology**. Husserl's work exerts a strong influence over Merleau-Ponty. In particular, Merleau-Ponty regularly expresses a critical stance toward Husserl's **transcendental phenomenology** and a positive taking up of his elusive later philosophy, **genetic phenomenology**. Many of Merleau-Ponty's central concepts are initially found in Husserl's work, as indicated in the index to this dictionary.

The Husserl Archives at Louvain

In late 1938, Father H. L. Van Breda transported some forty thousand pages of Husserl's unpublished (short-hand) notes to Belgium, along with thousands of pages of manuscripts produced by Husserl's assistants (including **Fink**). Given the intellectual climate in Germany and Husserl's Jewish heritage, this act likely saved these documents from imminent destruction, and these pages have been a continued source of inspiration for phenomenologists the world over. In March 1939, Merleau-Ponty was the first ever non-Louvain based researcher to visit the archive, where he consulted three unpublished transcriptions from Husserl's later work: *Ideas II*; Part III of *The Crisis of European Sciences and Transcendental Phenomenology*; and "Foundational Investigations of the Phenomenological Origin of the Spatiality of Nature: The Originary Ark, the Earth, Does Not Move." Cited in *Phenomenology of Perception*, these texts shape Merleau-Ponty's understanding of Husserl's late work, even reappearing in his final courses in the *Collège de France Lectures*. Although he spent little time at the Archives after 1939, Merleau-Ponty played a key role in bringing some of the transcriptions to Paris both in the mid-1940s and in the late 1950s.

Hyppolite, Jean (1907–68)

French philosopher and contemporary of Merleau-Ponty, particularly known for his studies of **Hegel**. Hyppolite and Merleau-Ponty have an extended exchange on the scope of Merleau-Ponty's project in *Primacy of Perception* (*PrP*, 39–41)

The "I can"

Merleau-Ponty adopts the phrase "I can" from **Husserl** as a way of describing our lived experience of bodily intentionality. The perceived world is structured not according to an "I think," but rather according to our body's capabilities and powers, a lived "I can." This is closely associated with our **motor intentionality** and the function of the **intentional arc**.

The Incarnate Subject: Malebranche, Biran, and Bergson on the Union of Body and Soul (1947–8) [*UBS*]

In the academic year 1947–8, Merleau-Ponty taught a course at both the Université de Lyon and at the *ENS* in Paris designed to prepare students for the *agrégation* in philosophy. The book consists in correlated and collected student notes, not Merleau-Ponty's lecture notes, and was published posthumously. Given the intention of preparing students for the exam, the course involves extensive "explanation of texts," but Merleau-Ponty also provides some critical response to the standard readings and several revealing interpretations.

Reading the History of Philosophy

The first lecture problematizes the possibility of an objective study of the history of philosophy. Taking **Brunschvicg**'s interpretation of Malebranche as a "failed Spinoza" as his example, Merleau-Ponty suggests that "two dangers" threaten the study of the history of philosophy. First, one might be tempted to analyze texts "literally," rendering the pursuit blind since the texts are never genuinely "re-thought"; second, one might be tempted (like Brunschvicg) to project one's own philosophy into the object of study (*UBS*, 30). For Merleau-Ponty, the **history of philosophy** must be pursued as both subjective and objective, through a personal resumption of the problems contained in the texts. That is, "[t]he history of philosophy is a confrontation, a communication" between the philosopher being studied and the philosopher seeking an understanding (31).

Lectures

The problem to be addressed in the course naturally emerges from **Descartes**' work, who in fact primarily discusses the *distinction* rather than the *union* of the soul and body. For Descartes, the union is *lived*, but cannot be an object of thought. The course begins with Malebranche's approach to the *cogito*, and considers his foreshadowing of **Gestalt psychology** and **phenomenology** in his commitment to something like lived experience. In the eighth lecture, the focus shifts to Maine de Biran, a philosopher known for his focus on embodiment. Brunschvicg attacks this position, suggesting that a return to the body is a negation of all of traditional philosophy. For Brunschvicg, suggests Merleau-Ponty, "[p]hilosophy consists of a conversion, clarifying, beyond psychological events, the pure relationship of the mind to the idea" (62). Biran's return to the body, however, limits itself to the "outside spectator," and never attempts to complete the account through a genuine phenomenological description of "corporeality, the lived world, and others in this new dimension" (75). Biran ultimately remains trapped within **psychologism**.

Turning to **Bergson**, Merleau-Ponty focuses on *Matter and Memory*. In the first chapter of this text, Bergson presents a theory of action of a "body in the presence of the world" (87). This living body is, he suggests, a "center of real action" that can "respond" rather than react, and its response is never wholly determinate and foreseeable. Moreover, as a center of action, the "objects which surround my body reflect its possible action upon them" (88). Perception thus cannot be reduced to a passivity; it is an "anticipation" of the body's potential responses. For Bergson, the world is an aggregate of perceived or unperceived *images*. This is a total being from which my perspective carves itself out according to its ability to act, and as such the problem of the *cogito* seems irrelevant within this realism of images. And yet, from where does Bergson tell this ontological story, logically divorced from the primacy of perception? This approach precludes any genuine return to lived perception.

Nevertheless, Bergson's utter disavowal of **constituting consciousness** is an important moment in the history of philosophy: a position that understands the "thing and consciousness of the thing" as linked without any priority given to either (89). Consciousness offers the possibility of "transcending" both realism and idealism (90), a possibility lost when Bergson retreats to his idiosyncratic realism of images. Despite his ultimate retreat, Merleau-Ponty is attracted to Bergson's recognition that the body is "a moment in the dialectic of time, and all consciousness of the past has a relationship with the body" (92). In the end, despite some gestures in this direction, Bergson refuses to let the body *be* the subject in the strong sense.

"Indirect Language and the Voices of Silence" (1952) [*S; MPAR*]

This essay was extracted and revised for separate publication from a manuscript that Merleau-Ponty abandoned in the early 1950s, published posthumously as **The Prose of the World**. The title of the essay alludes to its two main interlocutors. Merleau-Ponty's emphasis here on *indirect language* constitutes his answer to **Sartre**'s *What is Literature?*, while the bulk of his analyses relating to the theory of expression respond to **Malraux**'s *The Voices of Silence*. I have included some schematic section titles that do not occur in Merleau-Ponty's text.

[I. Structure in Speaking and Painting]

This essay opens with **structuralism**, exploring Saussure's definition of the meaning of each sign as the "divergence between itself and other signs" (*MPAR*, 76). Language, then, is a system of differences without any positive terms. To the question of how we can discuss a *difference* in meaning when the terms have no meaning in themselves, Merleau-Ponty alludes to Zeno's paradoxes and reminds us that lived gestures accomplish seemingly paradoxical activities all the time. Language is a structure in the process of evolution and internal articulation. It exists in the manner of a style, just as all of my gestures will unfold from my style, and yet are not "contained" in my style in advance. The child's first phonemic oppositions are a creative way of gearing into the spoken language surrounding the child, soliciting his or her voice and initiating the child into how signs can be meaningful through differences. These first gestures institute a style from which all speech will emerge, without thereby containing all of language in advance.

If meaning arises "at the edge of signs" and if "the genesis of meaning is never completed," then language cannot be a secondary operation in relation to thought (78, 79). Communication does not involve an act of interpretation, but rather a lending of ourselves to the movement of the signs. In the lived experience of language, there is never a pure meaning wholly transparent to a pure subject; meaning is forever "opaque." Not even the speaker has an "original text" of thoughts, his or her speech is satisfactory when it "reaches an equilibrium" (80). Thus, if "the idea of a *complete* expression is nonsensical" then "all language is **indirect** or allusive—that is, if you will, **silence**" (80). Even our most "direct" forms of speaking themselves do not admit of a one-to-one relation between words and ideas mapped onto a world in-itself, this is simply an illusion of the powerful structuring of our experience produced by the internal articulations of the language we speak (81).

Since the meaning of a word cannot be an associated "silent" thought, language itself must bear "the meaning of thought as a footprint signifies the movement and effort of a body" (82). That is, meaning is the other side of the lived and expressive gesture that takes it up, and into which this activity sediments for further expressions. Communication is possible insofar as we can lend our bodies to the gestures or traces of other expressive bodies, by walking in their footprints we gear into the *sense* of their movement and their world. Even if we can never fully recreate their expression, our performance is a **coherent deformation** that takes up the sense of their expression, which for that matter was never a pure and transparent possession of theirs either. Language appears to involve the indirect or oblique nature of embodied and lived meaning, which is to say "silence."

If this is the case, then "the writer's act of expression is not very different from the painter's" (82). One cannot simply say the painter speaks the silent language of color and line, but rather that both writer and painter are "silent" insofar as what they express is *beyond* the direct meaning of their gestures. This silent "beyond" is not an empty field, but is the latent and operative meaning of a particular lived experience, it is present as absent, haunting each word through the tone, pacing, context, and exclusion of all that is left unsaid. A writer's skill in using acquired significations does not guarantee a "direct" meaning, since "language expresses as much by what is between the words as by the words themselves" (82).

Consider the example of a film of Matisse **painting** viewed in slow motion. The video reveals a slight hesitation as Matisse's painterly gesture takes into account all that the stroke must respond to in the overall effect to bring about the painting that is in the "process of becoming" (83). This is a paradoxical response to the painting that does not yet exist, and each stroke establishes new relations on the canvas and carries itself into the whole as the stroke chosen over all the other possible one, even if now it looks to have been the only possible one for this painting. For "the truly expressive word and thus for all language in the phase in which it is being established," the writer too "gropes around a significative intention which is not guided by any text, and which is precisely in the process of writing the text" (83). The word the writer "comes down on" after their hesitation is not the one that has the right signification, but the one that responds to the situation, the past of language, and the future of that language that will be after its coherent deformation by this very act. These indirect sources of meaning are the "threads of silence with which speech is intertwined" (84). Thus, indirect language is the fundamental of language, and there is no genuine difference between the voices of speech and painting's voices of silence.

[II. Malraux and creative expression]

For **Malraux**, one can only compare painting and speech by going beyond their intended objects of representation (the world versus ideas) in order to discover a fundamental connection in "the category of creative expression" (84). Malraux identifies a parallel development in these two arts, from the classical attempt at an "objective" representation (exact language/faithful copies of Nature), to the "modern" return to "subjectivity" (84). Merleau-Ponty critiques this distinction by beginning with classical painting. Despite the "masters'" attempt at convincing representation, their paintings were nonetheless moments of "creative expression" (85). They may have thought they were only asking the world for its objective secrets, yet they were simultaneously expressing a way of responding to the world; that is, classical painting too is "the invention of a world" (85). Malraux's explanatory division between classical objective painting and modern subjective expression is not decisive, and the poles seem to "blend into one another" (86).

On the other hand, neither do painters such as Klee and **Cézanne** seem to fit the description of "modern" glorifications of subjectivity, since they are certainly not part of the "tribe of the ambitious and the drugged" (Malraux, cited by Merleau-Ponty, *MPAR*, 88). By contrast, Merleau-Ponty suggests that modern painting is marked by a rejection of the idea that a "complete" work is an objective representation convincing for the senses (88). For the modern painter, the work is complete when it communicates, when it "reaches its viewer and invites him to take up the gesture which created it and [...] to rejoin, without any guide other than a movement of the invented line (an almost incorporeal trace), the silent world of the painter, henceforth uttered and accessible" (88). So expressing the world is not the sole possession of classical painting; modern painting too can be an expressing of the world even if it doesn't limit itself to the "prose" of the senses. This is the problem of modern painting—not a return to the individual—but "the problem of knowing how one can communicate without the help of a preestablished Nature which all men's senses open upon" (89).

This leads to Merleau-Ponty's development of the notion of *style*. If the modern painter is not defined as the painter who puts his or her subjective experience into the work, he or she nonetheless does put his or her *style* there. The painter's style is what unites in an open trajectory the early works with the late ones, not because the painter returns to the early works to detect what will become of the late works, but because all of the earlier works *weigh* upon the present expression, containing the earlier attempts and taking them up in the direction of their *sense*. Completed expressions sediment into the painter's being as if "new organs," existing as a possibility for going further in unpredictable directions. Each new expression gears into an "inner schema" that becomes more solidified and mature, but never finalized or frozen insofar as the artist remains an artist. This *style* is not a decision, it "germinates" at the surface of the work, where the expressing body and the expression intertwine. A style, then, is not a set of procedures or technical applications, but "a mode of formulation that is just as recognizable for others and just as little visible to him as his silhouette or his everyday gestures" (90). As such, *style* is already at work in the painter's very perception of the world, indeed, "perception already *stylizes*" (91). As soon as the painter sees something *as something-to-be-painted*, the stylizing has already begun that will crystallize in the expression.

[III. Perception, History, Expression]

If a painter neither copies the world nor invests the canvas with an egotistical self-portrait, then the act of painting is an expression of the *encounter* between the painter and the world (93). Art has the never-ending task of expressing the world as a trajectory toward the truth that it can never reach. The activity of painting is not the pure work of an intellectual genius, but the effort to "advance the line" of the open trajectory of expression that takes up the painter's earlier works and all of her experience into a single gesture responding to the work that will only later exist—"without the painter himself [or herself] ever being able to say [...] what comes from him and what comes from things" (95). Even with **structuralism** bearing down on Merleau-Ponty's understanding, it is the phenomenology of expression that requires the **situated freedom** of painting as a paradoxical "response to what the world, the past, and the painter's own completed works demanded" (96).

Each moment of this trajectory accomplishes what **Husserl** calls a *Stiftung*, a foundation or an **institution**, which opens an entire future, an "unlimited fecundity." The *tradition* is that which, although *forgotten* as an explicit object of thought, is taken up and carried forward by our lived gestures.

For Malraux, the "tradition" is established by the museum or by the historical analysis looking at **history** from the outside. And yet this view fails to account for the open and allusive logic of **expression**. The expression is a new organ in an "open **field**" of possibilities we name "human culture" (96). The museum, then, does not create the unity of the history of painting, rather it is a secondary history, a history offered by a *pensée de survol*. There is another, deeper history in which the first wall paintings "set forth the world as 'to be painted'" and "called for an indefinite future of painting" (97). This is the lived and latent history of painting that tacitly weighs upon each stroke, each gesture, insofar as we attempt to express the world. This history is never the object of thought, but is carried forward by "each painter who revives, recaptures, and renews the entire undertaking of painting in each new work" (97).

The place of each painter in this history is that of an institution. "Vermeer" (the man, or his atelier) stands as an institution, an organ for having and expressing an encounter with the world. Vermeer too was an historical expression, taking up a past that was not "his" and yet not anywhere else than in his response. The museum, then, is an objective reduction of the history of painting, whereas only a **phenomenal reduction** would allow the underlying logic of painting to appear. Something is lost in the "museum's mournful light" (99). The value of the work is not its having reached the walls of the Louvre, but in its having expressed a human community, a manner of encountering the world. The museum presents only "fallen images," the lifeless traces of that rich encounter and expression of a world.

Is this approach an aesthetics of **psychologism**, reducing the painting to a product of the painter's life or community? In fact, the painter's life is a part of what the painter must respond to through his or her style while remaining oriented toward the future, and Malraux is correct to reject dogmatic psychoanalytic *explanations* of paintings. But one need not swing to the cult of the great artist as a pure and free intellect. As Merleau-Ponty argued in **"Cézanne's**

Doubt," the great artist does not transcend his or her situation, but succeeds in making it a means of expression of his or her encounter with the world (101).

Merleau-Ponty also critiques Malraux's discussion of "miniatures" and recurrent forms as discovered by historical science. According to Malraux, despite different scales or different cultures, one finds the "very same style" of expression (101). Thus, he concludes, there is a rational *telos* of art that unfolds in individual artists, although this does not require an overarching Hegelian Spirit. For Merleau-Ponty, such a conclusion is unwarranted. As he has argued, a gesture is not a rote mechanical set of movements; rather, it involves catching on to the *sense* of a movement that can be deployed in radically different contexts, such as singing a tune or playing it on an instrument. Thus, it is hardly surprising that the traces of the human world bear the style of human gestures, regardless of scale. Even our simple perceptual acts are stylizing ways of taking up the world, and the artist's gesture simply provides a more concrete trace of this style. As Merleau-Ponty writes: "All perception, all action which presupposes it, and in short every human use of the body is already *primordial expression*" (104). This same primordial expression is what connects, through a similar style, the works from distant cultures.

The unity of the history of culture begins, for Merleau-Ponty, at a level lower than isolated events and thereby needs no external synthesis. He proposes "to consider the order of culture or meaning an original order of **advent**" (105). Since every human gesture involves an indirect meaning as much as a direct signification, it follows that every human gesture has, as its horizon, the whole of human gestures, both past and *possible*. As he writes, the value of each gesture "exceeds its simple presence, and in this respect it is allied or implicated in advance with all other efforts of expression" (105). Thus, rather than some transcendent logic, culture is an open trajectory of expression in which each expression takes up and sustains the tradition while simultaneously creatively playing it forward. Drawing a key concept from Malraux, Merleau-Ponty concludes that each expression accomplishes a **coherent deformation** of the field of expression itself. At the moment of expression, the future of the expression is unknown, just as at the moment of birth or institution all that is certain is that "from now on something cannot fail to happen, be it but the end of what has just begun" (106).

Thus, the logic of **advent** offers an alternative to empiricist and idealist accounts of history. The trajectory of history is tied together by the simple fact that all gestures are "efforts to express" (106). The history of painting illustrates the genesis of *sense*, the taking up and altering of the past in an open trajectory toward the future, and "[a]dvent is a promise of events," not a destiny. Thus, **Hegel** was more correct when, in his *Philosophy of Right*, he emphasized the notion of **historical responsibility**. As Merleau-Ponty writes: "By action, I make myself responsible for everything; I accept the aid of external accidents just as I accept their betrayals" (109). If this notion is correct, then one should be judged not by intentions or consequences, but by *both*, or as Hegel says, by the work of the act and the actor's "success in making values become facts" (109). An act, then, is to be judged according to its success as an **expression**, as an institution or reinstitution in the field of culture and its ability to open a future. Merleau-Ponty concludes that this open **dialectic** is precisely the phenomenon of expression—a movement or trajectory for which there is no pre-existing plan, and yet which has a *sense*. In short, expression is the intertwining of the for-itself and the in-itself, and of the self and others.

[IV. Indirect Language in Literary Expression]

Merleau-Ponty considers what the above structure of expression reveals about *literary* expression. The novelist, he argues, does not speak to the reader's mind, but rather leaves expressive traces on the page soliciting the reader's body. These traces are less the description of some events, ideas, theses, or conclusions, than "the expression of style" (113). Language is not a set of ideas, but a manner of dwelling in the world that we "never stop developing" (114). But this essential incompleteness and **ambiguity** is the very essence of language, not a weakness to be overcome. The "meaning of a novel too is perceptible at first only as a *coherent deformation* imposed upon the visible" (115). We find the structure of expression to be the essential nature of our embodied and perceptual **being-in-the-world**, the very "existence" of the mind "in act" (115).

[V. Painting and Writing]

What might be said about everyday forms of expression? For Merleau-Ponty, it seems that in all cases, culture prolongs the past, but it does so in a manner that can fall either toward the side of a pure repetition, or toward a pure creation (116). On the side of creation, there is a further distinction between linguistic arts and painting. Whereas all paintings are *rivals*, the acquired language is a fecund reservoir for the writer. The Spirit of Painting is a product of the museum, since painting cannot paint painting; the trajectory of speech is able to turn back upon itself and thus able to move toward "truth" even if this means speaking of itself (117). As Merleau-Ponty writes: "Heraclitus's writing casts light for us as no broken statues can, because its signification is deposited and concentrated in it in another way than theirs is in them, and because nothing equals the ductility of speech. In short, language speaks, and the voices of painting are the voices of silence" (117).

Thus, "language is not meaning's servant, and yet it does not govern meaning" (*MPAR*, 120). Any attempt to step outside of the expressive activities destroys the expressive attempt, just as thinking about a gesture deprives it of its lived fluidity. The effort of painting, language, history, political action, and philosophy is to gear into the trajectories of culture, which "advance obliquely and not straight towards ends or concepts," and the only way to do this is to learn to "free their spontaneity"—speaking, then, is at once listening.

Ineinander

This German word drawn from **Husserl** means "intertwining" and is increasingly adopted by Merleau-Ponty to describe the ontological structure of the **flesh**. He characterizes it as a **chiasm** or as a relationship of **enveloping/enveloped** (*VI*, 268).

Institution

In "Indirect Language and the Voices of Silence" (1952), Merleau-Ponty begins to speak of *institution* in relation to **constituted** language, **expression**, and the **sedimented** structures of available significations. This emerges from **Husserl**'s use of the term *Stiftung* (foundation/institution). The institution is the establishing of a tradition as an open trajectory of future actions, and this function is possible insofar as the institution itself is forgotten and tacitly taken up and carried forward in new acts. An act of speech or **painting**, then, is to be judged according to its success in shaping a **field** of culture toward an open future. In his 1954–5 course of *The Collège de France Lectures*, Merleau-Ponty suggests replacing the notion of expression with that of institution, since institution avoids the problems of a philosophy of **consciousness** (*IP*, 76). Nevertheless, the logic of *expression* remains prominent in this course and afterwards, suggesting that institution offers a clarification rather than a replacement of expression. An institution is a **coherent deformation** of the past and present that opens a field of future expression, and in this course he identifies four levels of institution: vital/affective institution, institution of works, institution of language, and historical institution. For Merleau-Ponty, given the paradoxical nature of institution as *between* activity and passivity, philosophy must develop a form of **interrogation** that is able to gear into the open and contingent trajectory of sense.

Intellectualism (or idealism)

General category of philosophical approaches (opposed to **empiricism**) privileging *reasons* or explanations through the categories of the **constituting consciousness** or explicit intellectual acts. For an intellectualist, phenomena are the product of a pure and self-transparent consciousness which bestows meaning in the world and accomplishes the syntheses that give our experience its unity and its meaning. They conceive of the universe as a *pure interiority*. Given such a general description, this category includes Cartesian and Kantian philosophies, particularly when pursued as **reflective analysis**, as well as the underlying ontology of classical psychology.

Throughout his writings, Merleau-Ponty argued that Husserl's earlier formulation of a **transcendental phenomenology** was also caught up with a form of idealism that privileged the transcendental ego and constituting consciousness. But the very movement of phenomenological reflection led Husserl toward a **genetic phenomenology**: "The more he considered it," writes Merleau-Ponty, "the more Husserl recognized that reflection discovers not some eternal ideas, but rather an intellectual emergence of ideas, a *genesis of sense* (***Sinngenesis***)" (*CPP*, 334). Merleau-Ponty thereby recognized the importance of distinguishing the difference between intellectualism and phenomenology, and much of his careful analysis in ***Phenomenology of Perception***. See also "empiricism versus intellectualism (Merleau-Ponty's methodology)."

Intentional arc

Borrowing a term from Fischer, Merleau-Ponty suggests that any explicit conscious act "is underpinned by an 'intentional arc' that projects around us our past, our future, our human milieu, our physical situation, our ideological situation, and our moral situation" (*PhP*, 137). This **non-thetic** intentionality creates the unity of our experience and our world, and reveals the need for a new form of analysis of **consciousness—existential analysis** (138). The intentional arc is not an intellectual act, but an embodied and meaningful orientation toward the world according to the **dimensions** of our experience, including our **sexuality** (160).

Intentionality

Often identified as the "principle discovery of phenomenology," Merleau-Ponty argues that the recognition that "all **consciousness** is consciousness of something" is already present in Kant (*PhP*, lxxxi). Nevertheless, Husserl's phenomenology suggests two distinct modalities of intentionality: act intentionality, or the explicit act of judging or deciding, and **operative intentionality**— "the intentionality that establishes the natural and pre-predicative unity of the world and of our life" (lxxxii). This enriched notion of intentionality is necessary for us to understand our lived and embodied experience of a meaningful world that we sustain through our possible gestures and yet do not constitute through our intellectual acts.

Intercorporeality/intersubjectivity

Merleau-Ponty's discussion of intersubjectivity begins from Husserl's work on the experience of others, yet he shifts the emphasis from the epistemic challenge of experiencing others to the existential structures of a shared world through our bodies and our cultural objects. Thus, he stresses in **Phenomenology of Perception** that Husserl's investigations require we recognize not that transcendental subjectivity can discover others, but that it must always already "*be* an intersubjectivity" (*PhP*, lxxvi). The very structure of the **phenomenal field** is already infused with intersubjective structures. Simply, transcendental subjectivity is "an intersubjectivity" (378). One of the **dimensions** of our existence is the social world, and exists prior to any questions of knowledge. There is not first an isolated subject that must be related to others; rather, the isolated subject is derivative upon a prior intersubjective existence. As Merleau-Ponty writes, "the structures of the For-Others must already be the dimensions of the For-Self" (474). Through our **anonymity** and our **generality** we are always already in the world together.

This account is perhaps deepened even further through the structure of **reversibility** in *The Visible and the Invisible*. Merleau-Ponty suggests that the reversibility between my body and itself, and my body and others, guarantees a primordial *intercorporeality*, a shared belonging to the reversible **flesh** of the world. Touch with another is reversible in just the manner of touch between my two hands, and this offers an intertwining or **encroachment** at the level of **wild Being** prior to the distinctions of self and other (*VI*, 142).

Interrogation

In his late philosophy, Merleau-Ponty began to develop a critique of philosophical methodology that pointed toward a new mode of philosophical engagement. For instance, at the end of **"Eye and Mind"** Merleau-Ponty recognizes that the structure of **expression** and **history** indicate that humans are condemned to never complete the expression of Being. But rather than despairing of this conclusion, he suggests that philosophy seek a mode of *interrogation* that, like **painting**, takes up the open trajectory of sense that at once repeats and reshapes that sense through a **coherent deformation** (*MPAR*, 149). In *The Visible and the Invisible*, each of the first three chapters develops a critique of the history of philosophy and reveals just what philosophy needs for a genuine ontological interrogation. Leaving behind reflection, dialectic, and intuition, Merleau-Ponty argues that interrogation must not seek positive answers to perennial questions, but must remain committed to the absurd effort of expression that knows it can never fully complete its project; that is, interrogation must remain *expression*. Philosophical interrogation then is an "art," or an "inspired exegesis" that aims at nothing less than the attempt to express **wild Being** itself (*VI*, 133).

Intersubjectivity

See **intercorporeality/intersubjectivity**.

Intertwining

See **chiasm**, *Ineinander*.

Janet, Pierre (1859–1947)

French psychologist and neurologist. Janet's concept of the **"reality function"** of consciousness is discussed by Merleau-Ponty in relation to **Bergson**'s notion of **"attention to life."** See *SB*, 163; *PhP*, 81–2.

Jaspers, Karl (1883–1969)

German psychiatrist and philosopher. Although Jaspers is an important figure in German **existentialism**, Merleau-Ponty is primarily familiar with Jasper's early work in psychology, and cites this early work in *Phenomenology of Perception*.

Judgment

In Chapter Three of the Introduction to *Phenomenology of Perception*, Merleau-Ponty discusses whether the concept of "judgment" might allow **intellectualism** to insulate its approach from the critique of the **constancy hypothesis**. Intellectualism introduces the notion of judgment as *"what sensation is missing in order to make a perception possible"* (*PhP*, 34). Since judgment thus has the task of organizing **sensations**, intellectualism and **empiricism** must share the same **unquestioned belief in the world** that builds experience from punctual components. **Reflective analysis** accepts the role of sensations, and thus the only way to account for meaningful experience is by concluding that perception is ultimately judgment. Yet both common sense and phenomenological reflection indicate a genuine distinction between perception and judging. For instance, an illusion does not disappear the moment I understand it. Perhaps judgments might be interpreted as a form of lived or "natural" judgment, that is, a judgment "unaware of its own reasons" (44). Nevertheless, such a notion (drawn from **Descartes**) reduces judgment to a passive phenomenon. The inherent flaw of reflective analysis and transcendental philosophy is that "[b]etween myself, who is analyzing perception, and the self who is actually perceiving, there is always a distance" (45), and yet this distance is crossed in every human act. The impasses of transcendental philosophy are the very starting points of the phenomenology of perception, which waits on "the horizon of Cartesian thought" (46).

Kinesthetic sensations

Often associated with "proprioception," kinesthetic sensations are the sensations one has of the movement of **one's own body** or body parts. See *PhP*, 96.

Koestler, Arthur (1905–83)

Hungarian-born writer and intellectual. Koestler's experience as a journalist during the Spanish Civil War resulted in a disillusionment and rejection of his ties to the Communist Party, famously presented by his novel *Darkness at Noon*. This novel is the explicit subject matter for Merleau-Ponty first major political reflection: *Humanism and Terror* (1947). Koestler's novel depicts the trial of Nicolai Bukharin through the character of Rubashov in the famous Moscow Trials.

Koffka, Kurt (1886–1941)

German-born psychologist and cofounder of **Gestalt psychology**. Koffka was a student of **Husserl**'s. Merleau-Ponty was particularly influenced by Koffka's discussion of the perception of space and by his discussion of *Gestalt* as structure or configuration. See also *PhP*, 505n. 36.

Köhler, Wolfgang (1887–1967)

Born in Estonia, German psychologist Köhler was a key figure in the early development of **Gestalt psychology**. Although Merleau-Ponty explicitly agrees with **Goldstein**'s critique of Köhler's version of Gestalt psychology as overly committed to realism (see *SB*, 136–7), he does cite Köhler's descriptions of **behavior** as proof against **behaviorism** (i.e. 112ff.) and **sensation** as proof against the "**constancy hypothesis**" (*PhP*, 8). Merleau-Ponty also emphasizes that Köhler "assigns psychology the task of developing a 'phenomenological description'" (*PhP*, 506n. 60).

Kojève, Alexandre (1902–68)

A Russian-born student of Karl **Jaspers**, Kojève is responsible for having established the Hegelian spirit of French intellectual life through a series of lectures he presented in Paris in the 1930s.[12] Merleau-Ponty and many of his contemporaries, including **Sartre**, **Lacan**, Raymond Queneau, and Louis Althusser attended these lectures and incorporated Hegelian ideas into their own developing thought. Kojève's emphasis on **Hegel**'s approach to **history** is importantly reflected in Merleau-Ponty's work.

Lacan, Jacques (1901–81)

French structural psychoanalyst. Lacan and Merleau-Ponty, and **Levi-Strauss**, were close friends. Although Merleau-Ponty rarely mentions Lacan's work in his published books, his influence can be seen in the *Child Psychology and Pedagogy* lectures.

Lachelier, Jules (1832–1918)

French philosopher in the neo-Platonic and Kantian traditions, Merleau-Ponty repeats Lachelier's description of an object as "an intertwining of general properties" (*PhP*, 55, 365).

Lachièze-Rey, Pierre (1885–1957)

Influential contemporary Kant scholar during Merleau-Ponty's early career, and a strong voice (along with **Brunschvicg**) in establishing Kantian Idealism as the primary force in French academic philosophy. Lachièze-Rey's philosophy is explicitly discussed by Merleau-Ponty in Part Three, Chapter One ("The *Cogito*") of *Phenomenology of Perception*.

Lagneau, Jules (1851–94)

French philosopher and teacher of several French intellectuals, including **Alain**. Lagneau argued for an intellectualist style of philosophical inquiry known as **reflective analysis**. He did not publish his work, but his ideas have been preserved by a few collections of notes taken from his lectures. In *Phenomenology of Perception*, Merleau-Ponty critiques Lagneau's **intellectualism** (*PhP*, 507–9n. 53).

Lavelle, Louis (1883–1951)

Immediate predecessor in the Chair of Philosophy at the *Collège de France*. Merleau-Ponty discusses Lavelle in *In Praise of Philosophy*.

Lefort, Claude (1924–2010)

French political philosopher, Lefort was Merleau-Ponty's close friend and the posthumous editor of his unpublished manuscripts. The two met in the early 1940s when Lefort was Merleau-Ponty's student at *Lycée Carnot*, and this encounter inspired Lefort to continue in philosophy. In the late 1940s, Lefort contributed several political articles to *Les Temps modernes*. During the early 1950s, Lefort established an "anti-Stalinist" group known as Socialism or Barbarism, which exacerbated his deep conflict with **Sartre**. In 1952, when Sartre abridged Lefort's response to Sartre's own *The Communists and Peace*, and also slipped his own response into the same edition, Lefort broke all ties with *Les Temps modernes*, foreshadowing Merleau-Ponty's own imminent resignation.

Due to their continued friendship, Lefort was granted a privileged access to the deceased philosopher's working notes and personal papers. He oversaw the publication of two unfinished manuscripts, *The Visible and the Invisible* (1964) and *The Prose of the World* (1968). Lefort was also instrumental in bringing forth other publications, including some of the collections of lecture notes from the *Collège de France Lectures*.

Les Philosophes célèbres (1956)

Merleau-Ponty spent several years compiling and editing this beautiful volume that must be classified between an art book and a study in the **history of philosophy**. It includes contributions from nearly fifty philosophers addressing a wide range of thinkers from across the history of thought, ancient through contemporary. Some notable contributors include Bachelard, Beaufret, Deleuze (on **Bergson**), Gandillac, Pontalis, Schutz, and Ryle (on

Hume). Although the volume itself is untranslated, Merleau-Ponty extracted several of his section introductions and included them under the title "Everywhere and Nowhere" in *Signs*.

Les Temps modernes

This journal was founded in 1945 by **Sartre**, along with Merleau-Ponty, **Beauvoir**, and others. Primarily the political editor, in practice Merleau-Ponty acted as Sartre's general co-editor between 1945 and 1952. Merleau-Ponty often resisted having himself explicitly listed, and signed several of his contributions "T. M." He admitted later that he wished to avoid being characterized as merely a writer of current affairs.[13] After his rupture with Sartre, Merleau-Ponty resigned from the editorial board and began publishing his occasional political commentary elsewhere. Many of Merleau-Ponty's best-known articles appeared first in this journal, including **"Indirect Language and the Voices of Silence,"** as well as the chapters of *Humanism and Terror*. See **Sartre** for a discussion of Merleau-Ponty's resignation.

Lévi-Strauss, Claude (1908–2009)

French social anthropologist, structuralist, and long-time friend of Merleau-Ponty's. Merleau-Ponty is particularly attracted to Lévi-Strauss's "'brilliant' integration of **structuralism** with social anthropology" (*S*, 116). See also *CPP*, 236–8.

Lhermitte, (Jacques) Jean (1877–1959)

French neuropsychiatrist whose work on spinal cord and brain injuries, perceptual disorders, pain, and **phantom limb syndrome** were highly influential on Merleau-Ponty in *Phenomenology of Perception*. Lhermitte's book *L'image de notre corps* (1939) is a key to understanding Merleau-Ponty's use of the notion of **body schema**.

Logicism

The opposite of **psychologism**, which is the belief that all mental phenomena can be fully explained by external structures and causal relations, logicism is the belief that a realm of truths in themselves exists that is capable of resisting the skepticism of psychologism (*CPP*, 318). Merleau-Ponty follows the later Husserl in rejecting this position as incapable of explaining the **ambiguities** of lived and perceptual experience (*PhP*, 48, 509–10n. 60).

Lukàcs, Georg (1885–1971)

Hungarian-born Marxist philosopher. Merleau-Ponty considers Lukács's importance in *Adventures of the Dialectic*.

Lycée

In the French school system, *lycées* are secondary schools or "high schools." As a student, Merleau-Ponty finished his secondary education at *Lycée Louis-le-Grand*, a traditional "feeder" for the post-secondary study of philosophy at the *École normale supérieure*. As an instructor, Merleau-Ponty taught more or less consistently at the *lycée* level between the turbulent years of 1931–45 in Beauvais, Chartres, and Paris, before moving to post-secondary institutions.

[Madame Merleau-Ponty] Suzanne Berthe Jolibois

Merleau-Ponty married physician and psychiatrist Suzanne Berthe Jolibois (1914–2010) in late 1940. Their only child, Marianne, was born the following year. Between 1961 and 2010, Madame Merleau-Ponty remained involved in the slow release of Merleau-Ponty's notes and unpublished manuscripts, and several publications explicitly acknowledge her support.

Malraux, André (1901–76)

A writer, art historian, and later political figure, Malraux's book *The Voices of Silence* (1951) is the main focus of Merleau-Ponty's "Indirect Language and the Voices of Silence" (1952). Although he offers a subtle critique of Malraux's theory of art, Merleau-Ponty is particularly interested in Malraux's discussion of creative **expression** and the notion of **coherent deformation**.

"Man and Adversity" (1951) [S]

This essay takes as its lofty goal the establishing of the present and the future of philosophy. Merleau-Ponty argued that the present generation was called to repair the schism between **intellectualism** and **empiricism**, and he ventures that his century will be remembered as the one that "has gone beyond these antitheses" (*S*, 225). Such an accomplishment would involve reaching a **humanism** through ontology that would itself reconcile the very categories that establish humanism in classical thought (226).

The essay begins with a reflection on the impossibility of merely recording the advances in philosophy since 1900. This impossibility is not a result of a lack of time or the presence of incompatible streams, but rather of the fact that any *taking up* of the **history of philosophy** introduces a **coherent deformation**. As Merleau-Ponty writes: "A man cannot receive a heritage of ideas without transforming it by the very fact that he comes to know it, without injecting his own and always different way of being into it" (224). The history of philosophy is not a history of solved problems or universally *acquired* ideas, but a trajectory of various attempts at speaking the mysteries of being which is itself a meaningful trajectory without a predestined end; that is, every philosophy is **expression**. Offering the history of philosophy, then, is an "unlimited task" (225). Nevertheless, each philosopher who speaks carries forward this weight, it "is sedimented in us" and "is our substance" (225). The history of philosophy is sustained in the silence of what is said, and is carried forward without being explicitly thematized.

Despite these risks and the impossibility of the task, one must still speak, and he ventures that the *sense* of the century has been to go "beyond" the battle of **empiricism versus intellectualism** (225). The commitment to absolutes fuels this debate across the human sciences, "but what if it were precisely the case that the order of facts invaded that of values" (226)? Thanks to advances in philosophy, a new **humanism** can be sought from within the inseparability of body and mind, man and adversity. In a striking formulation given his own later philosophy, this results in a discovery at the heart of philosophy of "the notion of **flesh**, that is, of animate body" (227). The flesh, of course, will be a central component in Merleau-Ponty's late ontology nearly a decade later.

Before demonstrating the consequences for **humanism**, Merleau-Ponty first recounts the advances in terms of **psychoanalysis**, **structuralism**, and **history**. At the outset, psychoanalysis adopted a mechanistic understanding of the body through its focus on instincts, drives, and other impersonal forces. Yet **Freud**'s works suggested a deeper understanding, which was drawn out in clinical practice. The body evolves from a mere mechanism to the "enigmatic" vehicle where there is an intertwining of body and mind (229). Even the **unconsciousness** becomes an "ambiguous perception" that haunts our explicit acts (230), and the embodied individual is necessarily entered into intersubjective relations. Or again, the century has recognized the "strange relationship between consciousness and its language" (232). Repeating his argument that thought and language are not distinct, Merleau-Ponty suggests that language can no longer be viewed as a mere object or system from the outside; it must be taken up, with all of its ambiguities and latent meanings, in each gesture of speaking, and every speech will in turn be a **coherent deformation** of the system, altering it in the very moment of sustaining it. Thus, language and all systems of expression are condemned to be incomplete, and the twentieth century is marked by this discovery. Finally, the study of history too has been invaded by the "**ambiguity**" of incarnate political action. This moment, in 1951, finds Merleau-Ponty equally disillusioned with the empty declarations that mask liberal violence and the Communist failure to embrace **Marxist humanism** (236). Merleau-Ponty concludes that "[w]orld politics is confused because the ideas it appeals to are too narrow to cover its field of action," with the implication that a more robust philosophy of embodied political life and history is called for (one that Merleau-Ponty will offer in *Adventures of the Dialectic*).

If such is the *sense* of the advances of the twentieth century, they all are expressions of the fact that: "our times have experienced and are experiencing, more perhaps than any other, contingency" (239). The worst evils, it seems, emerge from the failure to embrace this contingency. If our efforts at understanding the other, or of establishing a society of equals "get bogged down in the paste of the body, of language, or of that world beyond measure which is given to us to finish, it is not that a *malin génie* sets his will against us; it is only a matter of a sort of inertia, a passive resistance, a dying fall of meaning—an anonymous *adversity*" (239). Without the adversity of sedimentation, there would be no friction for moving forward, but this necessary condition for expression is also the constant danger.

For this new conception, the humanism of the "inner man" has to be rejected, since this "inner man" "is only the phantom of our successful expressive operations" (240). Humanism no longer valorizes mind over body and power, but rather valorizes expressive embodiment. This new humanism is "the continued confirmation of an astonishing junction between fact and meaning, between my body and my self, my self and others, my thought and my speech, violence and truth" and the unwavering refusal to "explain" these poles through causal and separable factors (241). A failure to embrace this contingency leads to philosophical flights to classical dichotomies, political flights to fascism, and social flights to dogmatic religion—these powerful attempts to freeze history and rationalize contingency are the genuine threats to the future of expressive human existence, and such is "the menace of adversity" against which a genuine humanism must remain forever vigilant.

"Man, the Hero" (1946) [*SNS*]

This essay is a reflection upon the historical and contemporary meaning of "hero." Traditionally, the notion stems from a belief in an eternal world beyond lived experience where Good ultimately wins out over evil. In such a culture, the hero is the human guided by Providence, an agent of a world to come (*SNS*, 182). With **Hegel**, the figure of the hero evolves into a man of the present who can see, beyond the present, the emerging system or law that will only later be recognized as the truth. Like an artist's **expression**, the hero responds to the solicitation of the future, and thus brings about "the unexpected junction of reason and unreason" (183). And yet, if one adopts a philosophy that rejects *both* a divine law and a meaningful progression of **history**, does one reach a Nietzschean heroism that "lacks both rules and content" and is "interested only in power itself" (183)? The contemporary hero, however, is neither Hegel's nor Nietzsche's, but rather, the person who authentically embraces their contingency. In **Saint-Exupéry**'s *Pilote de guerre* (1942), the pilot risks his life not for absolute values or national pride, but because the mission or duty is "an intimate part of himself" as he lives in the thickness of the world (185). The contemporary hero simply embraces the contingencies of life and is absolutely committed to the movement toward the world and toward others that is the existential structure of human experience. Saint-Exupéry's hero can risk his life because it is the natural sequel of the existential movement of his life, an expressive and intersubjective humanism with no guarantee of progress.

Marcel, Gabriel (1889–1973)

Named a "Christian Existentialist" by **Sartre**, Marcel was a philosopher, writer, and a key figure in many intellectual circles in Merleau-Ponty's Paris. Merleau-Ponty's own thought extends Marcel's reflections on embodiment ("I do not use my body, I *am* my body"), and his second published article, "**Being and Having**," was a review of Marcel's book of this name. Merleau-Ponty was also deeply influenced by Marcel's distinction between **problems and mysteries**.

"Marxism and Philosophy" (1946) [*SNS*]

This essay is a study of the relationship between **existentialism** and Marxism. For Merleau-Ponty, the genuine direction of Marxism is against any form of reductive scientism or mechanism often associated with materialism. Rather, Marxist studies of the economy or society reveal the inadequacy of any universal or permanent laws for **history**. Each law that is identified depends upon a generalized set of conditions that must be maintained for the law to remain relevant. As such, social nature and history are effects and vary throughout history. In short, Marxism leads to the existential observation that existence precedes essence. History moves not according to Spirit, but through this ongoing lived struggle of humans appropriating nature in community with others (*SNS*, 129). Human nature emerges through praxis and community, and thus "Marxism is not a philosophy of the subject, but it is just as far from a philosophy of the object: it is a philosophy of history" (130). Connecting Marxism and existentialism, "[k]nowledge finds itself put back into the totality of human praxis" (134). Human beings have a paradoxical position in the world as neither the pure product of impersonal forces nor the pure legislator of rational order. They appear in the midst of the world as the "product-producer, the locus where necessity can turn into concrete liberty" (134). Such is the existential possibility to be found in Husserl's development of a *genetic* **phenomenology** (135), bringing Marxism, **existentialism**, and phenomenology together precisely with regard to the philosophy of history.

Marxist analysis

Similar to his reading of **psychoanalysis**, Merleau-Ponty interprets Marxism as a method of **existential analysis**. According to Merleau-Ponty, Marxism is not a reductive theory that reduces actions or history to an economic causality. Rather, it identifies economics as a **dimension** of our experience such that *every* human act is economic, and yet no single act is purely economic.

Marxist humanism

According to Merleau-Ponty, the unquestionable value of Marxism was to be found in its **existential analysis** and in its concrete humanism. The first involves its recognition that **history** is contingent and its commitment to examining all political or economic arrangements according to the actual systems of relations among men and between men and nature that they institute. This leads to a genuine humanism insofar as it recognizes the role of **historical responsibility** and the necessity of moving toward a genuinely less-violent relation between humans. For Merleau-Ponty, liberal politics obscured their violent structures through the mystifications of ideals, whereas Communist politics was violent but, through a recognition of its necessary violence, held the possibility for a "future of humanism" (*HT*, 107). This commitment led to Merleau-Ponty's early **wait-and-see-Marxism** that hoped to draw Communism toward a genuine humanist politics. Yet by the 1950s, Soviet politics had moved in the direction of Cold War politics (with the Camps and the Korean War), which led Merleau-Ponty ultimately to suggest that his Marxist humanist ideals would be best served by a **new liberalism**.

Mauss, Marcel (1872–1950)

French sociologist and anthropologist, famous for his original contributions to the study and methodology of ethnology and for working to clarify the connection between anthropology and psychology. His book *The Gift* (1924) is discussed in **"From Mauss to Claude Lévi-Strauss"** in *Signs*. He is also discussed at *CPP*, 235.

"Merleau-Ponty and Pseudo-Sartreanism" (1955)

Beauvoir's response to Merleau-Ponty's attack on **Sartre** in *Adventures of the Dialectic*. Beauvoir accuses Merleau-Ponty of deliberately mischaracterizing Sartre's position, calling it a "breach of confidence" that "must be denounced."[14]

Mésaventures de l'anti-Marxisme. Les malheurs de M. Merleau-Ponty (1956)

Although Merleau-Ponty never fully endorsed the policies or practices of the Communist Party, he nevertheless had expressed a preference for Marxism over capitalism and had adopted what he would term a **wait-and-see-Marxism**. After several ominous signs in Cold War politics, his break with **Sartre**, and his subsequent departure from *Les Temps modernes*, Merleau-Ponty significantly altered his political position. He focused his attention on what was correct in Marxism, and what was "non-Marxist" in Communism, and began sketching a **"new liberalism"** (*AD*, 227). Given his position at the *Collège de France* and his public profile as a political commentator, the Communist left was motivated to respond swiftly to Merleau-Ponty's text. Within the same year they organized a conference and published a collection of the contributions under the above title, which means: "*Misadventures of Anti-Marxism: The Errors of M. Merleau-Ponty.*" It includes long analyses and short rebuttals from thinkers such as Lefebvre and **Lukács**. Merleau-Ponty never explicitly responded to this collection, but did continue to contribute political commentary from the perspective of his "new liberalism."

"The Metaphysical in Man" (1947) [*SNS*]

This essay is a re-examination of the human sciences in light of the latent metaphysics that structures their practice. **Gestalt psychology**, for instance, does not question its ontological assumptions. Even where they recognize an internally organized whole (such as in **Köhler's** studies of animal behavior), they retreat to an **unquestioned belief in the objective world** in itself in order to populate the "real" world with the forms that will build up to the complex forms we perceive. Yet this betrays the spirit and the insights of the theory, blocking these theorists from recognizing how a phenomenological description demands a reconfiguring of the very categories of subject and object (*SNS*, 85).

Moreover, it seems as though all of the human sciences are moving toward this genuine reconfiguration. In linguistics, for example, the complete systematization of language as a causally structured system will fail to capture the experience of speaking (87). **Consciousness** does not exist in itself and possess language as a mere instrument, and thus language must be more than an impersonal system and less than a mere accompaniment of a pure thought. Language both surrounds and solicits the speaker and is sustained and reshaped by the speaking. Since language is neither a thing nor an idea, it requires a new form of reflection that will allow us to *understand* it rather than to *explain* it. Or again, sociology appears to be moving toward a similar insight, insofar as the social is recognized as more than a thing and yet less than a pure idea: it "envelops the individual" (90). This is the result of a sociology that takes **intersubjectivity** seriously and attempts to describe a lived sociality. The study of **history** too is moving in this direction. The historian no longer seeks a God's eye view nor a simple subjective response; genuine historical knowledge is won through *contact* beginning form our own historical existence. Understanding the past is possible only because our present is haunted by the past and our experience too is a lived experience by which we might communicate with the past.

Psychology, linguistics, sociology, and history reveal that phenomenologically inspired science leads us to "a dimension of being and a type of knowledge which man forgets in his **natural attitude**" (92). In short, they all reveal a certain latent *metaphysics in human existence itself*. Metaphysics, for Merleau-Ponty, begins with the commitment to describe the paradoxical structures that shatter the confidence of the natural attitude, and is "not a construction of concepts by which we try to make our paradoxes less noticeable but is the experience we have of these paradoxes in all situations of personal and collective history and the actions which, by assuming them, transform them into reason" (95–6).

"Metaphysics and the Novel" (1947) [*SNS*]

This essay is Merleau-Ponty's most explicit study of **Beauvoir**'s literary work. In addition, he suggests an identity between literary and philosophical expression and describes his understanding of existential humanism in relation to morality.

Initially, the gulf between literature and metaphysics may appear unbridgeable insofar as a philosophical rationalism believed it could exhaust experience through rational concepts and causal explanations. This attitude, which understands literary expression to be merely *explicitation*, leads to **transcendental idealism** in philosophy and "moral" literature of the classical style in which ideas pre-exist their expression and are simply translated into words. Yet despite such pretensions, writers such as **Stendhal**, Balzac, and **Proust** *express* their ideas, since their ideas only exist through their expression. Given the phenomenological and existential commitment to "formulating an experience of the world" through "contact" rather than explaining it through causal mechanisms or transcendental consciousness, these philosophies harmonize with the latent metaphysics of expression already at work in great novels. Indeed, philosophical expression must embrace "the same ambiguities as [those found] in literary expression" (*SNS*, 28)— that there is no pure idea or true morality that might serve as the standard for empirical expressions. And yet, even though the novel was always already expression, "existential" literature makes the metaphysical of literature explicit in the paradoxes of **expression**.

A paradigmatic example is Beauvoir's *She Came to Stay* (1943). Taking up the phenomenological emphasis on lived perception and the horizonal structure of experience, Merleau-Ponty considers the existential consequences, identified by Beauvoir, of this "perpetual uneasiness in the state of being conscious" (28). This is explored through the relation to the Other, and the resistance they present to our belief in the absolute distinction between Being and Nothingness. In particular, in the characters' attempt to establish a pure intersubjectivity, a being shared by two, the novel reveals the perpetual breaking through of some resistant individuality, even if not that of the pure Ego of classical "moral" literature. This has important implications of an existential humanism, and for a notion of **historical responsibility** such as he was concurrently developing in *Humanism and Terror*. We are caught between our intentions for acting and the effects of our actions, and our responsibility seems to emerge from both directions. From within the urgencies of lived experience, "[w]e have no other resource at any moment than to act according to the judgments we have made as honestly and intelligently as possible" (37), and yet even this cannot avail us of responsibility in the face of the historical reality of our actions. Thus, action and morality share the paradoxical structure of expression, and lead to the difficult position that "[t]here is no absolute innocence and—for the same reason—no absolute guilt," (37). Beauvoir embraces this resistance, resisting the extremes of existential optimism, and her work seems to lay the groundwork for developing a manner of living authentically, that is, of "actively being what we are by chance, of establishing that communication with others and with ourselves for which our temporal structure gives us the opportunity and of which our liberty is only the rough outline" (*SNS*, 40).

Minkowski, Eugène (1885–1972)

Psychiatrist influenced by **phenomenology**. Merleau-Ponty is particularly interested in Minkowski's studies of the psychopathology of schizophrenics in relation to the experience of *light* and *dark space* (*PhP*, 233, 301).

The Moscow Trials (circa 1936–8)

Also known as the "Purge Trials," a set of trials in the late 1930s and part of a larger purge effort that sent millions to prison or to camps. **Koestler** presents the "trial" of Bukharin in the character of Rubashov in the novel *Darkness at Noon* (1940). Merleau-Ponty's nuanced response to this novel and the trials themselves is the subject of *Humanism and Terror* (1947), where he attempts to re-read the trials according to the paradoxical structures of political action and **historical responsibility**.

Motivation

Merleau-Ponty discusses the concept of motivation, developed from the insights of **Gestalt psychology**, as an alternative non-causal way of understanding relations in the **phenomenal field** and in our experience. Motivated phenomena or **behaviors** are neither reducible to a third person causality nor to a rational decision of a **constituting consciousness**; rather, they are motivated by the background of the past, our body, or our world as they carry forward and reshape all of these relations. For instance, our perceptual experience is not caused by the apparent size of objects, but this motivates our experience of depth. Or again, our past does not cause our current behavior, but it motivates that behavior insofar as it shapes our possibilities and demands to be taken up in some way. For Merleau-Ponty, in contrast to causal thinking, there is in the phenomenal field an *internal* relation between a motivating phenomenon and a motivated phenomenon.

Motor intentionality

Contrary to cases of morbid **motricity**, Merleau-Ponty concludes that our normal **being-in-the-world** is oriented toward a world of possible actions and gestures, which solicit our body according to a **motor signification**. This is closely tied to Merleau-Ponty's understanding of Husserl's notion of the **"I can."**

Motor signification

For patients suffering from various forms of morbid **motricity**, it is found that they are unable to perform **abstract** gestures requested by doctors even though they are capable of performing almost identical **concrete** gestures in the course of their habitual actions. Nevertheless, they understand the instructions well enough that they recognize and take up the requested gesture when they happen upon it through some experimentation. This suggests to Merleau-Ponty that the instructions may still have a "intellectual signification," a **thetic** meaning, and yet have lost any "motor signification," that is, they no longer *speak* to the body. For normal subjects, the body itself is oriented toward a world of possible actions and gestures through a non-thetic **motor intentionality**, which is closely associated with Husserl's notion of the **"I can."**

Motricity [*motricité*]

This is a central notion throughout Part One, Chapter Three of *Phenomenology of Perception*, particularly in the discussion of **Schneider**. Primarily a *physiological* term drawn from the German word *Motorik*, the term can be translated as "motor activity," "motor function," or "faculty or power of movement." It is much more active than the English term "motility" or "motivity." In fact, Merleau-Ponty closely associates motricity with Husserl's notion of **intentionality** and of the **"I can,"** and the origin of the term is to be found in **Grünbaum**'s essay "Aphasie und Motorik." The chapter in question begins with an important study of several types of "morbid motricity" in which patients are incapable of performing **"abstract movements,"** while they remain capable of "concrete movements" performed in their daily lives or habitual situations. The patient, then, must develop a **thetic** relation to his or her motricity in order to, for instance, transport the body or take up a pre-determined posture; the normal person, however, carries their body toward the world according to an originary intentionality without any conscious interpretation (*PhP*, 139–40). The body is not under the power of an "I think," but is the seat of a lived **"I can."** Drawing directly from Grünbaum, Merleau-Ponty identifies our motricity as an originary manner of giving sense to our world (***Sinngebung***). This is also related to his evolving understanding of **sense**. Ultimately our motricity is one of the **dimensions** of the lived experience of **one's own body**, and rather than a knowledge of my body and its position, it becomes an expression of the scope of my **being-in-the-world** (*PhP*, 218).

Natural attitude

In our everyday or unreflective experience of the world, we are caught up in the world of objects and of our projects. And indeed, the very structure of intentionality is a *directedness* away from itself and toward its objects. As Merleau-Ponty writes, "[i]n the natural attitude, I have no *perceptions*, I do not posit this object as next to that other one along with their objective relations. Rather, I have a flow of experiences" (*PhP*, 293). This natural attitude necessarily leads to what Merleau-Ponty calls the **unquestioned belief in the world,** the source of many of the errors of classical philosophy.

For Husserl, phenomenology provides a suspension or *epochē* of the natural attitude through the **phenomenological reduction.** Rather than a simple form of introspection, this shift in attitude reveals the phenomenological structure of our lived experience and provides a foundation for the intuition of **essences**. For Merleau-Ponty, however, Husserl is overly optimistic in reaching a pure transcendental ego, and in fact "[t]he most important lesson of the [phenomenological] reduction is the impossibility of a complete reduction" (*PhP*, lxxvii). Merleau-Ponty's version of phenomenology is one that "suspends the affirmations of the natural attitude in order to understand them" without thereby breaking our "naïve contact with the world" (*PhP*, lxx).

"The Nature of Perception: Two Proposals" (1933/4)

The earliest traces of Merleau-Ponty's philosophical approach to the study of perception are captured in two research proposals. He received a grant for the initial 1933 proposal, but his request for renewal in 1934 was denied. Predating the completion of *The Structure of Behavior* by five years, these proposals offer insight into his initial reading of **Gestalt psychology** and some of the key notions and arguments that would shape the project of *Phenomenology of Perception*. The young Merleau-Ponty writes, beginning his first proposal, "It has seemed to me that in the present state of neurology, experimental psychology (particularly psychopathology), and philosophy, it would be useful to take up again the problem of perception, and particularly perception of **one's own body**" (*TD*, 74).

New liberalism

Having become disillusioned with the direction of Communist politics, Merleau-Ponty abandoned any optimistic **wait-and-see-Marxism**. In the epilogue to *Adventures of the Dialectic*, he concludes that all dialectical politics is at risk of freezing the movement and establishing a "**bad dialectic.**" Embracing the underlying politics of **expression** that emerged in his writing, Merleau-Ponty concluded that the political structure capable of remaining open to expressive movement would be a parliamentary structure. This would be to establish a non-Communist left politics capable of pursuing both historical struggle and a **Marxist humanism**. A new liberalism would thus institute open communication and exchange, forever increasing socialism and freedom from within the realities of intersubjective politics.

Noesis/noema

Ancient Greek terms used by Husserl in describing the intentional structure of **consciousness**. *Noesis* refers to the "intentional act," whereas *noema* refers to the "intentional content" or "intended meaning." Most generally, then, this refers to the two sides of any conscious event: the act of thinking or perceiving and that which is thought or perceived. This distinction is first developed at length in Husserl's *Ideas I* (1913), and is a central component of his **transcendental phenomenology**.

Non-thetic/pre-thetic/thetic consciousness or act

The adjective "thetic" stems from Ancient Greek origins where it means either "placed" or "laid down," and has evolved to apply to a positive statement or a thesis statement. Throughout the *Phenomenology of Perception*, Merleau-Ponty deploys a distinction between thetic (objective/explicit/act) **consciousness** and non-thetic (lived/operative) consciousness. The "thetic consciousness" is associated with intellectualist accounts in which consciousness involves an explicit positing of an object in an intellectual act or decision, whereas non-thetic consciousness is a form of **intentionality** revealed through phenomenological reflection upon lived experience. This non-thetic or *pre-thetic* consciousness is a more originary form of experience, and provides the material upon which thetic operations might be performed. For instance, I have a non-thetic awareness of the shape of the object I am reaching for, and a sort of gearing of my hand into the solicited shape of the object occurs without any interposed *thetic* or explicit act. Once the lived experience of the glass has occurred, I can ask "what did

I just pick up?" and thereby "thematize" or posit the object as an object in the world, characterized by objective properties such as size, weight, etc. "We uncover [through phenomenology], beneath act or thetic intentionality—and in fact as its very condition of possibility—an **operative intentionality** already at work prior to every thesis and every judgment" (*PhP*, 453).

"A Note on Machiavelli" (1949) [S]

This is arguably Merleau-Ponty's implicit answer to the reception of his political position as articulated in *Humanism and Terror*. The essay presents a reading of Machiavelli in light of Merleau-Ponty's own **Marxist humanism,** and the tone by which he describes Machiavelli suggests he himself feels misunderstood in the same way. "How could he have been understood? He writes against good feelings in politics [liberalism], but he is also against violence [communism]. [...] We do not like this difficult thinker without idols" (*S*, 211). In this essay Merleau-Ponty argues for a middle way that accepts the violence of human relations and yet remains committed to an **historical responsibility**. This approach, whereby the Prince must "define a political *virtue*" from within the "contingency and irrationality in the world," is nothing short of embracing the paradoxical place between freedom and determinism (217–18). Machiavelli recognizes that "**history** is struggle and politics a relationship to men rather than to principles," and this is precisely the fundamental structure of a Marxist humanism, one that remains on this side of liberal and Communist mystification. Perhaps returning to the autobiographical tone of the first lines, Merleau-Ponty concludes: "the repudiation of Machiavelli which is so common today takes on a disturbing significance: it is the decision not to know the tasks of a true humanism" (223).

Objective body

The body understood as a mere object in the world, subject to external forces or causal relations. See **phenomenal body,** *partes extra partes*.

"On Sartre's *Imagination*" (1936) [*TD*]

Merleau-Ponty's third publication offers a positive review of **Sartre**'s book *Imagination* (1936). The article reveals some of the underlying reasons for Merleau-Ponty's own initial attraction to **phenomenology**. Merleau-Ponty also defends **Bergson**, suggesting that he may be more charitably read as closer to **Husserl** (*TD*, 113), and discusses **judgment** in ways that will reappear in *Phenomenology of Perception*.

"On the Phenomenology of Language" (1951) [*S*]

This essay is one of Merleau-Ponty's most direct statements of his understanding of **Husserl**'s early and late accounts of language, and its potential relationship to **structuralism**.

Husserl and the Problem of Language

For Merleau-Ponty, Husserl's understanding of language evolved in important ways. In his initial formulation of **transcendental phenomenology**, Husserl sought an "eidetic of language and a universal grammar" that would provide some *a priori* knowledge of any possible language, allowing the phenomenologist to purify language so as to remove all **ambiguity** and to thereby reach the transcendental consciousness itself (*S*, 84). And yet, on this account language must be considered a mere accompaniment to thought, which itself must be pure and complete prior to its expression in language. The late Husserl, however, considered language not as derivative of intellectual intentionality, but as itself "an original way of intending certain objects" or as "the operation through which thoughts […] acquire intersubjective value and, ultimately, ideal existence" (85). This late work—illustrated by Husserl's "The Origin of Geometry"—is a return to a phenomenology of the speaking subject, which differs from linguistics insofar as it attempts to understand language not merely as a structure of spoken language, but in the lived experience of speaking and communicating, from within a system that transcends my hold and yet depends precisely upon its being taken up for its continued existence.

The Phenomenon of Language

The second part of the essay rejects the attempt to distinguish between language as an object for linguistic science and language as it is experienced in my own attempts at expression. Language is forever a play between its present (synchronic) structure and its developmental (or diachronic) movement, and thus the true phenomenology of speaking must "conceive of language as a moving equilibrium" that develops in a meaningful way. Moreover, language is a paradoxical structure that "never exists wholly in act" such that it contains, beyond the explicit meanings and relations, a whole host of "latent and incubating changes" by which it will move to a new equilibrium in unpredictable ways (87). In short, the phenomenology of language reveals not simply a description of how I experience languages psychologically, but rather something about the being of language itself, namely, "logic in contingency—an oriented system [...]—incarnate logic" (88).

This signals the continued role of embodiment and gesture for Merleau-Ponty's understanding of language, first established in his earlier works, now evolving under the influence of **structuralism**. Accepting that signs are indexes for differences to all other signs, they nonetheless solicit my voice as I attempt to respond to my situation or my intention to say something. As such, my spoken words are not translations of my thoughts: "my spoken words surprise me myself and teach me my thought" (88). My corporeal **intentionality** gears into the future by taking up the past in a paradoxical logic, and this does not require an explicit intellectual act or signification. My voice lends itself to words that are "pregnant with a meaning" without being contained in my mind or in the empirical gesture, but in the lived moment of speaking. The *sense* or meaning of the speech is "the excess of what I intend to say over what is being said or has already been said," an excess which always solicits further expression without ever being complete (89).

This paradoxical operation requires a rich notion of **sedimentation**. The expressive gesture is a creative operation that says something new by altering the very meaning of the words employed insofar as they are employed in this new context. As such, these "acquired significations" must be available in just such a way as to invite expression rather than mere repetition. Previous expressions sediment into the linguistic field, but not as self-contained ideas or clear sign-meaning relationships, for they were never this even in their initial statement. The sedimented expressions remain as nothing other than possibilities for future expressions. Just as a habit is not merely mechanical repetition, but the possibility for taking up the *sense* of the gesture again in a new context, the linguistic field orients us toward possibilities for speaking. In lived communication, an idea is acquired once I have taken up "a certain style" of speaking, once the idea has sedimented into my linguistic world through a **coherent deformation** of the available significations that contained it only as a possible transformation and reorganization of the whole (91). Sedimentation (and **institution**), then, is the engine of both "personal and interpersonal tradition," and the speaking subject is forever within traditions, taking them up, repeating them, and reshaping them in concert with others.

Consequences for Phenomenological Philosophy

What is the philosophical weight of this phenomenology of language? In Husserl, the relation is perhaps "not clear" (92), since sometimes he seems to reserve philosophy for a pure realm of thought and phenomenology for the description of the *Lebenswelt* [life-world]. Yet if phenomenology radically re-describes the subject and the world, this must have consequences for philosophy, and this is most clear in Husserl's late works on language. The paradoxical structures of communication and of intersubjective embodiment reveal to Merleau-Ponty that the findings of phenomenology require an entirely reworked philosophy. Foreshadowing his own reworking of philosophical categories, he suggests that the "subject" and the "object" in perception are not pure opposites, but rather intertwining through a solicitation and a gearing into in reciprocal relation. I am in the world not as an "I think," but as an "**I can**"; I experience the other not through analogy, but through **encroachment**; I speak in order to accomplish my thought—such disruptions of classical categories require a new philosophy of "my involvement in a 'pre-constituted' world," and thus a philosophy of an embodied, lived, and situated *Cogito* (95). Truth, on this new philosophy, would have to be a trajectory or a *sense* in history and in dialogue rather than an ideal to be achieved once and for all. As Merleau-Ponty writes: "Each act of expression realizes for its own part a portion of this project, and by opening a new field of truths, further extends the contract which has just expired" (95). Truth is the *sense* of the ongoing trajectory of expression and sedimentation. The essay concludes alluding to Husserl's late fragment **"The Origin of Geometry"** and invokes the possibility of a philosophy (not insignificantly attributed now to **Heidegger**) as "a unity exposed to contingency and tirelessly recreating itself" (97).

One's own body (*le corps propre*)

Throughout *Phenomenology of Perception*, Merleau-Ponty focuses his analysis of the experience of one's own body, by which he means the body as it is lived, always as my own, rather than the body thematized as an object in the world among others. As he writes, "[o]ne's own body is in the world just as the heart is in the organism: it continuously breathes life into the visible spectacle, animates it and nourishes it from within, and forms a system with it." (*PhP*, 209). Thus, it is not the body I *possess*, but the body that I *live* as my own, which has come to be called *the lived body*.

Operative intentionality

According to Merleau-Ponty, classical idealism has only focused on the form of intentionality that explicitly posits or thematizes objects through an intellectual act. He argues that such a form of "thetic" or "act" intentionality is only possible given a prior, originary form of intentionality by which we are in and toward the world in our lived experience. He names this **"non-thetic consciousness"** or operative intentionality (*PhP*, lxxxii, 441ff.).

"The Origin of Geometry" (1936) [*HLP*]

In his brief and fragmentary reflection, **Husserl** considers how individual intentional acts can establish ideal objectivities that are true for all speakers and all times, such as the truths of geometry. Husserl famously introduces an explicit role for *writing*, and discusses the manner in which expressive agents can take up the traces of expression. Merleau-Ponty first read this essay in 1939, and it influenced much of his reading of Husserl's "late" thought. It continued to influence Merleau-Ponty throughout his career, culminating in serving as the primary text in one of his final courses at the *Collège de France* (see *HLP*). It arguably shapes Merleau-Ponty's own theory of language and communication.

"The Origin of Truth" (or "The Genealogy of Truth," or "Being and the World")

These three titles refer to an unwritten project for which only allusive references or unpublished notes survive. Nevertheless, this project is generally believed to have evolved into Merleau-Ponty's last project, the manuscript published posthumously as *The Visible and the Invisible*. Conceived as the ontological phase of the project begun on expression in *The Prose of the World*, Merleau-Ponty writes, "[w]e experience in [the world] a truth which shows through and envelops us rather than being held and circumscribed by our mind" (*PrP*, 6). Perception maintains a certain primacy because it alone is our contact with the world and because it alone sees to it that we even have a concept of Truth.

Other(s) [*autrui*]

One of Merleau-Ponty's motivating questions is how to understand our relation to others. See, for instance, **Alter Ego**, *Child Psychology and Pedagogy* (course from 1951–2), **intercorporeality/intersubjectivity**, and the Index for other related entries.

Outside spectator

Merleau-Ponty's attempt to bridge the schism between **empiricism** and **intellectualism** required two complementary demonstrations of how each philosophy, taken in its pure form, necessarily leads to the same phenomenological perspective upon a **pre-thetic** experience. Although he discusses both sides in each of his first two book, *The Structure of Behavior* is primarily focused on pushing empiricism to its logical conclusions through the discovery of meaningful **behavior** through our perceptual experience. In contrast to the **phenomenal field** of *Phenomenology of Perception*, the first work proposes to begin "from below" the categories of any consciousness of perceptual experience in order to examine the furthest consequences of the perspective adopted by the scientist, the "outside" observer or spectator. This spectator is not, however, outside of the world and viewing it from above in a *pensée de survol*, but rather observing the emergence of meaningful behavior from within the world. Thus, the perspective reveals something that may be missed if the "short route" through reflective philosophy is adopted too quickly, namely, that *"behavior is not a thing, but neither is it an idea"* (*SB*, 127). One should note, however, that behavior reveals a form of **"consciousness"** at work in perceptual behavior that is *not* the consciousness discussed by classical intellectualism. As such, the second demonstration in the overall project is not a return to an "inside spectator," in the sense of an introspective philosophy, but rather a return to the lived experience of embodied perception that precisely reveals the presuppositions involved in this aspiration to a *pensée de survol*.

Painting

Merleau-Ponty was extremely interested in painting as a way of illustrating and furthering his philosophical projects, and his three essays on painting arguably represent the three periods of his thought—"Cézanne's Doubt" from his phenomenological period; "Indirect Language and the Voices of Silence" from his engagement with **structuralism**; and "Eye and Mind" from his ontological reflections. In addition, the figure of the painter or painterly expression serves as an example in almost all of his key works. In terms of particular painters, **Cézanne** is by far the most discussed, although there are also memorable discussions of El Greco (*SB*, 203), Matisse (*MPAR*, 83, 143–4), and Klee (*MPAR*, 143–4).

Paraphasia

Condition in which a patient alters or substitutes words or parts of words (*PhP*, 201).

Partes extra partes

The Latin phrase *partes extra partes* means literally "parts outside of parts," and is generally used by Merleau-Ponty to characterize a causal understanding of objects in the view explicitly adopted by **empiricism**, and implicitly remaining in **intellectualism**. The phrase is used by philosophers in the debate over the nature of extension or of an object and its relation to mind, including **Descartes**, Leibniz, and Locke, and to which Kant's second antinomy is perhaps meant to offer some transcendental response. In a rare citation of the phrase, Merleau-Ponty refers to it in one of Descartes' letters: "I call extended only what is imaginable as having parts distinct from one another [*partes extra partes*]" (*UBS*, 50). Although obviously connected to the mechanistic ontology of empiricism, Merleau-Ponty argues that intellectualism too asserts this ontology when describing the world in itself (*PhP*, 149).

Passive synthesis/transition synthesis

In *Phenomenology of Perception*, Merleau-Ponty follows Husserl in identifying a form of synthesis that is paradoxically accomplished through us rather than *by* us. Unlike the Kantian syntheses of the understanding, passive syntheses are accomplished prior to these reflective activities and are gradually constructed (*PhP*, 33). For instance, the experience of depth (276-7) or the experience of a complex object is not the result of various perspectives being juxtaposed or added together, nor is it the result of a thetic act of synthesis. Rather, "each perspective *passes into* the other" (344). Or again, this is particularly clear in the case of time. In my lived experience of time, I am clearly not the author of time, and yet I do not merely suffer the passing of time. Human subjectivity, then, is "Entirely active and entirely passive because we are the sudden upsurge of time" (452). This form is a feature of **operative intentionality**, and is necessary for a **genetic phenomenology**.

Péguy, Charles (1873-1914)

French Christian socialist, historian, and poet. Péguy was greatly influenced by **Bergson**'s early work. He is mentioned in both *The Structure of Behavior* and *Phenomenology of Perception*, and his notion of an historical event is discussed at some length in "Bergson in the Making" (1959).

Pensée de survol

This and similar formulations can be found throughout Merleau-Ponty's writings, and means "thinking from above," "high-altitude thinking," or more loosely "thinking from a God's-eye view." The notion of survol also has a connotation of surveying or dominating. Merleau-Ponty insists in the error of philosophical reflection to retreat from the concrete world of lived experience to the privileged standpoint of a pure, free, rational, and self-transparent **consciousness**. His philosophy of **ambiguous** lived experience and his notion of philosophical **interrogation** are at root attempts to think from with the paradoxical situation of human existence. As he recognized as early as *Phenomenology of Perception*, consciousness is ultimately **perceptual consciousness**, and thus the "fundamental philosophical act" would be to reject the *pensée de survol* and to return to lived experience through a new form of reflection (*PhP*, 57).

Perceptual consciousness

After the study of the notion of *Gestalt* and the **dialectical** relations between orders of reality in *The Structure of Behavior*, Merleau-Ponty concludes that we must expand the category of **consciousness** to include our lived and embodied experience of the world. This *perceptual consciousness* does not admit of the categories traditionally associated with consciousness in the intellectualist traditions, such as pure freedom and self-transparency. Merleau-Ponty's subsequent studies will go even further, suggesting that in fact "all consciousness is perceptual" (*PrP*, 13). (See *SB*, Chapter Four.)

Perceptual faith

In *The Visible and the Invisible*, Merleau-Ponty begins to speak of our **being-in-the-world** or our **natural attitude** as characterized by a *perceptual faith*, prior to the questions of proof or knowledge introduced by scientific or philosophical reflection. "[This] is our experience, prior to every opinion, of inhabiting the world by our body, of inhabiting the truth by our whole selves, without there being need to choose nor even to distinguish between the assurance of seeing and the assurance of seeing the true" (*VI*, 28). In short, our being in the world is a *faith in*, not a *knowledge of*, the world.

Phantom limb syndrome

A condition in which a patient continues to experience the presence of a limb that has been amputated. This is discussed alongside the parallel condition of **anosognosia** in *Phenomenology of Perception*. For Merleau-Ponty, neither empiricism nor intellectualism can explain this phenomenon, and he offers an alternative **existential analysis** of the experience that describes the phantom limb as an ambiguous phenomenon between presence and absence. The patient remains in the world structured according to the now-missing limb, yet the **habitual body** has not adjusted itself to the new **objective body** (*PhP*, 78–89).

The phenomenal body

The body as lived or as experienced in perception, as opposed to the **objective body** as an object in the world or as viewed by **science**. This distinction is discussed early in Merleau-Ponty's work (e.g. *SB*, 157), and structures much of his research.

The phenomenal field

The field of lived experience, as contrasted to the "objective" world discussed by **empiricism** and the pure "transcendental" field of **intellectualism**. The phenomenal field is capable of sustaining the positive indeterminacies of lived perception, and the paradoxical structures of embodied and expressive action that is always between **activity and passivity**. The field itself, however, must be seen also as a "transcendental field," not in the sense of the place of a universal knowledge, but in the sense that the field structures our experience as a field of possibilities according to contingent *a prioris*.

The analyses of *Phenomenology of Perception* offer a definitive way in which the phenomenal field of naive lived experience might become the "transcendental field" of **being-in-the-world**. Indeed, the phenomenal field sustains interweaving relations between objects and the landscape, between objects and the embodied perceiver, and even between the present and the past. Phenomenology, for Merleau-Ponty, is the attempt to grasp "sensing" as the "living communication with the world that makes it present to us as the familiar place of our life" (*PhP*, 53). Returning to the phenomenal world is, for Merleau-Ponty, "[t]he fundamental philosophical act" (57). Yet the phenomenal field must also be distinguished from any formulation that would turn it into an "inner world" of experience. The return to the phenomenal world is not to discover an isolated region of the universe, but to find **consciousness** intertwined with the world through the meaningful structures of experience and gestures, the "pre-scientific life of consciousness" of lived experience.

And yet, even if experience is recognized as such, the transcendental attitude quickly leads from created experience back toward creating or constituting experience. **Transcendental phenomenology** itself seems to follow this route. Merleau-Ponty argues that the phenomenal field "resists in principle being directly and completely made explicit" (61).

Phenomenological description

Merleau-Ponty regularly contrasts *description* with causal or rational *explanation*. **Science,** for instance, attempts to *explain* human experience as an intertwining of causal relations, whereas intellectualism attempts to explain experience beginning from the pure concepts of the transcendental intellect. Phenomenology, by contrast, recognizes that my existence does not result from causal factors, but rather "moves out toward them and sustains them" (*PhP*, lxxii). By bracketing off all beliefs we might have *about* the world through the **phenomenological reduction,** phenomenology attempts to provide a description of human experience as such, from the perspective of **being-in-the-world.** In contrast to causal explanations, Merleau-Ponty develops the notion of **motivation** from **Gestalt psychology.**

Phenomenological reduction (*epochē*)

After the initial discovery of **intentionality** in his earliest philosophical investigations, Husserl developed a "transcendental phenomenological approach" in his book *Ideas Pertaining to a Pure Phenomenology and to a Phenomenological Philosophy* (1913). When we experience an object in our everyday or "**natural attitude,**" we are captivated by the object or caught up in our activities. This fundamental condition involves, as Merleau-Ponty says, an **unquestioned belief in the world (in itself).** Phenomenology, as the attempt to *get back to the things themselves* in their appearing *as such*, requires that we break this natural attitude so that the appearing *as such* can appear. For Husserl, this necessary move involves an *epochē*, a bracketing off of our theories and beliefs *about* the world in order to be able to reach our genuine experience *of* the world in its appearing. From within the "reduced" experience, one can gain an understanding of the relationship between *noesis* and *noema,* and thereby have a genuine **Wesensschau** (intuition) of the *essence*. For Husserl, we thereby reach a purified realm of **consciousness**, the transcendental ego.

Merleau-Ponty endorses the **phenomenological reduction** as the necessary way of reaching our lived experience. Yet he remains skeptical of the purity of the transcendental ego as conceived by Husserl, and insists that "[t]he most important lesson of the [phenomenological] reduction is the impossibility of a complete reduction" (*PhP*, lxxvii). He prefers, following **Fink**, the characterization of the phenomenological attitude as a "standing in wonder" before the world, as a stepping back "in order to see transcendences spring forth" and a loosening of "the intentional threads that connect us to the world in order to make them appear" (*ibid.*). As a result, Merleau-Ponty remains more sympathetic to Husserl's final period of writing in which a **genetic phenomenology** attempts to take into account aspects of our experience that cannot be simply constituted by an isolated pure transcendental ego.

Phenomenology

Taken in its most literal sense, phenomenology is the study of phenomena, or as Husserl declares in a famous motto for the movement, it is the attempt to get "back to the things themselves." As such, phenomenology provides a description of human experience through the appearing of the world as such, without allowing what we believe *about* the world to shape that description. The result is meant to be neither an objective "explanation" of the world, nor a simple subjective description idiosyncratic to a particular subject. From this fundamental commitment, phenomenology seeks a place *between* or *prior to* the traditional dichotomies of subject/object, self/other, or idealism/empiricism. And yet it would be optimistic to call phenomenology a philosophical doctrine. Even within Husserl's own work, phenomenology admits of several internal divisions and debates, which is perhaps a natural outcome from a method that, as an attempt to describe experience, results in "infinite tasks" of description. One such task, of course, would be the phenomenological description of the experience of **one's own body**, which Merleau-Ponty took up as his own.

Indeed, as Merleau-Ponty himself says, phenomenology is not a doctrine but a style (*PhP*, lxxi). Merleau-Ponty's contribution to phenomenology came at a time when gaining access to **Husserl's** or **Heidegger's** texts was relatively difficult, and it is noteworthy that his *Phenomenology of Perception* does not provide any extensive exegesis of either Husserl or Heidegger. In 1939, Merleau-Ponty became more familiar with the evolution in Husserl's own thought from the **transcendental phenomenology** of *Ideas I* to the **genetic phenomenology** of his later and often unpublished writings. For instance, Merleau-Ponty was able to read Husserl's late fragment on **"The Origin of Geometry,"** which was published that year, and also to visit the newly established **Husserl Archives at Louvain** where he read several transcripts from Husserl's late writings. Prevented by the War from devoting further attention to Husserl's late text, one might marvel that *Phenomenology of Perception* emerges not as a study of phenomenological accounts of perception, but as a genuine phenomenological reflection taking off from a glimpse at the richness of Husserl's trajectory.

And yet, even if it is not a doctrine, phenomenology might well be considered a family resemblance term that includes some or all of the following components, identified by Merleau-Ponty in his preface to *Phenomenology of Perception*. First, phenomenology involves a commitment to **phenomenological description**. Empiricism errs in offering an *explanation*, intellectualism errs in attempting a *reconstruction*. As Merleau-Ponty writes, "the real is to be described, and neither constructed nor constituted" (lxxiii). This relates to a second component, namely, the commitment to **phenomenological reduction**. Although this method emerges in Husserl's transcendental phenomenology, and even if a "complete reduction" is impossible, it remains an essential attitude to adopt in any attempt at phenomenological description. Third, phenomenology involves adopting the concept of **essences**, but this should be carefully distinguished from idealism. For Husserl, the shift from the natural attitude to the phenomenological attitude involves a shift from objects according to their existence (*Dasein*) to objects according to their essence (*Wesen*). Yet the essence is not the goal of the investigation, it is the means by which the phenomenologist can understand human **facticity** or **being-in-the-world** (lxxix–lxxx). Fourth, phenomenology involves a commitment to the fundamental structure of **intentionality**, "all **consciousness** is consciousness of something," an insight that Merleau-Ponty recognizes in Kant (lxxxi). And yet, Kant's version of intentionality was what Merleau-Ponty calls "act intentionality," a thetic activity or intellectual act of explicit positing. Phenomenology recognizes a lived or **operative intentionality**—"the intentionality that establishes the natural and pre-predicative unity of the world and of our life" (lxxxii). Operative intentionality is, argues Merleau-Ponty, an existential structure and a lived or non-thetic *Sinngenesis* ("genesis of meaning") (lxxxiv). Finally, phenomenology involves the commitment to bring together "an extreme subjectivism with an extreme objectivism through its concept of the world or of rationality" (*ibid.*).

"Phenomenology and the Sciences of Man"

Published first in English in the collection *Primacy of Perception* (*PrP*, 43–95), this lecture has been republished in a more complete form in *Child Psychology and Pedagogy: The Sorbonne Lectures* (**1949–52**) (*CPP*).

Phenomenology of Perception (1945) [*PhP*]

A "classic" in twentieth-century thought, *Phenomenology of Perception* is Merleau-Ponty's central contribution to the history of philosophy. The book first served as Merleau-Ponty's primary doctoral thesis, and it presents a far-ranging exploration of the role of embodiment in human experience through both phenomenological and existential themes. The primary aim is to understand the "exceptional relation between the subject and its body and its world" (*PrP*, 4–5).

Preface

The preface, which his committee asked him to write given the relative unfamiliarity of the reading public with this new

German mode of thinking, begins with the simple question: "What is **phenomenology?**" (*PhP*, lxx). In fact, Merleau-Ponty's initial answer reveals that the deeper question was perhaps "Is phenomenology really philosophy?" The doctrine seems to resist all of the traditional categories of philosophical thought: it is the study of **essences** *and* existence, transcendence *and* immanence, an "exact science" *and* a return to our "lived" perspective. What philosophical value could be found in a field that urges the pursuit of truth and yet abandons all proven means of reaching it? Yet the *Phenomenology of Perception* is importantly the second stage of a more general project begun in *The Structure of Behavior*. Merleau-Ponty seeks to dissolve the schism between **empiricism** and **intellectualism** by pushing each to its logical conclusions, at which point they both lead back to phenomenology. Having unraveled empiricism in his first book, here Merleau-Ponty seeks to "find the unity of phenomenology and its true sense [*sens*] in ourselves" (*PhP*, lxxi). Introspection and **reflective analysis** ultimately fail, leading to the new understanding of reflection through **phenomenological reduction**, a pathway *between* absolute objectivity and absolute subjectivity. Such a method refuses to break our bonds with the lived world, and "[t]he most important lesson of the [phenomenological] reduction is the impossibility of a complete reduction" (*PhP*, lxxvii). At the end of the phenomenological reflection we find not a pure mind, but a **being-in-the-world**. In addition to these concepts, the *Preface* provides an excellent introduction to the phenomenological method of *description*, rather than explanation, the notion of a **non-thetic consciousness** or **operative intentionality**, and **Husserl**'s particular understanding of **essences**.

Introduction: Classical Prejudices and the Return to Phenomena.

Classical approaches to perception, suggests Merleau-Ponty, begin from a certain understanding of **sensation** as the discrete or "punctual" building blocks of perception. This understanding, however, results from the **unquestioned belief in the world**. Such a belief inevitably leads to some version of the **constancy hypothesis**, which posits a one-to-one relation between stimuli and our sense organs as the foundation for perceptual experience. Yet this definition of sensation cannot be maintained in light of the findings of **Gestalt psychology** and the fundamental **figure/ground structure** of all perception (3). Perception cannot be reduced to positive parts because its sense is always tied to its context and it often includes a "positive indeterminacy" (12).

On the one hand, might empiricism save the notion of sensation and the constancy hypothesis by introducing a process of **association** or a contribution from the **projection of memories**? The return to lived perception, however, reveals a spectacle that organizes itself intuitively and without the need for an auxiliary intellectual act. Describing a boat that he is approaching along the shore whose mast is indistinct from the trees flanking the beach, Merleau-Ponty writes: "I merely felt that the appearance of the object was about to change, that something was imminent in this tension, as the storm is imminent in the clouds" (18). On the other hand, perhaps intellectualism could insulate itself from the critique of sensation by introducing the faculties of **attention** or **judgment** into the structure of experience. Taking the mind to be a sort of spotlight that may or may not attend to the content of its experience or as a light that organizes experience according to a judgment, the intellectualist identifies **consciousness** with the scientific or epistemic gaze. This fails to recognize that the **field** is meaningful prior to its being attended to, and that judgment comes too late to explain the structure of the field of perception.

The notion of **the phenomenal field** offers an initial glimpse of how Merleau-Ponty takes up and enriches **Gestalt psychology**'s descriptions of perception and concept of **motivation**. This *field* is the location of our "living communication with the world that makes it present to us as the familiar place of our life" (53). Since consciousness, then, is ultimately **perceptual consciousness** rather than a detached *pensée de survol*, the return to the phenomenal field appears to be the "fundamental philosophical act" and the establishing of an entirely new theory of reflection (57).

Part One: The Body

The first part of this book establishes the central place of the body in the phenomenology of lived experience. In fact, the "problem of the body" itself stems from the very structure of intentionality. Forever directed away from itself and toward its objects, perception forgets itself in favor of the perceived, enacting the **unquestioned belief in the world**. Nevertheless, phenomenology reveals that perception is always temporally and spatially thick. When I catch sight of a **painting**, I might have in view the whole surface; when I move in to examine a stroke, I retain *in my very experience* of this stroke a sense for its place in the whole, anticipating or *intending* this whole through the horizons of present experience. The temporal thickness and spatial richness of this experience suggests experiential structures beyond those of classical thought, such as **retentions** and **protentions**, or **sedimentations** and anticipations. The experience of one object is particularly well suited to enrich our philosophy: **one's own body**. As he writes, "the body, by withdrawing from the objective world, will carry with it the intentional threads that unite it to its surroundings and that, in the end, will reveal to us the perceiving subject as well as the perceived world" (74).

The first chapter demonstrates why mechanistic physiology cannot explain the **ambiguity** of one's own body. For instance, it conceives of the body as an object, *partes extra partes*, related to itself and the world through *causal* relations. Having critiqued this position in *The Structure of Behavior*, Merleau-Ponty considers whether **Gestalt psychology** might offer mechanistic physiology a solution. Yet this approach necessitates a return to "the body I currently experience," a description that is never actually provided (78). As the experience of **phantom limb syndrome** demonstrates, such an approach could not provide an adequate description, and even **reflexes** demonstrate a form of **intentionality** and our fundamental **being-in-the-world**.

The second chapter considers intellectualist psychology, which indeed confers a special status on one's own body. My body is, for instance, *constantly* perceived, whereas all other objects come and go. And yet, my body is not *simply* an ever-present object—it is my "means of communication with [the world]" (95). Similar considerations apply to other special properties, such as "**affectivity**," "**double sensations**," or "**kinesthetic sensations**." In short, the special status of one's own body cannot be explained by the *content* of experience. Only by turning to the *existential* structures of the body—spatiality, sexuality, and speech—can one properly re-situate the body in a new philosophy.

Shifting to his positive account of embodied perception, Merleau-Ponty introduces the concepts of spatiality and **motricity**. Despite his critique of the body as an object, there is nevertheless something spatial about the body. This is initially introduced through the concept of the **body schema**, the non-explicit awareness of the positions and postures of our own body, reinterpreted as an existential expression of our being in and toward the world. As I initiate a task, my lived body already gathers itself together and rises up from where it is toward the task at hand. Thus, the *spatiality* of one's own body is not a positional or geometrical spatiality, but a "situational spatiality," and correlatively the phenomenologist must speak of "oriented space" as prior to the "homogeneous space" of **science** (102, 104). **Action** becomes not something that unfolds in space, but something that brings space about through an operative or lived intentionality. Spatiality thereby leads naturally to motricity, and Merleau-Ponty introduces **Gelb** and **Goldstein**'s case of **Schneider** to clarify lived action and spatiality. When asked to perform an abstract or imaginary gesture, normal subjects simply assume the required position and *perform* the action, wholly within the phenomenal field. By contrast, Schneider must compare the "intellectual signification" of the experimenter's instructions and compare it to his initial attempts; the instructions lack "motor signification, they do not speak to him as a motor subject" (113). Schneider must go through a "genuine act of interpretation" (133). It seems that normal subjects are oriented toward a meaningful world through an "**intentional arc**" (137), a non-thetic orientation that "projects around us our past, our future, our human milieu, our physical situation, our ideological situation, and our moral situation" (137). Rather than being bodies with the ability to move ourselves, humans are structured according to *motricity*, an originary mode of *intentionality*, and an oriented way of **being-in-the-world** of the "I can." Merleau-Ponty ends the chapter with an explicit account of the acquisition of **habit** and the incorporation of objects (such as the blind man's cane) into the **body schema**, both of which represent ways that the perceived world itself undergoes a reconfiguration. In conclusion, "we must not say that our body is *in* space, nor for that matter *in* time. It *inhabits* space and time" (140).

In the fourth chapter of Part One, "The Synthesis of One's Own Body," Merleau-Ponty asks how the lived body discovered above is *synthesized*, that is, experienced as a unity. Must there not be a transcendental ego performing this synthesis, and hence a return to intellectualism? For Merleau-Ponty, however, the unity of the body is not that of a constituted object, but that of the work of art. A work of art is neither simply a juxtaposition of colors or materials mimicking a real object, nor an idea imposed by the artist or audience upon the vessel of the work of art. It is something like the living trace of an expressive act, an embodiment of *sense*. The body too is "a knot of living significations," synthesized through the performance or possibility of gestures that gather it together toward its world.

Chapter Five turns to the question of **affectivity** and **sexuality**. Perhaps the approach to lived experience through the notion of spatiality leaves untouched the unquestioned belief in "objective" space as somehow primary. Here, "affective milieu" shows the same form of operative intentionality making objects exist for us through affectivity, and thus having "sense and reality only for us" (157). Through a study of **Schneider**, Merleau-Ponty rejects two opposite accounts of sexual experience, one that reduces sexuality to the elemental units of pleasure and pain, and one that posits a "thetic representation" of erotic ideas as bestowing meaning upon an ultimately neutral reality. Schneider has lost all *lived sexuality*, he "can no longer place himself in a sexual situation" (159). Through an **existential analysis**, we can see that sexuality is a **dimension** of normal experience, and thus haunts every experience without that experience being reduced to sexuality. This is also true of **Marxist (existential) analysis**, that economic position weighs upon every gesture or experience, and yet no single gesture is "purely" economic (174–8). Ultimately, sexuality (like the unity of the body) is a function of *expression*, since the body expresses sexuality just as "speech expresses thought," not as an "external accompaniment of it, but because existence accomplishes itself in the body" (169).

Part One, Chapter Six focuses on "The Body as Expression, and Speech." Even if the body has a certain spatiality and sexual intentionality, it is in the "phenomenon of speech" that one can finally transcend intellectualism and the classical "subject–object dichotomy" (179). For an empiricist, the process of speaking unfolds as a series of third-person causal processes, whereas for an intellectualist speech is merely an external accompaniment of thought. Yet the existence of **aphasia**, the inability to speak, reveals a realm of normal speech *between* that of **anarthria** (physiological inability to speak) and an intellectual decision to remain silent. When a patient is unable to sort color samples, this is not an isolated breakdown of the **categorial attitude**, but rather a disturbance in the existential structure of their world. Classical approaches cannot see this because "in the first there is no one who speaks; in the second, there is certainly a subject, but it is the thinking subject, not the speaking subject" (182). By contrast, Merleau-Ponty insists that *"the word has a sense"* because speech is not an external accompaniment of a thought that would be complete in itself; rather, thought is *accomplished* in speech (182). Even when I *listen* to a speech, the words accomplish my thoughts: they don't initiate a third person translation process. "Through speech, then, there is a taking up of the other person's thought, a reflection in others, a power of thinking *according to others*" (184). The words are meaningful not because of common dictionary meanings, but because they are a modification and a particular way of taking up the available significations in a new expression.

For this to be the case, words must bear a certain "gestural signification" which I, as a lived body possessed of language, must be able to take up and repeat, even if at first only according to their *style*. The analogy, then, is with movement. When I have learned a gesture, I do not need to represent external space and my body in order to complete the gesture (as **Schneider** does). I sense the possibility of my movements haunting my perceived world, and no sooner than do I have the intention does my body gather itself up toward the task. Through the **intentional arc** I project (non-thetically) a certain field of possible actions. As the power of adopting styles, the body is a "natural power of expression" and the locus of all communication. This suggests to Merleau-Ponty the necessity of a **gestural theory of meaning**. This is not to reduce meaning to sensations, but to recognize that thought and speech are not separable aspects of my experience. In terms of affective experience, "[t]he gesture does not *make me think* of anger, it is the anger itself" (190). The same is true of linguistic communication, as the speaker's words accomplish my thoughts and initiate me into his world (though never fully).

Thus, the study of speech reveals "the enigmatic nature of **one's own body**" (203). The body, then gives birth to *sense* in the world, and communicates sense to other body, and this expressive structure of the body simultaneously shapes the world as that which is meaningful and which solicits the body's powers. The perceived world of nature and of culture emerges as a result of the miracle of expression, so long as we remember that expression is not a purely intellectual act. Thus, the two objects of Part One (the body) and Part Two (the perceived world) are already found to be intertwining, and this is precisely because "*everything resides within the world*" (204). This body necessitates a rethinking of the Cartesian *cogito* and the union of the soul and the body. **Existential analysis** discovers that the body is "always sexuality at the same time as freedom, always rooted in nature at the very moment it is transformed by culture; it is never self-enclosed but never transcended" (205). I do not possess my body, rather I *am* my body; the body, and not the mind, is the natural subject of perception. The discovery of the enigmas of "one's own body" reveals a certain "obscurity" that in fact "spreads to the perceived world in its entirety" (*PhP*, 205).

Part Two: The Perceived World

Introduction to Part Two: The Theory of the Body is Already a Theory of Perception

In the second major part of this work, Merleau-Ponty's concern is to offer a description of the perceived world not insofar as it might exist in itself, but rather *as perceived*. The discovery that **one's own body** is not "in" the world like a mere object, but rather "breathes life into the visible spectacle" (209), suggests that any theory of the body must also be a theory of the perceived world. And yet, in order to describe this perceived world, one must disavow any attempt to describe the world "from above," from a *pensée de survol* of reflective analysis; that is, one must "plunge into the thickness of the world" (210). The perceived world and one's own body are "two sides of a single act" (212). Through **Aristotle's illusion** and **Stratton**'s experiments, we can see that classical conceptions of the body fail because one's own body is, rather, an "expressive unity that we can only learn to know by taking it up."

As such, the body is not a mere object, it is more of a "natural myself," or again, "the body is the subject of perception" and the perceived world it always already implicated (213).

Chapter One: Sensing

Thus, the error of classical approaches was a failure to recognize "**one's own body**" as more than a simple component in the system of experience. A return to the perceiving body offers a chance to overcome the crippling distinction between existence *in itself* and existence *for itself*, showing the body as nothing less than "the living relation of the one who perceives with both his body and his world" (216). Consider the *sensing* of a certain blue. For Merleau-Ponty, "Blue is what solicits a certain way of looking from me, it is what allows itself to be palpated by a specific movement of my gaze. It is a certain field or a certain atmosphere offered to the power of my eyes and of my entire body" (218). The color then is not something grasped in my mind, it is something intended through my **behavior,** and this is why there is an imminent presence of "blue" from the moment I adopt an intentional "blue attitude" (219). The relationship between perceiving subject and perceived world s one of question and response, *solicitation* and *gearing into*. Sensing occurs *between* passivity and activity, as my body finds jut "the attitude that *will* provide it with the means to become determinate and to become blue; I must find the response to a poorly formulated question. And yet, I only do this in response to its solicitation." (222). Because sensing is an *intentional* activity, it cannot be the case that the subject of perception is **Hegel**'s "hole in being" or **Sartre**'s "nothingness"—rather, each perception is a moment of my personal history and is situated within a thick set of relations and horizons, and thus responds to the past and the present, and the lived body is a "fold" in Being (223).

Perception thus takes place *between* a passive event and an active accomplishment, and as a result it is characterized not by a central "I" or ego, but through a certain **generality** and **anonymity**. All experience unfolds within a **field**, and sensation is never an isolated "punctual jolt." I am open to a system of which I am both a part and that I sustain, but not through an intellectual act. There is a "connaturality" between the perceiving body and the perceived world, and this requires not an absolute or pure subject, but one that is "made and remade by the course of time" (225, 228). For instance, space is not *a priori* unified, but is taken up as unified through the intertwining of the sensory domains. There is a fundamental "communication between the senses" that allows them to be both distinct *and* united, an ambiguity in lived experience that fuses the sensible "domains" together into a whole that is greater than its parts. Our fundamental structure of lived perception, then, is first and foremost **synesthesia**. The senses gear into each other and "translate each other without the need for an interpreter; they understand each other without having to pass through the idea" (244). This allows Merleau-Ponty to embrace **Herder**'s notion of "man as a *sensorium commune*," since one's own body is "the common texture of all objects and is, at least with regards to the perceived world, the general instrument of my 'understanding'" (244).

But is there, nevertheless, a transcendental act of synthesis? After all, "what is it to live the unity of the object or the subject, if not to create that unity" (248)? This is not necessary for Merleau-Ponty because the bodily synthesis itself is itself a temporal synthesis: "Subjectivity, at the level of perception, is nothing other than temporality, and this is what allows us to leave to the subject of perception his opacity and his history" (248). Each perceptual act presumes to reach the thing, yet its synthesis is forever surrounded by horizons of absence, and thus this subject is forever pre-personal in the sense that it is never the pure self-conscious "I" of intellectualism. Perception is a **dialectic** between constituted and constituting time, and in a sense time is "self-constituting" *through us* (250). The "self" only knows itself insofar as it takes up the impersonal or ambiguous self of lived experience, like an "original past, a past that has never been present" (252).

Chapter Two: Space

But might the intellectualist point to *space* as the *a priori* "form" of knowledge. In contrast to classical definitions of space as either the relations among the content of space, or the abstract set of spatial dimensions of a homogeneous field, our experience of space in fact exhibits a different form of synthesis. Thus, rather than looking for space through things *in* space or through some pure activity of intellectual connecting (i.e. geometry), Merleau-Ponty argues that "we must seek the originary experience of space prior to the distinction between form and content" (259).

The first region is our experience of orientation of our visual field. In a famous experiment, Stratton devised a pair of goggles that would "correct" the inversion of the image on the retina. At first, the visual field is experienced as inverted, but after several days Stratton found that the visual field would begin to regain its orientation. This reorientation is not an intellectual act, but reveals "an immediate equivalence between the orientation of the visual field and the consciousness of one's own body as the power of this field" (212). Through a new habituation, an orientation is established despite the upheaval of the contents of the visual field. Thus, "we cannot understand the experience of space through the consideration of the contents, nor through that of a pure activity of connecting, and we are confronted by a third spatiality" (258). In an analogous experiment with a visual field oriented at a 45-degree angle, subjects quickly reorient their grasp of up and down, Merleau-Ponty argues that this reveals how perception begins from a certain "spatial level" (259). In short, the **phenomenal body** is a system of possible actions, "a virtual body whose phenomenal 'place' is defined by its task and by its situation. My body is wherever it has something to do" (260).

What about the experience of depth? Again, Merleau-Ponty suggests that classical approaches fail to capture our lived experience. And yet, in the experience of depth the alleged signs from which depth is to be interpreted are not causes of our experience, but rather **motivations**. Consider the experience of visual illusions, which cannot be reduced to simple errors in judgment. Nevertheless, this raises the question of synthesis. For Merleau-Ponty, the experience of depth is the result of a synthesis accomplished by the body not by the mind, and in fact, this perceptual synthesis is already a temporal synthesis and the expression of a certain relationship from me to things. Depth is the expression of the scope that our gestures might have in the phenomenal field, what Merleau-Ponty calls the "hold" of the phenomenal body upon its milieu, and in fact the same **existential analysis** goes for height and breadth as well (279). Or again, consider the perception of movement. Despite the categories of classical thought, "I perceive movements without an identical moving object, without an external reference point, and without any relativity" (281). One can neither compose movement out of static perceptions nor reduce movement to an intellectual judgment. The moving object is a phenomenal reality, and it is this phenomenal reality of movement that is destroyed by the thematization of movement. Phenomenal movement is a function of temporality, things "coexist in space because they are present to the same perceiving subject and enveloped in a single temporal wave" (288). Only by accepting a non-thetic consciousness can we avoid our logic destroying the phenomenon of movement, as it had for Zeno.

These considerations suggest an entirely different understanding of space, lived space, which is closely tied to how I can immediately experience wholes greater than their parts. The fact that spatiality is tied to our being within the world is reinforced when we consider different experiences of spatiality, such as the spatiality of night or that of mythical space. This dynamic understanding of spatiality does not presuppose a geometrical space, but rather quite the opposite—lived space is that from which geometrical space is deduced. There is a layer of "expressive experiences" prior to the level of intellectual or thetic consciousness. Moreover, these different spaces are not purely isolated, as psychologism would require, but rather open to each other through their horizons (307). This world, that haunts all of my experience without thereby being the object of my experience, is the inexhaustible natural world into which I am inserted at all moments of my life.

In the conclusion of this chapter, Merleau-Ponty takes up the question of illusion, and the consequences that the phenomenon of illusion might have for perception and knowledge. There is an absolute **evidentness** of our lived experience which is a type of lived certainty prior to knowledge but above the level of mere experience—phenomenology is the attempt to "stand in wonder before the world and cease to be complicit with it in order to reveal the flow of motivations and carry me into it, in order to awaken my life and to make it entirely explicit" (309). In order to understand illusions, one needs to discover a new *cogito*, prior to revealed truth and illusion. To perceive, writes Merleau-Ponty, "is to believe in the world. It is this opening to a world that makes perceptual truth possible or the actual realization of a ***Wahr-Nehmung***" [perception, or literally "truth-taking"] (311). Perception is a process that moves from illusion to truth and is oriented toward a complete grasp that can never be achieved.

Chapter Three: The Thing and the Natural World

Classical thought believes that the thing is a collection of properties, or alternatively, that the thing is what is constituted by consciousness, but how might we understand the thing given the above analyses? What is the internal relation between perception and the things or the world of perception? A perceived color, for instance, is not merely an objective and passively received phenomena; rather, it is the function of a body taking a position and orienting itself according to a certain color level. In fact, an experience of constancy itself is related to our manner of taking up the world: "[s]moothness is not a sum of similar pressures, but rather the manner in which a surface makes use of the time of our tactile exploration or modulates the movement of our hand" (329). And indeed, the unity of the thing is a result of being the single pole of a unified gesture of exploration. Moreover, given that our senses cannot themselves be conceived as isolated worlds or dimensions, each "contact of an object with a part of our **objective body** is thus in fact a contact with the totality of the actual or possible phenomenal body" (331). And indeed, the unity of the thing is itself the manner in which all of these aspects gear together into its unique style through my embodied engagement with them, "[t]he thing is constituted in the hold my body has upon it" (334). And yet, the thing presents itself as transcending our experience of it; it nevertheless remains foreign and hostile to us, a resolutely silent other (335). Through insights from **Gestalt psychology** or from the work of **Cézanne**, Merleau-Ponty suggests that the sense of the thing is not something built up out of individual parts, nor something imposed by a mind perceiving it. In the real world, "sense and existence are one" and the sense of the thing exists nowhere else than in the sensible configuration that solicits the powers of our body. As Merleau-Ponty concludes, "there is a logic of the world that my entire body merges with and through which inter-sensory things become possible" (341). But, paradoxically, the thing is not actually given in perception; it is lived by us and yet transcends us.

The second part of this chapter deals with the constitution of the natural world in general. Just as we saw with the thing, the world has a certain unity without there having to have been the result of an intellectual act unifying its various parts. Although the world has a certain style, if forever remains on the horizon of my explicit perceptual acts. Nevertheless, the world never fails to have a perspectival character, but this comes from the fact that "each perspective *passes into* the other and, if one can still speak here of a synthesis, then it will be a "**transition synthesis**" (344). Lived experience emerges through operative intentionality, and the natural world is the ultimate pole of this network of intentionalities: "The natural world is the horizon of all horizons, and the style of all styles, which ensures my experiences have a given, not a willed, unity beneath all of the ruptures of my personal and historical life" (345). This again is possible only because the synthesis of the perceptual field is itself a temporal synthesis. That which is present before me is only present presumptively present given its network of intentional horizons: "my life slips away from me on all sides and it is circumscribed by impersonal zones" (346). Time, like the world, is the type of being in which we can only gain access to it by "occupying a situation within it, and by grasping it as a whole through the horizons of the situation" (347). In order to provide some verification of this account of things and the natural world, Merleau-Ponty concludes this long chapter with an analysis of the phenomenon of hallucination. Against classical attributions of hallucination to perceptual or intellectual errors, Merleau-Ponty suggests that this pseudo-presence is enacted through my body, and not through an intellectual judgment: "the hallucination is not a perception, but it *has the value of reality* [...] And this is what we will never understand if we turn the hallucination into an intellectual operation" (358). In short, the study of perception and of the world reveals that "I only know myself in my inherence in the world and in time; I only know myself in ambiguity" (360).

Chapter Four: Others and the Human World

How are we to describe the perception of others and of cultural objects? Merleau-Ponty opens with a reflection on the way in which experience is temporal. Although a "natural time" incessantly carries my personal experience away according to an utterly **anonymous** life, I also carry forward with me the **sedimentation** of my personal life and the ability I have to perceive the marks of humanity borne by the cultural objects in my field. My entire experience unfolds within "an atmosphere of humanity that might be only vaguely determined (when it is a matter of some footprints in the sand), or rather highly determined (if I explore a recently evacuated house from top to bottom)" (363). Within my experience, my intentional orientation structures the world according to the sedimentation of previous human actions, and this is the basis for communication between individuals, whether it be through language or through gestures, or between present individuals or across time. Thus, it is essential to understand just how this sedimentation is possible, and for Merleau-Ponty the answer is our embodied relationship to cultural objects. When I see a pipe or a spoon, it immediately invokes the near presence of others as the anonymous users of these tools without any interpretive act. This same structure occurs in the perception of others: "If my consciousness has a body, why would other bodies not 'have' consciousnesses?" (367). For instance, when an adult playfully bites the finger of a child, the child is capable of moving his or her mouth in imitation, sensing from within his or her own embodied experience the possibilities for movement that are presented on the outside—being "immediately capable of the same intentions" (368). Humans are capable of entering into "internal relations" rather than merely external relations of interpretation. This is the primary structure of communication and of being in the world together. Indeed, my own perspective on the world is one that leaves the world transcendent and open, and it is therefore not necessary to enclose the other person within my perspective— we are "together in a single world in which we all participate as anonymous subjects of perception" (369). In other bodies, I discover an extension of my own intentionality, a "familiar manner of handling the world," but this is only another anonymous living being, not yet another person (*PhP*, 370). Human communication through the privileged cultural object of language completes this picture, constituting a common situation of which neither interlocutor is the sole creator or master.

But is this anonymous ego really "the Other" we set out to discover? Given that all consciousness begins from its own perspective, there must be some truth to the problem of solipsism, and yet nevertheless there is communication. In short, phenomenology reveals that solipsism and communication are two sides of the same phenomenon. In perception, things and the world transcend my hold upon them as well, and others thus can appear in the world and yet be forever beyond my absolute possession. As a result, the social world (like the natural world) is not an object to be perceived or to be constituted by a transcendental ego. Rather, it is a **dimension** of our being itself, and there is a lived communication with the social world and a virtual communication with others that exists "silently and as a solicitation" in our very being, prior to our awareness or thematization of them (379). The social world, as an existential modality, shares the difficulties that arise in all of the other modes of transcendence: "My body, the natural world, the past, birth or death" (381). The existential structure of my experience unfolds within an atmosphere of horizons that ultimately reach my own birth and my own death without their ever being presently experienced for themselves. Ultimately, "[t]he question is always to know how I can be open to phenomena that transcend me and that, nevertheless, only exist to the extent that I take them up and live them" (381). Phenomenology thus reveals that the transcendental ego must be replaced by a transcendental "ambiguous life where the *Ursprung* of transcendences takes place" (382). This locates an ambiguity at the heart of philosophy, and the need for a new *cogito* and a new study of time: "if we uncovered time beneath the subject, and if we reconnect the paradox of time to the paradoxes of the body, the world, the thing, and others, then we will understand that there is nothing more to understand" (383).

Part Three: Being-for-Itself and Being-in-the-World

Chapter One: The *Cogito*

What, then, is subjectivity? Taking the structure of consciousness and the nature of ideas as his starting point, Merleau-Ponty begins by considering the example of the Cartesian *cogito* itself as an idea: "made up of so many thoughts that occurred to me while reading **Descartes**, but that are not currently present, and the other thoughts that I vaguely sense in advance, thoughts that I could have but that I have never developed" (389). Having an idea involves being oriented not merely toward a pure meaning or thing, but toward all of these complex horizons and sedimentations. Yet these are never thematized. On the classical understanding, this orientation would have to be accomplished by a transcendental ego in touch with eternal ideas. And indeed, in reading Descartes it is this pure self that I must be in touch with in order to understand the mediation unfolding. This pure power of thought, argues intellectualism, is the center of all of my experience, a core of my subjectivity itself outside of the world and outside of time. But is this God-like subject necessary to account for lived experience? In short, phenomenology seeks to find "a path between eternity and the fragmented time of empiricism," a new *cogito* or subject that responds to lived space and lived time (392).

The return to lived experience establishes that thought and perception are not as distinct as they appear in classical thought. In fact, prior to the categories of error and truth, there is a more fundamental being in the world that is the ground of both. Vision, for instance, is accomplished within the visible world, and visual consciousness is only aware of itself as the forgotten operation through which it has reached its object (395–6). The *cogito* never wholly transcends this manner of **being-in-the-world**. But might one still believe in a pure core of consciousness free of the perspectival nature of **perceptual consciousness**? No, for even affective intentionality requires the thickness of perceptual consciousness. The feelings of love are not something that we possess all at once in a simple moment. They begin to take shape in the arrangement and the unfolding of my actions and my thoughts over days and months, they are "a synthesis that was *in the making*" (400). There is a lived certainty that emerges from this experience. I accomplish my existence in my gestures and my actions and therefore I am "certain because I am the one who *does* them" (402). Since this unfolds on the level of action rather than on the level of thought, it is a synthesis that is never complete, and yet that is necessarily self-affirming. This lived certainty is essential even for "pure" activities of mind, such as geometrical thinking, since the spatial experience and language to match is "implicated in my general hold upon the world" (405). For Merleau-Ponty, even the proofs of geometry are genuine expressions of possibilities rather than the discovery of pre-existing truths, and are based upon concepts generated in embodied experience (407).

In fact, for Merleau-Ponty, our body is the condition of possibility not "merely of the geometrical synthesis, but also of all of the expressive operations and all of the acquisitions that constitute the cultural world" (408). Returning to the paradoxes of language discussed earlier, Merleau-Ponty insists again that speech is not merely the external accompaniment of thought. Speech takes up the system of significations and expresses a new thought through an embodied and paradoxical operation, and this thought does not, strictly speaking, pre-exist its expression. Ideas, then, are the strange existence that is neither eternal and indifferent to the means of expression, nor reducible to the fragile pages upon which they are jotted down. Rather, "ideas endure or pass away, and the intelligible sky subtly changes color" (410). Although "[l]anguage transcends us," we are the ones who speak, and every gesture ensures that "the new intention takes up the heritage of the past; it is, in a single gesture, to incorporate the past into the present and to weld this present to a future" (410, 413). There is no place at the heart of the phenomenological *cogito* for an eternal and pure transcendental thought. Thus, between eternity and time Merleau-Ponty discovers a **Fundierung** or "founding" relation, a paradoxical relation in which neither term related pre-exists the relation. Each is tacitly named with its other, and thus being-in-the-truth and **being-in-the-world** are synonymous (415). The seeming self-evidence of truth, what Merleau-Ponty calls **evidentness** [*évidence*], is a fact just like perception, and this is thanks to the fact that "every consciousness is, to some extent, perceptual consciousness" (416). Not that we have absolute certainty, but that we live within the truth through the necessary perceptual orientation toward truth, *habemus ideam veram*. The world remains the inexhaustible real as a general solicitation for our further attempts at understanding it.

In reading Descartes' meditations, I learn about the *cogito* in a general way and according to the sense of the words in the thread of ideas he has placed there. Language performs its habitual task of pointing away from itself toward that which it intends. And yet, the *cogito* that we reach by reading Descartes' texts is merely a "spoken *cogito*," or a *cogito* that exists as an idea in constituted language, a second-hand *cogito*. Descartes was hoping to draw our attention to the "tacit *cogito*" that animates all of our "expressive operations" and yet that slips through our fingers because of the interposed "thickness of cultural acquisitions" required to bring it to explicit awareness (424). As Merleau-Ponty writes, "beyond the spoken *cogito*, there is clearly a tacit *cogito*, an experience of myself by myself" (426). Phenomenological description has determined that this subjectivity does not constitute the world or the word and can thus never come to a pure self-transparency, yet paradoxically "the tacit *cogito* is only a *cogito* when it has expressed itself" (426). Thus, Merleau-Ponty is careful to not reject all forms of subjectivity and self-consciousness, insisting only that the pure transparency of the self—what he calls thetic consciousness of the world and of itself—is what must be rejected from classical thought. Subjectivity is not that which constitutes the world or observes it from above, but rather is "the **project of the world**" insofar as consciousness is not separate from the world, but accomplished in the world and remains forever worldly. This leads Merleau-Ponty to the following definition of subjectivity: "I am a field, I am an experience. One day, and indeed once and for all, something was set in motion that, even during sleep, can no longer cease seeing or not seeing, sensing or not sensing, suffering or being happy, thinking or resting, in a word, that can no longer cease 'having it out' with the world" (429). My birth is the appearance *in the world* of "a *new possibility of situations*" (429).

Chapter Two: Temporality

Adopting the words of **Claudel** and **Heidegger**, Merleau-Ponty begins this chapter with the claims that time is the sense of life and that "the meaning of *Dasein* is temporality" (432). Yet the focus of this chapter is Husserl. To understand how the subject can be understood as temporal, we must first "forge a conception of the subject and of time such as they communicate internally" (432). In fact, it seems that time requires an observer either placed outside of the flow of time or placed within it and carried along by it. As such, time can be neither "a real process nor an actual succession that I could limit myself simply to recording. It is born of *my* relation with things" (434). Time is not, then, a property of the objective world, where all there could be are juxtaposed now-points related externally. And yet, neither is time a product of consciousness. In order for there to be a genuine relation of temporality, the actual present "must already announce itself as an impending past; we must sense weighing upon it the pressure of the future that seeks to depose it" (437). The very essence of time demands that it be incomplete, and eternity itself must be discovered on the horizon of our very experience of time, just as language is on the horizon of every particular speech act and yet never itself possessed as an object of thought. In short, time is "not an object of our knowledge, but rather a dimension of our being" (438).

Phenomenological description reveals the "field of presence," which includes a thick moment bordered by horizons. A memory is not a repetition of an isolated now-point, but rather a moment that brings with it the past and the future horizons of this previous field of presence as it was experienced then. Taking up Husserl's terminology, Merleau-Ponty introduces the language of **protention and retention**. As point A goes by to point B, it is retained as point A in its pushed-backness, and point A thereby continues to weigh upon point B; and indeed, point B itself is only understood if one includes the anticipation of point C, if not in its content then in its style. One should be careful however, not to assume that time in phenomenology is reducible to a simple line. For Merleau-Ponty, this diagram is simply an abstract presentation of "a network of intentionalities" (440). And again, it is important to note that this holding of the past in hand is not an explicit intellectual act. As he puts it, "I am presented with A as seen shining through A'" (441).

The constitution of this temporal thickness is not accomplished by and explicit synthetic act of identification, but rather through a lived "interlinking of successive horizons" that "gradually connects me to the whole of my actual past" (441). My present is oriented toward the immediate future and toward the recent past without thereby needing to posit them in explicit consciousness. Thus, following Husserl, Merleau-Ponty introduces the notion of **"passive synthesis"** by which temporality is nothing but a "single phenomenon of flowing" (442). Just as objective space was secondary to a lived spatiality, objective time is secondary to lived temporality. Our nature as an **ek-stase**, a self outside of self, and the resulting "overlapping of the past and the future is what makes objective time possible" (443). Time then is neither a continuity (as **Bergson** thought) nor a discontinuity (of objective now-points). Time is a subjectivity, insofar as it is forever the same and different, just as I am both the same person across my life and yet wholly different as I take up my past in order to create a future. Time, then, has the unity of a "cohesion of a life" (444). Time, then, must be understood to have the structure of the subject, and "the subject must be understood as time" (445). Thus, it is not correct to say that subjectivity is "in" time, nor "outside" of time. Through the privileged present, I engage with all of time, and eternity remains as the horizon that haunts my every experience without itself ever appearing. Thus, the most fundamental form of subjectivity is not an eternal subject that "catches sight of itself in an absolute transparency" (448). Rather, ultimate consciousness is our "consciousness of the present" in which my being and my consciousness are one in a fundamental structure of "being toward ..." that includes a tacit understanding of ourselves as present in and toward the world. Subjectivity is this very transition from one present to another, what Merleau-Ponty names ek-stase, a self-constituting overflowing of itself—in order for subjectivity to be itself, it must "open up to an Other" and take up a movement by which it emerges from itself (450).

The importance of this moment in the text is marked by Merleau-Ponty's conclusion, in which he in fact summarizes the overall project of his first two books. Bent upon reconciling empiricism and intellectualism, he has uncovered the paradoxical relationship between *non-sense* (the universe of independent facts, empiricism) and *sense* (the universe given meaning by **constituting consciousness**). Phenomenological analysis "of one's own body and of perception revealed to us a deeper relationship to the object and a deeper signification than this idealist one" (453). Beneath every intellectual synthesis is a more primordial operative synthesis accomplished through lived experience and through our body, gearing into what Husserl calls the "*Logos* of the aesthetic world" (453). And the world is nothing less than the "cradle of significations [...] the sense of all senses, and [...] the ground of all thoughts" that remains upon the horizon of all of our individual experiences and as "the unique term of all of our projects" (454). The analysis time confirms this new notion of sense, since time is nothing other than the sense of our life, that by which all things can have sense. For Merleau-Ponty, subject and object are revealed, through the study of time, to be two poles of a single relation—a thick presence that is essentially haunted by the absent, a visible lined with invisibility.

Chapter Three: Freedom

What role might freedom play in this existential and phenomenological analysis? If we begin from a classical understanding of consciousness, then "all things are within our power, or none of them are" (461). If the subject remains free in each subsequent action from her earlier commitments, then nothing is ever actually done, and yet, as Merleau-Ponty writes, "[t]he very notion of freedom requires that our decision plunges into the future, but something has been done by it" (462). And yet, even beyond the difficulties posed by the explicit categories of objective thought, one can see that our entire field of possibilities has been previously structured by lived and tacit decisions. The only genuine choice, then, is "the choice of our whole character and of our way of being in the world" (463). But does such a move in fact reduce to a type of determinism? To resist this consequence, Merleau-Ponty analyses the fundamental power of giving-sense (*Sinngebung*) of intentionality. Such acts are not intellectual or thetic *decisions*, but emanate from my embodied gearing into the world. The lived subject anticipates herself in relation to things, and the sense of the world is established through the exchange, both real and virtual, between the world and our embodied existence. Our milieu, then, is structured according to values we have given to it according to our lived engagement with it, and this is the form of valuation that occurs in all aspects of human experience. Merleau-Ponty calls this the "**sedimentation** of our life," indicating how experiences or attitudes from our past sediment into the very structures our present experience and our possibilities. This does not reach the pitch of an absolute determinism, but acknowledges that our present possibilities are weighed upon by our past. When an obstacle appears to me as insurmountable, this reveals an embodied commitment to a certain way of being toward the world; the cultivation of an inferiority complex over twenty years expresses a commitment to inferiority that weighs upon my body, not as the sum of these past experiences, but rather "as the atmosphere of my present" (467). Freedom is born in our manner of taking up this past in this situation, navigating the possibilities of the landscape and potentially even reshaping them. Ultimately, freedom is never wholly outside of the gravitational pull of the past and the present.

The same conclusion can be reached by considering freedom within historical or political action. **Historicism** explains action through a network of determinisms (e.g. economic), or grants the historical actor a pure freedom of decision. And yet the lived category of "worker" is not merely an economic category, nor simply something I can decide to be. To *be* a worker, I must embody this "mode of communication with the world and society" and genuinely live within the world in this way. Or again, how do different groups come to share a class-consciousness when their lives are materially different? Neither through external causes alone, nor through free intellectual decisions; the Revolution "was prepared for by a molecular process, it ripens in coexistence prior to bursting forth into words and relating to objective ends" (471). Freedom is always situated, and thus is limited to beginning to reshape our lived possibilities, and it never has the power to simply make me into what I *decide*. My embodied life is not an intellectual project, but a project of the world, an existential project "that merges with our way of articulating the world and of coexisting with others" (473). Our life is neither free nor determined, it is *motivated*.

This existential theory of situated freedom offers Merleau-Ponty the chance to discuss the question of **history**, since the above discussion confirms that there indeed can be "situations, a sense of history, and an historical truth" (474). The sense of history emerges through us, but is not our doing. The individual does not move history through an intellectual decision; rather by gearing into history through an embodied taking up of the past toward future the individual can shape the sense of history without giving us the illusion that history has a single direction and a predetermined end. Just like a human life, or a gesture, history is motivated.

Thus, subjectivity can never be a pure and self-transparent constituting consciousness. As an existence, it brings forth a halo of **generality**. As Merleau-Ponty writes: "We thus recognize, surrounding our initiatives and ourselves taken as this strictly individual project, a zone of generalized existence and of already completed projects, significations scattered between us and the things" (476). This is only possible because of the generality and **anonymity** of consciousness As a concrete subject within the systems that I nonetheless constitute, the flow of time, independent existence of language, or the transcendence of the world appear to me according to my perspective and from within the present, and indeed the present "actualizes the mediation between the For-Itself and the For-Others, between individuality and generality" (478). From within this perspective, freedom is possible—without stripping consciousness of everything to the point of it being a nothingness capable of choosing anything—because although the world is always already constituted, it is never completely constituted. Insofar as it is constituted, we are less free than determined; insofar as it remains open to our expressive gestures and coherent deformations, we are less determined. Yet what is clear is that we are never absolutely free, never absolutely determined. Thus, if there is freedom, it is born within situations and within lived experience, and "the hero" speaks not from a *pensée de survol*, but expresses the non-thetic decisions that give meaning to one's life. Thereby ending his treatise with the words of the hero (**Saint-Exupéry**) that might well serve as a motto for Merleau-Ponty's philosophy: "Man is a knot of relations, and relations alone count for man" (483).

"The Philosopher and His Shadow" (1958) [S]

This relatively late essay is an important illustration of Merleau-Ponty's reading of **Husserl**, and incorporates several components of his previous readings. Privileging Husserl's later works over his earlier **transcendental phenomenology**, Merleau-Ponty here seeks to identify a certain "un-thought" in Husserl's work by which one can take him further. It is thus important that the essay begins with a reflection on the status of **tradition** and practice of *reading* in the **history of philosophy**. Merleau-Ponty rejects either an "objective" reading (which would repeat the past without touching it) or a "subjective" reading (which reveals nothing but the subjective contribution of the philosopher who is reflecting). Rather, "there must be a middle-ground on which the philosopher we are speaking about and the philosopher who is speaking are present together, although it is not possible even in principle to decide at any given moment just what belongs to each" (S, 159). This would be to recognize that no system of thought is a thing in itself, but always contains latent and un-thought elements, and always "opens out on something else" (160). A *responsible* reading, then, would gear into the thought in order to re-think it and to take it further. Reading is not deciphering a thought hidden in the texts; it is a creative expression of taking up a tradition in order to found it and to reshape it through a **coherent deformation.**

The first part of the essay focuses on Merleau-Ponty's understanding of the **phenomenological reduction** as at once a returning to oneself and a distancing from oneself. By reflecting upon the unreflected, I change lose is *as* unreflected, and this is the paradoxical fate of any transcendental phenomenology. The reduction thus shifts us out of the **natural attitude** of intending the world, but without thereby breaking our contact with the world as transcendent; the reduction does not wholly isolate a pure **consciousness** (162). In short, phenomenology is not simply a move from the objective to the subjective, since it problematizes this very distinction. A certain "primordial faith" in the world can never be transcended, and thus is not grounded in reflection, but rather in our very existence as an *Urdoxa*, an originary opinion at the heart of our existence itself. Phenomenology's task is to "to unveil the pre-theoretical layer on which both of these idealizations find their relative justification and are gone beyond" (165). And yet, if phenomenology points beyond the categories that it nevertheless employs, should one not simply leave off phenomenological reflection for something else? For Merleau-Ponty, Husserl's turn to the body and to the categories of the "always already constituted" and "never completely constituted" reveal that phenomenology itself unveils the ultimate structures of experience and blocks the transcendental movement of the earlier formulations. Husserl's thought, then, contains the traces of an unthought ontology that Merleau-Ponty's philosophy is an attempt to interrogate.

The second part of the essay explores the implications of these intuitions of a phenomenological interrogation beyond the realm of the **constituting consciousness**. For instance, in exploring the **"I can"** and the importance of perspective in perception, Husserl invokes the image of **touching/touched**: "I touch myself touching; my body accomplishes 'a sort of reflection'" (166). This insight explodes the classical categories of subject–object, and initiates "an ontological rehabilitation of the sensible" (167). My body and the world are blurred, they are of the same fabric or **flesh** that merely turns back upon itself and thus institutes an *opening* by which Being appears. Moreover, the body accomplishes the synthesis of time, not as an active synthesis, but as "the transition that as carnal subject I effect from one phase of movement to another" (167). But given this primordial intertwining, ought we to abandon **intentionality**? For Merleau-Ponty, the notion retains its value insofar as the intertwining requires also that we speak of intersubjectivity. In touching or gesturing-with others, we establish a "single intercorporeality" (168). The notion of intentionality is essential for our understanding of others: since "I" am not a constituting consciousness, but rather a certain divergence or folding back in the flesh of the world, the other too can appear as a **behavior** that intends my world and makes me visible for another (170). As Merleau-Ponty suggests: "Sensible being is not only things but also everything sketched out there, even virtually, everything which leaves its trace there, everything which figures there, even as divergence and a certain absence" (172). Husserl's ultimate unthought, then, requires that we think through how humans are present both horizontally and vertically, visibly present yet also "hollowed out" by a certain absences which "also count in the sensible world" (172).

And yet, do these advances drain all meaning from the distinction between constituted and constituting? What is the relation between the pre-objective order and the logical objectivity that thematizes it? For Merleau-Ponty, this leads to the phenomenological relation of *Fundierung* and the resulting paradoxical logic of expression. By expressing the unreflected, embodied intersubjectivity, one falsifies the object one wanted to express and reshapes the very nature of the object through this expression. Each level of constitution repeats this paradoxical logic, suggesting that they are the "adventures of constitutive analysis—these encroachments, reboundings, and circularities" for which Husserl's early intuition of "a reciprocal relation between Nature, body, and soul" had prepared him (177). Thus, phenomenology pulls both toward the pre-thetic and pre-objective world of Nature and toward the world of thought as understanding that nature, and the solution to this double-direction is to be found within us by discovering a phenomenology of our relationship "to non-phenomenology." **Wild being** must not be rejected, but brought within phenomenology. This is the shadow of the philosopher, a shadow that haunts his every philosophical move, and the "philosopher must bear his shadow" (178). The shadow of Husserl's thought swallows up his original intention of revealing constituting consciousness, but the process of exploring the light is necessary in order to show us what remains "left over: these beings [**quasi-objects**] beneath our idealizations and objectifications which secretly nourish them and in which we have difficulty recognizing *noema*" (180). Despite his best efforts, Husserl's thought "awakens a wild-flowering world and mind" that undermines its own intentions (181).

"The Philosopher and Sociology" (1951) [S]

Despite a long separation between philosophy and sociology, the spirit of phenomenology calls for a "reexamination of their relationships" (*S*, 98). In practice, neither **science** nor philosophy are diametrically opposed, and one must discover an inquiry that is not a simple co-exploration of two rigidly separated objects, but involves two intertwining pursuits in the context of lived intersubjectivity. Merleau-Ponty suggests that Husserl's later philosophy offers a pathway toward the intertwining of these two disciplines, since reflection does not take place outside of the world and outside of time, but rather within the "field of presence" and the life-world (105). By the time that Husserl writes in his final works that the "transcendental subjectivity is **intersubjectivity**," he is committed to erasing the distinction between the empirical and the ideal, between philosophy and sociology (107). Thus, philosophy is less a realm of knowledge than an attitude of "vigilance" bent upon uncovering "rationality in contingency" (111). In short, phenomenology is called to short circuit the scientist's faith in object or causal thinking (112).

"The Philosophy of Existence" (1960) [*TD*]

Making a distinction in a late interview between **Sartre**'s **existentialism** and what he calls "the philosophy of existence,"

Merleau-Ponty sought to include a diverse set of thinkers (**Scheler, Jaspers, Marcel,** and **Husserl**) under this later rubric. This text also discusses Marcel's distinction between **problems and mysteries** at some length, which arguably shapes many of Merleau-Ponty's questions. See **existentialism**.

Piaget, Jean (1896-1980)

Swiss psychologist known for his influential studies in child psychology and his theory of child development stages. Although Merleau-Ponty mentions Piaget in his early studies, he solidifies his criticism of Piaget's methodology in *Phenomenology of Perception*. Piaget argues that the child does not understand the "problem of the other" until the age of twelve, when the child "accomplishes the *cogito* and obtains the truths of rationalism" (*PhP*, 371). Yet the world of child perception remains on the horizons of the objective worldview of the adult, which can be sensed in lived or intersubjective experience. Child consciousness is itself a **structure**, and not merely a deficient mode of adult consciousness (*CPP*, 40, 132–3, 141ff.).

In Praise of Philosophy (1953) [*IPP*]

Merleau-Ponty's "Inaugural Lecture" at the *Collège de France* was given on 15 January 1953. Being the youngest member ever to hold the chair, and having been subject to a controversial nominating process, Merleau-Ponty devotes the lecture to the spirit of philosophy itself, both past and future. The lecture was dedicated to his mother, who, though nearing the end of her life, was proudly in attendance. Although less central to his English reception, the *éloge* is a well-known text in France, and often figures as part of the philosophy curriculum in *lycée*. Merleau-Ponty's address begins with a veneration of the institution itself. Sensing his own research as an ongoing and unfinished disorder, he can hardly see himself as the "heir of the distinguished men whose names he sees on these walls" (*IPP*, 3). And yet, philosophical "ignorance" captures the mission of the Collège. The decision to even maintain a chair in philosophy calls, then, for a reflection on the "function of the philosopher" (4), through the history and the future of philosophical inquiry. A philosopher "possesses *inseparably* the taste for evidence and the feeling for **ambiguity**" (4). Philosophy, then, is an art; the philosopher must never lose sight of the ambiguity of the world in favor of absolute knowledge, and must never renounce knowledge in favor of equivocation: "from knowledge to ignorance, from ignorance to knowledge, and a kind of rest in this movement" (5).

Louis Lavelle

The address begins by considering Merleau-Ponty's immediate predecessor, **Lavelle**, who held the chair between 1941 and 1951. Despite Lavelle's orientation toward a philosophy in contact with pure Being, Merleau-Ponty detects the art of the philosopher. Lavelle preserves a paradoxical relation between "total being" and "our own being" (5). Nevertheless, Lavelle ultimately remains committed to idealism, and thus never fully embraces the **ambiguity** of the world.

Henri Bergson (and Edouard Le Roy)

If Lavelle begins from spiritualism, **Bergson** begins from "the world and constituted time" and moves in the opposite direction in order to discover the inseparability of "happening and meaning" (10). Thus, in the opposite direction, one finds in Bergson the "ambiguous sparkle" of a genuine philosopher. Nevertheless, even in his early discovery of **duration**, Bergson tends toward absolute knowledge, which eventually culminates in a sort of "cosmological consciousness" of which each individual **consciousness** is merely a more or less developed part. Positing a divine thought excludes the opposite and institutes a "pure" positivity in which no "non-Being" could appear (11). Humans contain the seeds of the divine, but can never in fact reach it, but must seek it through coincidence or fusion. Nevertheless, Merleau-Ponty detects the insistent reappearance of the negative in the "interior movement which animates [Bergson's] intuitions" (13). For Bergson, the philosopher's role is not passive, for the philosopher *invents* both its problems and their solutions. In short, Bergson's philosophy is oriented toward a philosophy of **expression**, and if this is the case then the notion of coincidence or fusion is misleading. The idea of separation itself must be the target, and the philosopher must aim (as duration) to gear into the duration of the universe. This universal duration is nothing other than me, and yet it transcends me; the "absolute is 'very close to us and, in a certain sense, in us'" (15). To reach the absolute requires, paradoxically, plunging deeper into the human situation that we are (16). Bergson's method is a particular form of intuition, which Merleau-Ponty argues is **expression**. Intuition orients the philosopher's speech without "containing it in abridged form" (18), and his or her voice is solicited by what "is not achieved before it has been said" (19). As a process of expression, that which is expressed only exists after the expression, and is only contained in advance in the manner of a style. Philosophy, then, is the open and endless pursuit of bridging the unbridgeable gap between "mute being" and "meaning" (19).

As such, philosophy, **history**, and even Being itself are not the unfolding of an idea that pre-exists its expression, but rather an *orientation* that must be actualized in struggle and cannot be fully known in advance or from the perspective of an absolute spectator. Thus, "the internal movement of Bergsonism" is "the development from a philosophy of impression to a philosophy of expression" (28). Emphasizing the importance of Bergson's notion of the "retroactive effect of the true," Merleau-Ponty concludes that the "exchange between the past and the present, between matter and spirit, silence and speech, the world and us, this metamorphosis of one into the other [...] is [...] the best of Bergsonism" (29–30). Returning to the theme of the philosopher's art, the philosopher must not judge from the position of a *pensée de survol*: he or she must take up his or her place in life, the world, and history and yet oriented toward the true. The philosopher must be patient and never "go beyond what he sees himself" (32). As such, the philosopher cultivates a "rebellious gentleness, the pensive engagement, the intangible presence" that may be disquieting to those who prefer positive projects and definitive research plans. Alone the philosopher, in his or her art of expression, is the sole judge of where his or her "activity loses the meaning which inspired it" (33).

Socrates

What is the relationship between the art of philosophy and his or her society? Bergson cultivated a certain "uneasiness" between the philosopher and others or life, yet the structure of the academy can turn the thinker into a "functionary" decidedly "cut off" from life and others (33). Not that philosophers should not write academic books, which are after all *expression*, but they should resist the solid and closed systematic philosophies that books tend to present. Hence, a look to Socrates, the perennial patron of philosophy who spoke with others and never wrote. Socrates occupies a position *between* others and the Gods, and yet he believes in the Gods for the wrong reasons and is loyal to Athens for the wrong reasons. Socrates believes through reason, not faith; he is loyal to the laws because of reason, not because he believes they are "good."

When Aristotle flees Athens seventy-five years later to save the city from committing a second "crime against philosophy," he reveals that philosophy has become a "thing," possessed and guarded by philosophers (36). For Socrates, philosophy only existed "in its living relevance to the Athenians [...] in its obedience without respect" (*ibid.*). The philosopher is the one who remains in contact with the human world, and yet takes a distance in order to understand it, in order to obey the spirit or values of the city, rather than the empirical or historical formation of them. Yet rulers are fearful of this internal distancing, for the philosopher may not conclude that obedience is the answer, and may inspire others to resist. The ruler demands blind faith and loyalty. As Merleau-Ponty writes, "it is already too much to have reasons for obeying" (38). By standing trial, Socrates pleads the case not for himself, but for the City able to embrace the philosopher within as the genuine spirit and value of the City itself. To put Socrates to death is a crime against the values of Athens itself, the ideal of a just city whose laws embrace reason and truth rather than blind obedience. The philosopher must remember Socratic irony: "Socrates does not know any *more* than [his interlocutors] know. He knows only that there is no absolute knowledge, and that it is by this absence that we are open to the truth" (39). This would require a city open to **historical responsibility**, since the laws mistakenly assume that each individual is purely autonomous and that guilt is all or nothing. "In so far as we live with others," writes Merleau-Ponty, "no judgment we make on them is possible which leaves us out, and which places them at a distance." In a melancholy tone, Merleau-Ponty wonders if society again is in the process of rejecting the philosophers who "dwell within it" (41).

Religion and History

Philosophy itself risks warranting this rejection if it becomes a dogmatic debate between positions rather than a return to the living questions of the human world. For Merleau-Ponty, this danger is particularly acute in philosophies of religion or of history, and appears when theology declares all philosophy *atheism* and Marxism declares all philosophy *ideology*. What is required, implies Merleau-Ponty, is a *philosophy* that refuses the absolutes of knowledge, a phenomenology of the lived movements of experience and history.

A step forward is achieved through **structuralism**. According to Merleau-Ponty, the theory of signs points toward an account of living language in which the speaking subject takes up a paradoxical or ambiguous position by *at once* demonstrating his or her "autonomy" or freedom in speaking and yet, "and without contradiction," responding to a linguistic structure and community upon which his or her language is dependent (54–5). There is a paradoxical logic between the individual and the institution that works reciprocally and according to an imminent or lived logic established in the temporal movement of the cultural phenomenon. As such, Merleau-Ponty here identifies a certain generalizability of structuralism from linguistics to history and politics, although only given the insistence that the structure not be given explanatory authority outside of the lived process of its taking up—a certain "post-structuralist" tendency in his phenomenology of expression.

Philosophy

The philosopher's art—remaining in contact with life and history as they are being born, and yet distancing herself in order to *understand* them—is thus a paradoxical one. The philosopher, then, is never truly at rest, and never truly at home in life or in history. For the man or woman of history, a person can simply *be* guilty for being an opponent. The structures of these categories insist that we simply obey on faith (59). The philosopher must remain open to the contingency of these laws or these actions, for the criminal may *become* an ally. The genuine respect for **historical responsibility** draws suspicion from the men and women of history. As Merleau-Ponty writes, "even if [the philosopher] had never betrayed any cause, one feels, in his very manner of being faithful, that he would be able to betray" (60). And yet, the philosopher must continuously reveal the divided structures in each person that makes up the contingent and ambiguous nature of human experience, and this is nothing but a human capacity to radically reflect upon oneself in order to be authentically oneself. Thus, the least philosophical move would be the attempt to isolate philosophy from life in favor of some fictional absolute knowledge. "The philosopher is the man who wakes up and speaks. And man contains silently within himself the paradoxes of philosophy" (63–4).

"The Primacy of Perception and Its Philosophical Consequences" (1946 [1947])

In the year following the publication of *Phenomenology of Perception*, Merleau-Ponty was invited to present and defend his research before the *Société française de philosophie*, and a transcript of the event was published the following year. The text offers an important condensed statement of his main arguments, as well as a defense against some of the initial criticism leveled at his phenomenological psychology.

Written Overview

The study of **Gestalt psychology** reveals that perception is an "originary mode of consciousness" (*PrP*, 12). Irreducible to a passive recording of sense data or an active constitution of the perceived spectacle, perception must be an existential structure of inhabiting our world. Perception gears into a spectacle that is already "pregnant" with form, and this takes place in a lived world (rather than in the universe as conceived by classical science). Thus, perceptual experience involves embodied actions and gestures within the world such that any interpretive distance or third person perspective would falsify this "quasi-organic relation" between the world and the perceiver, a relation that bursts the categories of immanence and transcendence.

But do these descriptions carry any *philosophical* weight? Merleau-Ponty resisted the interpretation that they amounted to nothing more than psychology. The consequences of phenomenology in fact belie any hope for a "timeless" or unchanging world of ideas that might provide a solid foundation upon which perception can be built up through **judgment** or the understanding. In short, the objection presupposes the very *pensée de survol* that Merleau-Ponty's philosophy renders impossible. Taking on the idealism of French academic philosophy, Merleau-Ponty doubles-down on perception itself: "all **consciousness** is perceptual, even the consciousness of ourselves" (13). That is, even the supposedly pure transcendental consciousness meant to establish intellectualism is itself *perceptual*, structured according to **horizons**, and only ever presumptively in possession of its objects of thought. The return to perception is nothing other than the discovery of the proper level of philosophy itself, and that level is *phenomenology*. As such, Merleau-Ponty can conclude: "The perceived world is the always presupposed foundation of all rationality, all value and all existence. This thesis does not destroy rationality or the absolute. It only tries to bring them down to earth" (13).

Oral Presentation

The presentation begins with a clear phenomenological description of perception. Each momentary perceptual given is internally related to an entire **horizonal structure** that is only present *as absent*, present *as intended*. The unseen side of an object is not merely unseen, it is present as "in my vicinity" thanks to something like a tacit givenness (14). This presence is not the result of an intellectual act (judgment or projection), but of a "practical synthesis" that comes from the fact that I can (intentionally) gear into the object as something to be seen. Given this description of lived perception, the studies by **Gestalt psychology** merit the name of phenomenological descriptions. Since perception, prior to any intellectual acts of synthesis, discovers a **field** that is already pregnant with a form, one must conclude that intellectual (or Kantian) synthesis is not foundational in perception. Rather, perception must be characterized by Husserl's notion of an **operative** or **transition synthesis**, a "horizontal" synthesis that anticipates in the present the fullness of the object and its temporal place in my experience. Perception, then, is accomplished by my body, not by my mind, and the perceived is "a totality open to a horizon of an indefinite number of perspectival views which blend with one another according to a given style" (16). Merleau-Ponty concludes that perception is the paradoxical intertwining of immanence and transcendence and that the world, as the totality of perceived things, is not the sum of separable objects, but "the universal style of all possible perception" (16). Finally, the experience of **others** definitively confirms these descriptions and the impossibility of intellectualism (18).

Merleau-Ponty considers and answers two objections. First, one might claim that psychological descriptions remain contradictory because it is precisely the task of philosophy to "think," and thereby to move to the world of thought and of ideas where truth is to be found—"[w]hen we think it," they suggest, "its contradictions disappear under the light of the intellect" (18). Merleau-Ponty suggests that the assumption that there is a non-contradictory realm of thought is itself a presupposition worth questioning. The pure ego presupposed by this objection is itself a perspective that can never in fact be reached. The second objection is to Merleau-Ponty's entire project—asking us to return to lived experience, to the perceived world as we experience it, suggests that reflection or thought (that is, philosophy) is unnecessary. How could such a disavowal of the very method of philosophy itself still *be* philosophy? To this charge that a return to the "unreflected" is a renunciation of reflection, Merleau-Ponty responds that his return to the unreflected is not a rejection, but an attempt to reveal that reflection itself is never pure and never complete. Moreover, lived perception reveals structures that shape all other forms of intentionality, since even intellectual acts include horizons, operative syntheses, and meaningful wholes prior to their parts (19). The discovery of the primacy of perception is a result of the fact that ideas, as much as perceptions, involve future and past horizons, and even the possibility of having a pure sense of myself is itself perspectival and bodily, temporal and lived (21). After rehearsing his criticism of **Gestalt psychology** for not raising their insights to their philosophical status, he admits that "reason" must attempt to rise above its historical, social, or psychological influences, but this must never be the pretension to rise above all perspectives to the level of a *pensée de survol*. The "primacy of perception" is a recognition that philosophy must begin from the world, from our natal bond with the world, and not pretend to reject this world in an illusory rise to a God's-eye view. A phenomenology of perception thus involves "getting closer to present and living reality" (25), and sets the stage for a study of morality and aesthetics from within the world and beginning from our "common situation," such that "at the very heart of our most personal experience [...] is the remedy to skepticism and pessimism" (26). What the primacy of perception rejects, then, is not the world of rationality, meaning, and value, but simply the characterization of such a world as pure and wholly separated from the ambiguities and contradictions of experience.

In addition, the transcribed discussion provided at the end of this publication helps to situate Merleau-Ponty's place in French intellectual life, between **Bréhier** (his advisor and an historian of philosophy), **Hyppolite** (a Hegelian), and Beaufret (a Heideggarian).

Problems and mysteries (Marcel)

Following **Marcel**, Merleau-Ponty drew the distinction between *problems*, which are questions that I might pose and solve by considering some set of facts or concepts that are external to me, and *mysteries*, which are questions that the embodied person asking is inextricably caught up in, that is, philosophical and existential questions (see *PhP*, lxxxv; *TD*, 104, 133).

Project of the world

Through the analysis of the *cogito* in the final part of *Phenomenology of Perception*, Merleau-Ponty establishes that subjectivity cannot be the constituting source of the world, nor a *pensée de survol* that observes it as if from above. Rather, subjectivity is a *project of the world*, or a *worldly project*. This is to define subjectivity not as a thing or as a private sphere, but as a **field** within the world and open to the world, and this is perhaps a precursor to his notion of **flesh**.

Projection of memories

In Chapter Two of the Introduction to *Phenomenology of Perception*, Merleau-Ponty considers whether introducing memories into perceptual experience might insulate classical theories from the critique of the **constancy hypothesis**. If the perceptual data actually recorded on the retina is incomplete, perhaps empiricists might claim that memories must be projected into that experience. And yet, the selection of *which* memories to project implies that I already recognize the present organization as calling for just these memories, but such an *active* account of memories is incompatible with empiricism (*PhP*, 21).

The Prose of the World (~1952/1968) [PW]

In a letter related to his candidature at the *Collège de France*, Merleau-Ponty announces that he is working on two related books: *Introduction to the Prose of the World* and *The Origin of Truth*. The first was to provide the structure of **expression** through a study of the literary use of language, and the second was to offer the metaphysical foundations of such a philosophy of expression. The first project was abandoned (or held to the side) in early manuscript form around this time (see **Lefort's** explanation, *PW*, xi–xxi). Merleau-Ponty did extract and revise a significant portion of this manuscript, published in *Les Temps modernes* as "Indirect Language and the Voices of Silence" (1952). The second project evolved into a different phenomenological ontology, *The Visible and the Invisible*, also remaining incomplete upon Merleau-Ponty's death. The reader should bear in mind that this book was not intended for publication in its now available state. For Merleau-Ponty's own summary of his goals in this manuscript, see "An Unpublished Text by Maurice Merleau-Ponty" (1952) (*PrP*, 9–11).

Chapter One: The Specter of a Pure Language

Is there such a thing as a pure language that would "leave nothing to be desired, contain nothing which it does not reveal, and thus sweeps us toward the object which it designates" (*PW*, 3)? In a language purified of all **ambiguity** and all equivocation, speakers could be assured of reaching truth and achieving a complete communication. And indeed, in both common sense and the exact sciences, "[w]e all secretly venerate the ideal of a language which in the last analysis would deliver us from language by delivering us to the things" (4). After all, what is **science** if not a purified language, free of the ambiguities of natural languages. On such a picture, algorithm becomes the essence of language, and expression involves precise signification for which the speaker can be held responsible. Nevertheless, such a picture is "a revolt against language in its existing state" (5). *Communication* on this picture is simply an illusion, since words can never thereby contribute anything new to thought, whereas the experience of language gives birth to a "mute faith in the secret virtues of communication" (8)? To answer these questions, one would have to seek a genuine phenomenology of lived language or speech.

Chapter Two: Science and the Experience of Expression

When I see an object, I am barely aware of my *seeing*, but rather wholly engrossed by the object. The same intentional structure prevails in prosaic uses of language. When an expression is successful we are caught up with the meaning, not the signs by which it is brought about (10). On the other hand, systematized and adequately removed from the context of speaking, language can appear as a lifeless system. This recalls the important distinction between *speaking speech* and *spoken speech*, or as he says here: "voice and echo" (10). There is a **dialectical** relationship between these two sides to language, and spoken speech is a personal or public reservoir for creative repetitions: the book may catch like a fire, but it is a fire that is not solely fed from the author's materials—it "feeds off of everything I have ever read" (11). The meaning or *sense* of the book will evolve across the trajectory of its readings, since indeed the reader is always both "receiving and giving in the same gesture" (11). Expression does not sediment fixed meanings or ideas; rather, "it makes use of everything I have contributed in order to carry me beyond it" and such that there can be a genuine communication insofar as the author and I come together in the same world as set out by the text, though we undoubtedly inhabit this world differently. Thus, "spoken" or sedimented language is the one brought to the text by the reader, and the one both the author and the reader share, and yet this expression will shift and remake that very language, and once it has become sedimented in the community, this book too will be a part of the cultural acquisition. Nevertheless, "speech" or expressive language will remain a "call to the unprejudiced reader" (13), and meaning and expression are never complete, despite the pretenses of spoken speech.

Communication is thus possible because I am "a speaking subject capable of linguistic gesticulation" (14). For Merleau-Ponty, then, language "*is* signification before *having* a signification," that is, language is first and always enacting its primary expressive function as the "vehicle of truth" rather than a "statement" of truth. Merleau-Ponty identifies two ways of erring with regard to language. As Merleau-Ponty writes, "language is the gesture of renewal and recovery which unites me with myself and with others" (17). Whereas "I think" allows room for doubt, "I speak" presupposes the system of self-other-world, not a "pure 'I,'" and as an embodied subject in a system of embodied subjects, we are all exposed to others (18). Language, then, must be nothing other than "the reverberation of my relations with myself and with others," or again, language is the "medium of human relations" (20). Merleau-Ponty argues that between a pure **consciousness** that is indifferent to language and a pure determinism by the external history of language, there is an "I speak" in which the two systems cross in our lived experience. For language to have a meaning I do not need to posit a universal or pure language "hovering over history," since it is as an open and expressive being in the living present that I can gear into the traces of others. This embodied expressive being, then, is the principle of resolving the traditional debates between the intellectualists and the empiricists, of finding a sense born in the contingency of history.

In fact, the structure of expression is present even when language *seems* to be working "directly or prosaically, where grammar operates more than style" (30). Yet in any speech act, I communicate "[w]ith my throat, my voice, my intonation, and, of course, with the words, with my preferred constructions and the time I allow each part of the phrase" (29). And it is precisely Saussure's understanding of a language less as a sum of signs and significations than as a system of differences, which themselves result from the functioning of speech (31). Saussure compares the effect of a new expression to the effect that would result from a change in the mass of one planet in a solar system: "this isolated fact would generate general consequences and displace the equilibrium of the entire solar system" (34). The new expression is, to echo Merleau-Ponty adoption of Malraux's phrase, a **"coherent deformation"** that leads to a new equilibrium, and this process of disequilibrium–equilibrium is driven by nothing other than speaking subjects and their desire to communicate. Expression, then, is forever a "paradoxical enterprise" since it must at once respond to and take up a sedimented past or spoken language and yet "detach itself and remain new enough" to genuinely express something" (35).

Chapter Three: Indirect Language

A separate entry has been provided for the authoritative version of this material: see **"Indirect Language and the Voices of Silence" (1952)**.

Chapter Four: The Algorithm and the Mystery of Language

The enigmatic yet necessary relationship between speech and thought is "the mystery of language" (116). But how can one even study this mystery when language resists all who focus on it, but appears in its fullest to those who simply take it up and use it? The moment I speak *about* language, I am no longer the one *using* language as I was, and language will always overflow whatever I might say about it. If one needs to return to the lived experience of language as the genuine evidence of expression and communication, what mode of reflection can "restore what is paradoxical and even mysterious in this evidence" (117)? How is speech "pregnant with a meaning" (118)? As Merleau-Ponty here says, signs are but the "visible trace" of a movement of thought, and communication is the gearing into the movement of another thought through the re-performance of its traces.

Nevertheless, something happens in the truths of science that involves an experience of touching some "truth" that "did not begin with me and will not cease to signify after me" (121). In short, the experience of scientific expression reveals the powerful moment of **institution**. The error is in assuming that the signs that touch upon this universal sense are somehow themselves unambiguous and universal. The truths only appear within a system of other premises and definitions, and it is the system itself that is the vehicle of truth. Moreover, the system that offers mathematical truths a seemingly timeless truth is itself a developing system, and therefore not "timeless" (122). Since we are necessarily embodied, we are always within the world, and our knowledge is never going to legitimately adopt a ***pensée de survol***. Even the truth of mathematics emerges from a subject already "immersed" in the world "and benefits from the carnal ties which unite them both" (123). This is the basis for the functioning of the algorithm, which is not the discovery of the articulations of the universe, but the establishing of an "ensemble of relations" and "*an open horizon of relations that can be constructed*" (125). The algorithm is an institution inviting an open trajectory of expressions within a given mathematical culture that will be true, until questions that remain latent are addressed to the system so as to alter its structure once again in the development of knowledge. Even mathematical thought "is creative," and the algorithm, *expression*. What is revealed, then, is the "becoming" or "development" of meaning, which is the accomplishment of sense in contingency from within horizons of sedimentation. Thus, although the very activity of lived expression leads us to forget this orientation in favor of some spoken "truths," "truth" itself is nothing "but anticipation, repetition, and slippage of meaning" (129). Truth is that toward which we are oriented through language, just as the world is that toward which we are oriented through our embodiment, and this understanding of truth is the radical consequence of the theory of expression.

Chapter Five: Dialogue and the Perception of the Other

Turning to consider dialogue, Merleau-Ponty suggests that even scientific uses of language and communication require speech, which "accomplishes those anticipations, encroachments, transgressions, those violent operations" that transform the system through expression. But this expression is not enough in itself: it must speak to a community in which it reconfigures the spoken toward a horizon of future expression. Expression is a form of *empiétement*, trespass, of "oneself upon the other and of the other upon me" (133), and it is this transgressive relation that we call dialogue. First, there is a silent relation with others, who is *nowhere else* than in this embodiment before me, not reducible to their body, but the body as a "singular existence, *between* I who think and that body, or rather, near me, by my side" (134). The body of the other is not an object in my environment; it "haunts" my world. As a source of meaningful **behaviors**, or as the initiation of an unexpected response, the body of the other reveals that I am not in a private world, not through *intellectual* analogy, but in *lived* experience. In this experience, the "self" is "decentered."

Communication thus requires the notion of *field*. A perceptual object in my phenomenal field is not my private object, and my experience of it does not have the rigid borders of absolute thought—unlike the structures of **transcendental idealism**, *fields* are not exclusionary. "Rather, a field tends of itself to multiply, because it is the opening through which, as a body, I am 'exposed' to the world" (138). There is a **generality** to my experience, and this also allows others to populate my world through the carnal relations that are never "intruding from outside upon a pure cognitive subject" (139). With this *perceptual* presence of the other, a dialogue with this other becomes possible. Insofar as we have similar enough bodies and sedimented histories, we can "encroach upon one another" (139), but this is not made possible by the common institutions, but rather by our common general practice of expression itself. Through the **"anonymous"** (because pre-thetic) structures of corporeality that place me in the same world as the other that an open communication with them becomes possible. As a practice, then, expression establishes not a "community of *being* but a community of *doing*" (140). Thus, linguistic communication is not possible simply because we share a common lexicon of cultural sedimentation; it is possible because we share the expressive existence that can take up this past toward an open future, and because we can and do together.

Chapter Six: Expression and the Child's Drawing

What is the relation between "objective" art and more "primitive" forms of art (child drawings, primitive art, art of "madmen") (147)? It may seem that objective art and literature map on to the world in itself, while the other forms are subjective or fantasy. Yet the above considerations suggest an underlying ability for expression that grounds human actions, and that objective art is not different in kind any other cultural expressions. Even if objective art seems to capture the world, this is only because we are solicited by it through well-sedimented institutions, and it too is not without "contingency" and "risks" (148). For Merleau-Ponty, in any expression, "the aim is to leave on the paper a trace of our contact with this object and this spectacle" (150). The expression leaves the other side of how this spectacle made us vibrate, it leaves a "testimony," and the trace can be taken up again by another lived body in a genuine **communication**. As such, the child's drawing is not a failed expression, but the testimony of a different world and different relation to space and time, the possible co-existence *in* the world of what is both "visible and invisible" (151).

Protention and retention

Drawn from **Husserl**'s discussion of the constitution of inner time, Merleau-Ponty makes use of the notions of protention and retention in his discussion of temporality. Rather than invoking a notion of memory, Husserl suggests that as each moment passes by I retain it in my experience in its pushed-backness. Similarly, I also anticipate the arriving moment in a protention that is present in its imminent arrival. This account allows for a thickening of **consciousness** beyond the punctual now-points of scientific time, and reveals how subjectivity is a temporal structure.

Proust, Marcel (1871–1922)

French author and important intellectual figure. Merleau-Ponty mentions Proust in several places, in both his early and later texts. In terms of specific analysis, Proust's notions of memory and **affectivity** figure in *Phenomenology of Perception* (see, for instance, *PhP*, 83, 88, 410), and Proust figures prominently in the 1954–5 courses from *The Collège de France Lectures* (*IP*, 28–40). In *The Visible and the Invisible*, when describing the aspect of the flesh that Merleau-Ponty calls "the most difficult point, that is, the bond between the flesh and the idea," it is Proust's descriptions that occupy the final pages of the text. For Merleau-Ponty, no one had been more successful in "fixing the relations between the visible and the invisible, in describing an idea that is not the contrary of the sensible, that is its lining and its depth" (*VI*, 149).

Psychoanalysis

Theory and therapy developed by **Freud**. Merleau-Ponty often discusses psychoanalysis alongside Marxist analysis. In both cases, Merleau-Ponty is critical of a "narrow" version of the theory that attempts to offer a *causal* explanation of human behavior or experience, and favors a "broad" interpretation in which **sexuality** or the past is understood as a motivating **dimension** of our experience (*CPP*, 73–4). For Merleau-Ponty, then, the weight of the past is not determinism; rather, the claim that emerges from **existential analysis** is that every human act is sexual, yet no human act is purely sexual. Thus, even if it fails to provide a science of behavior, psychoanalysis is "better suited than rigorous induction to the circular movement of our lives, where the future rests on the past, the past on the future, and where everything symbolizes everything else" (*MPAR*, 75).

In a late statement about psychoanalysis (the Introduction to **Hesnard**'s 1960 book on Freud), Merleau-Ponty acknowledges that Freud's work opens up the possibility for a new philosophy, namely, **phenomenology**. In fact, phenomenology offers psychoanalysis a language by which it can fully articulate its discoveries, and might indeed give rise to a "'humanism of truth' without metaphysics" (*PSY*, 67). And yet, phenomenology does not simply say more clearly what psychoanalysis sensed; and psychoanalysis does not offer a doctrine of science that might ground the metaphysical aspirations of the phenomenologist. Rather, they share and intertwine in how they take up human being as an object of study, as a *field*, or as a certain "*latency*" (71).

Psychologism

A theory in psychology that assumes all psychic phenomena can be fully explained through external structures and causal relations. Merleau-Ponty, following Husserl, understands this as leading to a radical skepticism that ultimately undermines even its own claims, since its own claims must themselves be the effects of external and contingent causes. This is contrasted with a **logicism**, the positing of truths in-themselves capable of withstanding the radical skeptic. This position is definitively left behind through the development of **phenomenology** (*PhP*, 60–4, 418–19).

Pyrrhonism

This is a term for skepticism, stemming from ancient Hellenistic skeptic Pyrrho.

Quale (pl. *qualia*)

Closely related to sense-data theories of perception, this Latin term is used by philosophers to pick out the subjective or qualitative experience of having a sensation. *Qualia* are typically assumed to be available to reflective or introspective **consciousness**. A return to a genuine description of the **phenomenal field** reveals that a "pure *quale*" is impossible because the structure of perception is not one relating the body as a mere mechanism to an impartial mind. Perception is in fact a "living communication with the world" (*PhP*, 53).

Quasi-object

A category of objects discussed in **Husserl**'s "Foundational Investigations of the Phenomenological Origin of the Spatiality of Nature: The Originary Ark, The Earth, Does Not Move." The Earth is a perceptual object that haunts every experience we have of movement, and yet it does not itself appear and never itself "moves." For Merleau-Ponty, the body too is such a *quasi-object*. See *HLP*.

"Reading Montaigne" (1947) [S]

This essay discusses **Montaigne**'s skepticism in the third book of *Essays*. For Montaigne, doubt leads one to affirm not that everything is false, but that perhaps *anything* is true, and thus there is what Merleau-Ponty calls an "ambiguous *self* [...]—the place of all obscurities, the mystery of all mysteries, and something like an ultimate truth" (*S*, 198).

"Reality function" (Janet)

Similar to **Bergson**'s notion of **"attention to life,"** Janet posited a notion of the "sense of reality" or the "reality function" by which **consciousness** was tied to the world in normal experience, and which was missing in pathological experience. As such, Janet is able to describe how emotions can be experienced as a genuine "flight from our world and, consequently, from our **being in the world**" (*PhP*, 514n. 23). Nevertheless, Merleau-Ponty follows **Sartre** in critiquing Janet's underlying dualism between mind and body (*PhP*, 81–2).

Reflective analysis

Cartesian- and Kantian-inspired philosophical methodology that, rather than describing experience, works backwards from experience to discover its conditions of possibility, ultimately leading to absolute structures of **constituting consciousness** (*PhP*, lxxiii). In particular, by turning from the world toward a pure center, reflective analysis remains "unaware" of the problems of the world or of others (lxxv). Although Merleau-Ponty sometimes uses the term interchangeably with **intellectualism** or critical philosophy, and criticizes the position at length (40–3; 227–8), he does explicitly link it to **Alain** and **Lagneau**, who ultimately foreshadow **Gestalt psychology**'s call back to the description of phenomena (507–9n. 53).

Reflex

Often described in mechanistic terminology of triggered reactions, the reflex provides classical physiology with an ultimate foundation for its studies of **behavior**. Yet **Gestalt psychology** denies the possibility of a one-to-one correlation between stimulus and response, and even suggests that reflexes are a form of **intentionality** (*SB*, Chapters One and Two). As Merleau-Ponty writes, "reflexes themselves are never blind processes: they adjust to the 'sense' of the situation, they express our orientation toward a 'behavioral milieu' just as much as they express the action of the 'geographical milieu' upon us" (*PhP*, 81).

Repression

Merleau-Ponty's particular understanding of repression emerges through his discussion of the **phantom limb**, which is a phenomenon that cannot be understood as exclusively physiological or as purely psychological (*PhP*, 80). As a result, repression is characterized by the manner in which a person continues to carry with them a failure or a trauma in a non-explicit part of their being or experience. The structure of the repressed is sustained not as an **unconscious** representation, but in the manner in which it reshapes the subject's experience and possibilities. And in fact, just as one event can be generalized through repression to a structure that shapes my entire life, our organic bodily being "plays the role of an *innate complex* beneath the level of my personal life" (86). In short, my personal existence *represses* its inherence in a body, which is to say that it turns away from its body and yet never transcends this bodily being. The **ambiguity** of embodiment is a result of an "organic repression" that has the structure of an ambiguous presence that cannot be explained by physiology or by psychology (87).

Reversibility; sensing/sensed; sensibility

Merleau-Ponty's late ontological reflections discuss a fundamental principle of **reversibility** that he names the "ultimate truth" (*VI*, 155). This notion emerges from his earlier explorations of the **ambiguity** of **being-in-the-world** and the enigmas of **touching/touched** and **seeing/seen**. He explores the notion of *Ineinander*, or **intertwining**, and the paradoxical structure of **enveloping/enveloped** as the fundamental fact that the body is at once a power of exploring the world and is necessarily *of* the world. This suggests that the body is the place of a fundamental **encroachment** between sensing/sensed, a fundamental Sensibility by which Being itself and others can appear. In **"Eye and Mind"** he discusses how **painting** has a privileged access to the reversibility between seeing/seen (*MPAR*, 129), as well as the possibility of understanding a reversibility between **dimensions** (140). This structure of proliferating reversibilities is repeated in *The Visible and the Invisible* such that a fundamental element of **flesh**, as the place of all **chiasmatic** relations, is able to structure an entire ontology and a new understanding of **intersubjectivity** as **intercorporeality**. In all of these cases, the reversibility must be recognized as in principle possible but as never in fact completed, since a *coincidence* between the two poles would negate the spacing or *écart* by which Being appears as the invisible of every visible.

De Saint-Exupéry, Antoine (1900–44)

French writer, journalist and pilot, killed in 1944 while flying a reconnaissance mission. In *Phenomenology of Perception*, Merleau-Ponty quotes from Saint-Exupéry's novel *Pilote de guerre: Mission sur Arras* (1942), even offering this "hero" the final words of the treatise, a highly symbolic gesture given that this "hero's" novel was banned by collaborationist censors in Occupied France and became a key text in the underground literature of the *Résistance*.[15]

Sartre, Jean-Paul (1905–80)

Perhaps the most famous existential thinker of the twentieth century, Sartre was a philosopher, a writer, and a political activist. He is often associated with **Beauvoir**, his long-time intellectual and romantic partner, and a philosopher and writer in her own right. Sartre and Merleau-Ponty met as students and after 1940 developed a personal and working relationship until a major rupture in 1953. Nevertheless, despite their political and personal differences, they shared a commitment to the study of **Husserl** and **Heidegger**.

Sartre was older than Merleau-Ponty by two years, meaning that their overlapping time at the *ENS* did not necessarily result in much interaction. Rather, they "knew each other without being friends."[16] In a famous anecdote, Merleau-Ponty reports that their first meeting involved Sartre coming to his aid when he and another student were being accosted by a group of fellow *normaliens* for having objected to some anti-Christian songs the boys had been singing. Sartre intervened and managed to broker a resolution "without concessions or damages" (*SNS*, 41), but afterward their relationship remained one of an acquaintance. Two years later, Beauvoir's and Sartre's opinions of Merleau-Ponty soured when, according to Beauvoir, Merleau-Ponty cowardly ended a courtship of her close friend "Zaza" because her friend's mother objected to the relationship.[17]

Although they had only rare contact in the late 1930s, one of Merleau-Ponty's first publications was **"On Sartre's *Imagination*"** (**1936**). Merleau-Ponty was also sympathetic to Sartre's criticism—in *Transcendence of the Ego* (1936)—of Husserl's transcendental version of phenomenology, often echoing Sartre's argument when expressing his preference for Husserl's later work. In 1940, Sartre and Merleau-Ponty formed a literary resistance group under the banner of two ideas that Sartre (who was not yet a committed Communist) believed should structure modern society: **"Socialism and Liberty."** This would be a prelude to their later journal

Les Temps modernes, a journal meant to establish a middle position between Communism and the Christian or capitalist right. Merleau-Ponty also responded philosophically to Sartre's ***Being and Nothingness*** (1943) at length in ***Phenomenology of Perception*** (1945), particularly on the notions of temporality and freedom in Part III.

Nevertheless, political and philosophical discord led to a significant falling-out. As early as ***Humanism and Terror*** (1947), Merleau-Ponty had expressed some reservations about the direction of the Soviet Union, although he remained optimistically committed to **Marxist humanism**. By the early 1950s, the emerging accounts of the Camps and the Soviet involvement in the Korean War led to Merleau-Ponty's rejection of this earlier optimistic attitude. In "The U.S.S.R. and the Camps" (1950), he declared: "What we are saying is that there is no socialism when one out of every twenty citizens is in a camp" (*S*, 264). In a surprise move in 1952, Sartre published a pro-communist series of articles (*The Communists and Peace*) in *Les Temps modernes* without showing them in advance to the political editor, Merleau-Ponty, who would nevertheless be perceived as associated with their appearance. Merleau-Ponty demanded that a rebuttal also be published, to be supplied by **Lefort**. When Lefort's piece, "Marxism and Sartre," appeared in 1953, it was abridged and was accompanied by Sartre's own counter-rebuttal. Lefort broke all ties with Sartre and the journal over the incident. For his part, Merleau-Ponty did not resign until months later when Sartre unilaterally removed a "disclaimer" that Merleau-Ponty had felt necessary for a one-sided anti-capitalist article that Sartre had accepted. These personal conflicts, along with a brooding discord over the very nature of the relationship between politics and philosophy, reached the tipping point, and Merleau-Ponty resigned his position with the journal. Merleau-Ponty's most explicit response to Sartre's political philosophy is the chapter "Sartre and Ultrabolshevism" from ***Adventures of the Dialectic***. Sartre did not personally respond to this attack, but Beauvoir did publish a response: **"Merleau-Ponty and Pseudo-Sartreanism."**

After 1956, Merleau-Ponty and Sartre maintained a distant but respectful relationship. Sartre's philosophical work remained a key interlocutor for Merleau-Ponty. For instance, Sartre is discussed at length in the Preface to ***Signs*** (1960), and the longest chapter ("Interrogation and Dialectic") of ***The Visible and the Invisible*** is an extended discussion of **Being and Nothingness**. Upon Merleau-Ponty's death, Sartre wrote a lengthy and often touching eulogistic piece, which remains the main source of our understanding of their relationship.[18]

De Saussure, Ferdinand (1857-1913)

Swiss linguist whose work on linguistic **structuralism** lay the foundations of structuralism and post-structuralism (both within linguistics and beyond). Merleau-Ponty began to become familiar with Saussure's work in the late 1940s, and his most explicit writings influenced by structuralism are found in *The Prose of the World* (*PW*, Chapter Two) and "Indirect Language and the Voices of Silence" (*MPAR*, 76–81).

"A Scandalous Author" (1947) [*SNS*]

This essay is a lively defense of **Sartre**'s integrity and his literary work against a series of misunderstandings and unfair criticisms. It represents a positive moment in the relationship between Merleau-Ponty and Sartre.

Scheler, Max (1874-1928)

German-born phenomenologist whose work on intentionality, sensible expressivity, and **affectivity** had a significant impact on the young Merleau-Ponty. Merleau-Ponty's first published article, "Christianity and *Ressentiment*," was a review of Scheler's book *Ressentiment*.

Schilder, Paul (1886-1940)

Austrian neurologist who emigrated to the United States and continued his work in English. Schilder's notion of körperschema or "body image" was highly influential on Merleau-Ponty's work in *Phenomenology of Perception*, contributing to his understanding of the existential structure of the **body schema (image)**.

The Schneider case

In Part One, Chapters Three to Six of *Phenomenology of Perception*, Merleau-Ponty makes repeated use of the famous case in neuropsychology of **Gelb** and **Goldstein**'s study of Johann Schneider (sometimes referred to by the abbreviation *Schn.*). Schneider had suffered a deep wound to the back of his head while serving in the German army. The wound reached the occipital region of his brain and likely damaged his visual cortex. As a result of the injury, Schneider suffered from systematic impairments, showing symptoms of several disorders including visual **agnosia, alexia,** and loss of **body schema**. Leaving aside the validity of the diagnosis or the potential errors in Gelb and Goldstein's methodology, the validity of the reports is less of a concern in terms of the role Schneider plays in Merleau-Ponty's argument. Even if the pathological behavior attributed to Schneider is idealized, it nevertheless can still lead to insights into the genuine structures of "normal" lived experience insofar as it serves as a contrast. For Merleau-Ponty, Schneider's gestures must pass through consciousness, which reveals the importance of **motor intentionality** and the **"I can"** for understanding normal **being-in-the-world**.

Science

Merleau-Ponty is often critical of the underlying ontological presuppositions of classical science, and yet these perhaps obscure his own underlying respect for modern science. Not only does he consistently engage with **Gestalt psychology** and other theories of perception, he also devotes a significant portion of his research to asking questions about nature. As he asserts in an early text, the "only thing under attack is the dogmatism of a science that thinks itself capable of absolute and complete knowledge"

(*WP*, 36). His insistence on **phenomenology** is not a negation of scientific research in favor of purely subjective descriptions, but rather a recognition that human experience is not *merely* a product of nature or history. Rather than offering us the "truth" about the world, scientific perspectives are in fact "naive and hypocritical" because they do not recognize the *prior* perspective of **consciousness** "by which the world first arranges itself around me and begins to exist for me" (*PhP*, lxxii). The only genuine way to engage in philosophical reflection requires a return to lived experience. Thus, **phenomenology** aims to return to the lived world that is prior to the scientific descriptions of the world, which themselves must necessarily remain secondary or abstract. Even in his late work Merleau-Ponty remains committed to balancing science and philosophy through his lectures on nature. Nevertheless, philosophical **interrogation** or the efforts of **painting** illustrate an attempt to gear into the unreflected or brute Being of lived experience, that of which science is but a secondary expression (*MPAR*, 142–3).

Sedimentation

In *Phenomenology of Perception*, Merleau-Ponty suggests that our gestures must *sediment* into a cultural acquisition, yet this notion of sedimentation should not be mistaken for an "inert mass at the foundation of our **consciousness**" (*PhP*, 131). Rather, our past sediments into the present structure and atmosphere of possibilities of our landscape, and the structure of consciousness involves the double movement of expression and sedimentation. Language, for instance, is a sedimented structure of previous acts of speech (202), and our personality and memories are a sedimentation of our life (466–7). Both of these structures only exist insofar as they shape our present experience. As Merleau-Ponty becomes more influenced by **structuralism**, he begins to discuss sedimentation as a structure that emerges through speech, by which each expression is a **coherent deformation** of the sedimented language, paradoxically taking it up and reshaping it (*S*, 89–92). Sedimentation, then, is the necessary friction or **adversity** against which **expression** is possible (239).

Seeing/seen; visibility

In *Phenomenology of Perception*, Merleau-Ponty discusses the relation between seeing/seen alongside that of **touching/touched**. Just as my body can in principle reverse its attitude between touching and being touched, such as between my two hands, my body is also a power for seeing and in principle itself visible. Yet this potential **reversibility** is never accomplished, and my body is not itself visible insofar as it is seeing. Invoking the power of a mirror, I can "glimpse" my "living gaze when a mirror on the street unexpectedly reflects my own image back at me" (*PhP*, 94). Our visible nature structures how Merleau-Ponty thinks through **intersubjectivity** insofar as "I must be my exterior, and the other's body must be the other person himself" (lxxvi). The other appears through this visible body's behaviors, without actually being contained there, and vision is "the gaze gearing into the visible world, and this is why another's gaze can exist for me" (367). There is an **ambiguity** here that is not a "reasoning from analogy." Another person can appear precisely because I am an embodied vision, and "not transparent for myself" (368).

In **"Eye and Mind"** the experience of the mirror again appears, and reveals the in principle possibility of seeing ourselves seeing, a reversibility that suggests "the metaphysical structure of the flesh" and that converts "myself into another, and another into myself" (*MPAR*, 129–30). The body is at once seeing/seen, **touching/touched** (124). This reversibility lights the spark of an incessant "crossover" or **encroachment** between activity and passivity. **Painting** is nothing other than the expression of the enigma of this in terms of seeing/seen, or Visibility. This leads Merleau-Ponty to place seeing/seen at the heart of his ontology, reflected even in the title of *The Visible and the Invisible*. The reversibility of seeing or touching reveal what he calls a "carnal relation" with the "flesh of the world" (*VI*, 83) that draws philosophy back from the extreme categories of, for instance, Being and Nothingness. These categories remain forever on the horizon of a more primordial intertwining of the visible and the invisible, of seen and seeing (100). Yet the impossibility of actualizing this reversibility, of being simultaneously seeing and seen, is what opens the space or *écart* of Being to appear. Hence, the **chiasm** between seeing and seen institutes a reversibility in the flesh of the world, named in this case Visibility.

Sensation

Merleau-Ponty offers several criticisms of what he calls the "myth of sensations" (*SB*, 165). Following **Gestalt psychology**, which demonstrates that the most basic components of perception are "concrete stimulus wholes," he suggests that the notion of a "punctual" sensation or datum is based upon the prejudices of classical thought. This criticism appears again in *Phenomenology of Perception*, where this "seemingly clear" notion of sensation is shown to render perception itself incomprehensible (*PhP*, 3). In fact, the notion of sensation is a product of the **unquestioned belief in the world** and leads to the notion of a point-by-point connection between stimuli and perceptions, the basis of the **constancy hypothesis**. The notion of sensation should not be "saved" through auxiliary hypotheses, but rather rejected as "[t]he premise that obscures everything" (23).

Sense (sens)

One cannot stress enough the importance of Merleau-Ponty's use of the French word *sens*, which can be translated variously as "meaning," "sense," or "direction." As such, when Merleau-Ponty is discussing meaning in relation to language, he has this rich notion of *sens* in mind, and not the perhaps more narrow usage of "meaning" in English to denote an idea. Understanding this rich notion of sense or meaning is decisive for understanding Merleau-Ponty's account of language and expression, as well as the overall continuity of his work from perception to ontology.

In his earliest works, the notion of *sense* emerges through **Gestalt psychology** as a way of describing the *sense* of the whole that is irreducible to its parts, and hence the emergence of meaning in experience without any **thetic** intervention by consciousness (for instance, *SB*, 50). When I recognize a behavior, I grasp its *sense* (99), and higher-level behavior itself is a response to the *sense* of a situation. The notion takes on a further importance in **Phenomenology of Perception**, and particularly in relation to speech and **expression**. Merleau-Ponty argues classical approaches mistakenly assume that speech is merely an *external accompaniment* of thought, such that thought is the source of the meaning as an "idea" that could just as well exist in itself. For Merleau-Ponty, "*the word itself has a sense*" and speech *accomplishes* thought. This leads to a **gestural theory of meaning** in which the manner in which gestures embody their *sense* is offered as an explanation of how linguistic gestures too embody their sense. As such, meaning is not a "thing" that might be possessed in the mind of a speaker or listener, it is a paradoxical trajectory of lived performances of speaking and hearing, and it emerges in the place of taking up the **sedimented** language toward a new speech. This is, then, an intertwining between literal and figurative language, and a new theory of meaning as an open trajectory of performance.

Merleau-Ponty also explores the consequences of this rich notion of sense in relation to painting, politics, and history. **History**, for instance, can be understood not as a simple juxtaposition of events, nor as the unfolding of a pre-determined plan. Just like expression, history is a trajectory that has a *sense*. For additional examples, see the related pages indicated in the Index of this dictionary.

Sense and Non-Sense (1948) [SNS]

This collection contains essays written between 1945 and 1948, divided into three general parts: I. Arts, II. Ideas, and III. Politics, and includes a brief Preface. The collection is essential for understanding Merleau-Ponty's existential and Marxist directions of thought, as well as his original contribution in phenomenological aesthetics. Each essay has been discussed in a separate entry in this dictionary.

In the opening line of the Preface, Merleau-Ponty suggests that what unites the cultural movements of the twentieth century was the attempt to express the "revolt of life's immediacy against reason" (*SNS*, 3). Wary of the rationalism of classical intellectualism, from the structure of knowledge to politics and ethics, Merleau-Ponty is drawn to authors who enact a return to the "concrete" experience of "the fervor of the moment, the explosive brilliance of an individual life, the 'premeditation of the unknown'" (*SNS*, 3). Such an attitude draws together theories as diverse as phenomenology, **existentialism**, **Gestalt psychology**, Marxism, the practice of artists (**Cézanne**, or **Proust**), and **psychoanalysis**. Non-sense, then, is not to be excluded as the opposite of sense or rationality. Rather, an honest study of lived experience demands that we understand the **ambiguity** and paradoxes of experience, between *sense* and *non-sense*. The language or reason we have is a contingent fact of our birth, and through the experience of war, of art, or of the breakdown of reason, there occurs something of a phenomenological reduction that leads us to consider these structures themselves. And from this, "[t]he experience of unreason cannot simply be forgotten: we must form a new idea of reason" (*SNS*, 3).

This new understanding of reason unfolds in this collection through **painting**, novels, history, and politics, insofar as each repeats a certain logic of expression. The creation of the work of art is an event in which meaning is brought into the world, and yet the meaning cannot be separated from its expression. Neither the writer nor the reader is wholly "master" of the meaning, the work itself is an event of meaning belonging to many across time, and its meaning is a trajectory of the performances of this trace, a history of the lending of lived bodies to its movement. In short, the structure of expression is not the structure of a translation from a world of ideas existing in itself, mechanically translated into the shared language of, say, English. Rather, "[e]xpression is like a step taken in the fog—no one can say where, if anywhere, it will lead" (*SNS*, 3). Since what is expressed and the expression exist in an internal relation, expression must be embodied, and thus in can never be complete in the sense of a pure idea thought or expressed by a pure mind. Even "sense," then, borders on non-sense (*SNS*, 4). From this, one can see the deep importance of the first section of essays devoted to the *Arts*, where Merleau-Ponty tests out the paradoxical structures of **expression** in painting and writing. The same paradoxical structures reappear for Merleau-Ponty as he considers the role of morality given the contingent nature of action. Finally, the same paradoxical structures of expression shape Merleau-Ponty's politics. He already recognizing the failures of *both* capitalist and communist politics, he chides his own **wait-and-see-Marxist** optimism as expressed in the essays in this very collection. Nevertheless, there is room for optimism, since political men can learn from Cézanne, in whose hands the necessary failure of complete expression is turned into a powerful embracing of the paradoxical and contingent nature of life itself. Thus, thanks to the paradoxical logic of expression, a "human world is possible" even if never guaranteed (*SNS*, 5).

Sensorium commune

The center or place of intertwining of the senses. **Herder** suggests that man is a perpetual *sensorium commune*, "sometimes affected from one side, sometimes from the other" (*PhP*, 244). For Merleau-Ponty, this notion clarifies how the senses communicate and structure our pre-predicative experience of a unified world, as well as how **one's own body** is the locus of expression and of the unity between expression and signification. Thus, my body must itself be "the common texture of all objects" and also that which gives *sense* to cultural objects as a "general system of symbols" (245). This leads Merleau-Ponty to embrace Herder's insight: "I live the unity of the subject and the inter-sensory unity of the thing, I do not conceive of them in the manner of reflective analysis and science" (248).

Sexuality

The most explicit discussion of sexuality occurs in Part One, Chapter Five of ***Phenomenology of Perception***. In this context, Merleau-Ponty argues that **psychoanalysis**, understood as **existential analysis**, reveals that sexuality is a **dimension** of human experience. As such, *every* human act is sexual, and yet no human act is wholly reducible to sexuality.

Signs (1960) [S]

Including essays spanning from the late 1940s until 1960, *Signs* was the last book published by Merleau-Ponty during his lifetime, and the essays are an essential sampling of Merleau-Ponty's thought as it evolved during these turbulent years. Politically, for instance, these years saw Merleau-Ponty break with his **wait-and-see-Marxism** in favor of a **new liberalism**. Or again, these years represented a deepening engagement with **structuralism**. Throughout these essays one finds Merleau-Ponty's unmistakable philosophical style of drawing together such diverse pursuits into his singular trajectory of **interrogation**. This dictionary contains entries for each of the philosophical essays from this volume. The volume also contains a "Preface," discussed just below, which is an important illustration of Merleau-Ponty's late thought that should be read alongside **"Eye and Mind"** and *The Visible and the Invisible*.

Preface

"How different—how downright incongruous—the philosophical essays and the ad hoc, primarily political observations which make up this volume seem!" (*S*, 3). Rarely does Merleau-Ponty employ an exclamation mark, but here it seems appropriate given the diversity of essays in this volume. And indeed, beyond their topics, the content of his position had undergone some significant shifts during the years represented by this volume. As he had written a few years earlier, while prefacing the road he would travel with the dialectic, "one must tie all this together, and that is the object of this preface" (*AD*, 3). Even if it fails to tie all of this together, the Preface to *Signs* establishes the *sense* of the texts that had been written and their movement toward the one that would not be finished (*The Visible and the Invisible*). In any case, it certainly gives one the appreciation for what this collection in fact gathers together, which is "philosophy and **history** as they are being made," and one philosopher's genuine attempt to think from within their becoming, accepting all of the dangers of prognostication and **historical responsibility** that ensue.

The tone of this preface begins to the pessimistic side of a reflection on the very possibility of a relation between theory and practice, philosophy and politics. The burning questions that consumed him and the thinkers of his generation may well burn out, leaving only a series of distant "facts" that hopefully point the way toward a better future. This connection to history, however, must be maintained, so that old ideologies do not re-infuse the State with a "bad" philosophy—a worry Merleau-Ponty directs at de Gaulle's shift from critiquing elite powers to establishing his own; the Church's attempt to return to State power; and Communist politics, for failing to move toward a politics of both freedom and humanism. On all three accounts the effort is again to suppress "the spirit of inquiry and the confidence in truth" (5). Thus, what good is it to have been right, or to be right, when philosophy seems to have no effect on history? Why have a political philosophy when politics arises from practice and practice forever turns to dogmatisms?

Merleau-Ponty detects this pessimism "on all sides," but perhaps most strikingly among those who are or were "Marxists," and who thus had genuinely attempted to unite theory and practice in their lives. For Merleau-Ponty, the shift in Marxist politics to communist politics resulted in a non-expressive politics, one that was "purely tactical" as "a discontinuous series of actions and episodes with no tomorrow" (6). Such was to adopt the worst of philosophy (**historicism/psychologism**) and the worst of politics (the freezing of the dialectic). But can one remain a Marxist without being a Communist? One might declare oneself Marxist on some select list of "essential points," or one might demand a "new doctrine" altogether, but both approaches are likely impossible (7–13). For Merleau-Ponty, Marxism has entered a new stage in which it is true as critique or analysis, but false as a political doctrine (9). Marxism has become a "classic" in the history of thought, which means it shapes the world in which things can be true or false. Marxism thus ceases to be a political practice or structure, and becomes rather a philosophy, a generalized style of action. For Merleau-Ponty, then, "Marxism is […] an immense **field** of sedimented history and thought where one goes to practice and to learn to think" (12). Philosophy as engagement, then, is called to disclose "exactly the Being we inhabit," and the paradoxes and contradictions it finds there (13). This would be, then, the philosophy of intertwining to which Merleau-Ponty was headed, at once philosophy and politics, ethics and metaphysics.

Shifting to his own late philosophy, Merleau-Ponty turns to questions of expression in language, art, and history in order to declare the death of an historical epoch in philosophy, namely, the *pensée de survol*. He detects in philosophy today a return to a question **Heidegger** famously poses: "What is Thinking?" Yet even if it thus begins from the "desert island" of a pure and unconditioned self-presence, philosophy quickly discovers it has a milieu that conditions its very possibility. There is an indeterminacy in lived experience by which latent meanings are carried forward, by which each self is open to its outside and to a future it only senses. Through my experience, the past and the future "encroach legitimately upon one another" (14). A careful return to lived experience suggests that "[t]he whole description of our landscape and the lines of our universe, and of our inner monologue, needs to be redone. Colors, sounds, and things—like Van Gogh's stars—are the focal points and radiance of being" (15). Such intertwining and radiance, encroachments and entanglements, are the stuff of an entirely new ontology.

Consider the appearance of **others** in the world. For Merleau-Ponty, even before I might make a judgment about the other by analogy to myself, I must already be oriented toward others as "outlines, deviations, and variants of a single Vision in which I too participate" (15). As embodied within a world that I see and by which I am seen, they are my "twins" or the "**flesh** of my flesh" because they are equally reversible folds in the very heart of the visible. I may never fully "overlap," since each fold is unique, yet I can experience proximity insofar as I and the other "haunt" the perceptible together. The other human is not "one thing among others," it is a visible that suddenly alters into a power for looking at me, and from then on we share an opening to a Visible that neither of us can claim to possess as a **constituting consciousness**. Thus, "our glances are not 'acts of consciousness' [...] but openings of our flesh which are immediately filled by the universal flesh of the world" (16). The entire ontology of bodies is, for Merleau-Ponty, thus dependent upon the reversibility of perception, that the lived body is at once a power for touching and itself tangible, a power for seeing and itself visible. The visible other is the surface of a depth; I "see" nothing but colors, but I catch sight of her in her style and her particular way of modulating the world and the situation. She is not her body *plus* her "soul," she is wholly embodied.

When we speak, however, it seems that we "interrupt this fascination" of bodily communication, and yet this appearance results from the classical distinction between speech (as a system or code) and thought (as pure meaning in itself), a distinction that Merleau-Ponty has several times thrown into question through the phenomenological description of speaking, listening, reading, conversing, etc. For Merleau-Ponty, there is an inescapable intertwining of thought and speech, because "[e]xpressive operations take place between thinking language and speaking thought; not, as we thoughtlessly say, between thought and language" (18). Thoughts are not "things" at all, but networks of available significations that remain latent when we speak, and thus expression proceeds according to a **coherent deformation:** "reorganizing things-said, affecting them with a new index of curvature, and bending them to a certain enhancement of meaning" (19). This creative repetition does not remove us from bodily communication, it varies and amplifies "intercorporeal communication as much as we wish" (19). Moreover, if this is the case, we are never walled off from others, for "[a]ll those we have loved, detested, known, or simply glimpsed speak through our voice" insofar as we are a trajectory of communication and expression (19). And in all of this, there is no separate realm of ideas, a second positivity or world; rather, "[i]deas are the centers of our gravitation" insofar as they weigh upon the real and virtual gestures and actions of living bodies, and exist nowhere else than as the invisible of the visible, as its depth.

Thus, for Merleau-Ponty the subject must be neither pure positivity nor pure negativity, but rather the thickness of a being that is both in the world and takes up the world through what he calls "'verticality'—the present" (21). In the lived present there is an intertwining of past and present, self and other, subject and object, and this intertwining can never be understood from within the oppositions of classical philosophy. Rather than the contradictions between "Being" and "Nothingness," one must speak of the intertwining and reciprocal relation between the "visible" and the "invisible," where the visible is never completely present and the invisible is never *in principle* invisible. In every moment of visibility, there is an interplay between the visible that is seen and the invisible that is *seeing*. Thereby rejecting the ***pensée de survol***, philosophy must return to a genuine interrogation of embodiment as the **chiasma** between the visible and the invisible (21). This would be a philosophy that "plunges into the perceptible, into time and history, toward their articulations" (21); one that "seeks contact with brute being" through rigorous interrogation of lived experience and following the example of the best moments of literature, art, and the practice of life.

Despite the difficulty of the task and the ruinous state of affairs, Merleau-Ponty offers a hint of optimism that others will come along to take up the sense of history from where he will leave off, and their new energy and new "bearings" will shape a currently unpredictable future. In the paradoxes of embodied intersubjectivity and in politics, there is at least a growing though still mute "expectation," even a "hope" (23). The essay ends with a more attainable goal, a study of the interpersonal intertwining of **Sartre** and Nizan. Merleau-Ponty detects in Sartre's "Preface" to Nizan's novel *Aden Arabie* a genuine recollection that finds a young Sartre and a mature Sartre in a paradoxical discussion in which "one comes to suspect [...] that there is only one Sartre" (23). The discussion is an illustration of a "Merleau-Pontian analysis," which entails an exacting requirement that the **ambiguity** of the past be respected by the present. He demands that we recall both what Sartre reports explicitly and what remains on the horizon. Each person is more than their explicit declarations, and one's decisions neither change one instantly nor negate one's past. For Merleau-Ponty, Nizan is a man who came to realize the reality of **historical responsibility** since history may well turn one's expected heroic role into that of the traitor, and since in "Communist life as in the other nothing is ever irrevocably accomplished" (31). The failure of a *politics of survol* suggests the paradoxical situation in which there is no truth but the one to be accomplished, and that "no man is alone" (34). If there is no grand scheme of history and no pure intellect responsible for intentions, if historical responsibility is correct and we are all guilty for the evils that are "born in this web that we have spun about us—and that is suffocating us," then what is called for is a politics of expression that Merleau-Ponty here characterizes as "an unremitting *virtù*" (35).

Philosophical Essays and "Ad hoc, primarily political observations ..."

Entries have been provided for each "philosophical" essay. At the end of *Signs*, Merleau-Ponty includes a selection of some diverse political essays, primarily from after his departure from *Les Temps modernes*. The selection of essays paints the portrait of a philosopher who not only wanted to speak to the academic audience at the *Collège de France*, but who also felt the need to direct his insights into the world where they might make a difference in history.

Sinngebung

German term meaning *sense-giving* or *sense-bestowal*. Used by Merleau-Ponty to characterize transcendental approaches to **consciousness** that understands its role as the active operation that intends and organizes the world (*PhP*, lxxv).

Sinngenesis

German term meaning "genesis of sense," drawn from Husserl.

Situated freedom

In the final chapter of *Phenomenology of Perception*, Merleau-Ponty argues that human action can be considered neither purely free nor purely determined. Rather, our freedom is born within our situation. The past structures my action not according to a causality, but insofar as it shapes my present possibilities and haunts the landscape as the "atmosphere of my present." As a result, "[o]ur freedom does not destroy our situation, but gears into it: so long as we are alive, our situation is open" (*PhP*, 467).

"Socialism and Liberty"

In 1940, Merleau-Ponty and **Sartre** formed a small resistance group and published several editions of "Socialism and Liberty," named for the two ideals Sartre believed necessary for a modern society (prior to his conversion to Communism in the early 1950s). The group only lasted a short time, but set the stage for their subsequent journal, *Les Temps modernes*, established in 1945.

Sociologism

The approach to sociology that interprets social phenomena according to external structures and causal relations. See **psychologism**.

Speaking speech versus spoken speech

In *Phenomenology of Perception*, Merleau-Ponty is not yet directly influenced by **structuralism**, and yet he adopts what he calls the "famous" distinction between languages [*langages*] and speech [*parole*]. Thus, he distinguishes between a *spoken speech*, by which he means **constituted language** as a structure of available significations held as the **sedimentation** of previous acts of expression, and a *speaking speech*, in which the expression cannot be separated from the expressed since this is an authentic act of expression, a *sense* that is coming into being. He stresses that the authentic acts of speaking speech are only possible against the background of spoken speech, foreshadowing his adoption of the notion of **coherent deformation** (*PhP*, 202–3).

Stendhal, Henri Beyle (1793–1842)

French author. Stendhal was one of Merleau-Ponty's key literary examples in several texts, alongside Balzac, **Proust**, and **Valéry**. Stendhal plays an important role in Merleau-Ponty's account of **expression** as presented in his 1953 course "On the Literary Use of Language" (*Collège de France* Lectures) and in "**Indirect Language and the Voices of Silence**" (for instance, *MPAR*, 113).

Stratton, George Malcolm (1865–1957)

American psychologist famous for his experimental work on vision "without" retinal inversion. Stratton designed and donned goggles that turned his retinal images upright, and recorded his experience. Although at first the entire world seems itself inverted, as Stratton lives in this "inverted" environment he begins to experience his own body as upright and the visual objects begin to take their place in his experience where they belong (see *PhP*, 254ff.).

Structuralism

Method of analysis by which an object of study is viewed and analyzed in terms of the structural relations between its elements, and in which the elements have their meaning or value according to these relations. Merleau-Ponty is particularly influenced by **Saussure**'s structuralism in linguistics, although he mentions **Lévi-Strauss**'s structuralism in **anthropology** and **Lacan**'s structuralism in **psychoanalysis**. His understanding of structuralism is also importantly related to his understanding of **structure** in **Gestalt psychology**.

In terms of language, Merleau-Ponty became familiar with Saussure's approach in the late 1940s, and he accepted Saussure's description of language as a system of differences. Yet he carefully placed a special emphasis on the return from language as a mere system of signs to the experience of inhabiting the system from within as a speaking subject. For Merleau-Ponty, Saussure's insight reveals the paradoxical relationship between the individual and the social, or the speaking and the spoken. Language does not exist except insofar as it is spoken, and yet the speaking subject "does not own language" (*CPP*, 63). Linguistics, then, would only be a first step in a general *semiotics* that requires a phenomenological approach to all cultural realities. Saussure's insight rests on the recognition that a word does not "mean" or "signify" a single idea. Rather, each sign marks a *difference* from all other signs in the system, and it signifies this difference. "Words," writes Merleau-Ponty, "are systems of power that are interconnected with one another" (63). Thus, language "transcends the habitual distinction between pure meaning and pure sign" (64). Merleau-Ponty finds it "hard not to think of Saussure when Husserl insists that we return from language as object to the spoken word" (*S*, 106), showing again the phenomenological reading of **structuralism** that is at the heart of Merleau-Ponty's middle period. This phenomenological structuralism also reworks the relationship between philosophy and **history**.

Structure

The notion of "structure" (or "form") in Merleau-Ponty is first and foremost a reference to **Gestalt psychology**, and not to **structuralism**, which he only adopted later. The experiments of Gestalt psychology had revealed that all experience is *structured* according to a primary relation of **figure/ground**. Moreover, everything that might appear necessarily appears as a whole that is greater than the sum of its parts. Nevertheless, Merleau-Ponty critiques the Gestalt theorists for failing to reach a genuine **phenomenological reduction** because they believed in a natural or "real" level of structures that might ground structured experience (*SB*, 140ff.). Merleau-Ponty argues, rather, that the notion of structure requires a reworking of the very concepts of "real" and "ideal," and thus demands a return to a genuine description of perceptual experience and the presence of irreducibly meaningful structures. Structure is precisely "the joining of an idea and an existence which are indiscernible, the contingent arrangement by which materials begin to have meaning in our presence, intelligibility in the nascent state" (206–7).

In the middle period of his career, Merleau-Ponty became increasingly interested in **structuralism**, although his understanding of structuralism remains importantly influenced by his study of Gestalt psychology. Although he perhaps moves further away from structuralism in his last works, he never abandons the importance of the notion of structure.

The Structure of Behavior (1938/1942) [*SB*]

In 1938, Merleau-Ponty completed his first or minor doctoral thesis, "Consciousness and Behavior," which was published in

1942 as *The Structure of Behavior*. From the opening lines, he defines his goal as the attempt to understand "the relations of consciousness and nature" (*SB*, 3). Across his early work, Merleau-Ponty is committed to bridging the schism between **intellectualism** and **empiricism**, and he believed this could be accomplished by demonstrating that each philosophy eventually leads back to the phenomenological description of **pre-thetic experience**. *The Structure of Behavior* begins this reconciliation by adopting the viewpoint of the **"outside spectator"** in order to reveal how empiricism, with its mechanistic ontology, fails to genuinely account for our lived experience. For Merleau-Ponty, **behavior** is "neutral with respect to the classical distinctions between the 'mental' and the 'physiological' and thus can give us the opportunity of defining them anew" (4). The careful description of behavior demonstrates how **consciousness** emerges in the world as a **structure**, and neither as a mechanism reducible to its parts nor as a pure mind. Though the study of how **Gestalt psychology** undermines psychology's (and its own) presupposed naturalistic ontology, Merleau-Ponty is able to present the relation between consciousness and nature as one of **understanding** or as **intentionality**.

Reflex and Higher Forms of Behavior

Merleau-Ponty begins by studying classical empiricist approaches to behavior by which behavior is reduced to **reflex**. Given that the body is itself understood as a mechanism, its behavior must be understood resulting from a "stimulus–response" relationship, with higher forms of behavior being a complex set of elementary reflexes. And yet, **Gestalt theory** reveals that the behavior of organisms is not simply a triggering of reflexes by external stimuli. Rather, "stimulus often acts much less by its elementary properties than by its spatial arrangement, its rhythm, and the rhythm of its intensities" (10). The organism is meaningfully oriented toward its *Umwelt* ("milieu"), and thus the study of behavior requires the notion of form or **structure**. The appearance of an irreducible *sense* through the emergence of meaningful behavior in a particular milieu confirms the fundamental principle of Gestalt theory, that the whole is greater than the sum of its parts (50). This requires nothing less than a new theory of **reflex** (52, 56). The necessity of this approach is confirmed by Merleau-Ponty first analysis of **Gelb** and **Goldstein**'s study of **Schneider** (65–73).

Higher-level behaviors must be understood as possessing a *sense*, which might be considered a melodic unity. The melody is not the sum of separate notes, since the same notes in a different context are not "the same," and since the melody is "the same" even if transposed so as to have not one of the previous notes. Similarly, behaviors are not reducible to an automatic mechanism, since they are "improvised, actively constituted at the very moment of perception" (88). Since behavior cannot be understood at an atomistic level below the structure of **figure/ground**, Merleau-Ponty has here established the primacy of the perceived or phenomenal world over the "real" world in terms of understanding living organisms. On such a theory, the learning of behavior cannot be accounted for according to Pavlov's account of conditioning through "trial and error." Such a theory requires that pre-existing elements be reorganized through repetition, yet learning behavior is rather established according to value, which cannot merely be present as a simple causal factor. Learning a behavior involves investing a certain multiplicity with a *sense*, and this requires "a general alteration of behavior which is manifested in a multitude of actions, the content of which is variable and the [signification] constant" (96). Just as I can sing a melody in any key, or pick it out on different instruments, learning a behavior involves grasping the *sense* and being able to take that form into other situations. Learning, then, is not a "*real* operation" (99), but a general alteration of the phenomenal or perceptual world.

Thus, the various levels of behavior are not linearly structured from elementary to complex, but through **dialectically** related structures in terms of how the form relates to the content of the behavior. "**Syncretic forms**" are behaviors are those tied directly to certain types of situational content that, as a whole, motivates an instinctual response. "**Amovable forms**" consist in behaviors that respond to what is signified or indicated by the content of a situation, enabling structures such as "means–end" behavior (105–20). "**Symbolic forms**" of behavior make possible creative response to the *sense* of the situation, transposing meaning from one structure to another and opening up expressive and symbolic behavior, such as language. With these three dialectically related forms, the study of behavior reveals that consciousness can be described not simply as an intellectual or epistemic principle, but primarily as "a certain manner of treating the world, of 'being-in-the-world' or of 'existing'" (125–6). These first chapters thus demonstrate that the value of the notion of behavior is to be found in its paradoxical structure as *between* idea and thing, a positive **ambiguity** that will undo traditional approaches to philosophy.

The Philosophical Significance of Structure

In Chapter Three, Merleau-Ponty aims to establish the philosophical significance of these discoveries in behavioral psychology, teasing out the underlying ontology of dialectically related orders of reality: "The Physical Order, The Vital Order, and The Human Order." The world in itself is not the same as the *milieu*, and each organism expresses a meaningful set of behaviors that he calls the *a priori* of the species. This *a priori*, because it is a structure, is a contingent fact rather than universal or necessary form. Learning behaviors, then, introduces new *a priori* structures, yet **Gestalt psychology** has failed recognize its own philosophical consequences, and ultimately falls back upon the "realistic postulates which are those of every psychology" (132). **Koffka** and others attempt to locate form "among the number of events of nature; it is used like a cause or a real thing; and to this very extent one is no longer thinking according to 'form'" (136–7). Properly understood, form reveals the relation between consciousness and nature because it expresses "the synthesis of matter and idea" (137). And indeed, even **science** requires a concept of "physical structure" that must borrow from "the universe of perceived things," that is, the **phenomenal world**.

Shifting to "vital structures," we move to the order of **action**. Rather than establishing an equilibrium in a field of forces, living systems respond to virtual conditions brought into existence by the system itself (145). Moreover, each organism develops a *style* characteristic of its dialectical relation to the milieu, its manner of "taking a bait, of walking toward a goal, of running away from danger" (151). This **dialectic** relation suggests that the manner in which the organism is oriented toward the milieu shapes the manner in which the milieu appears, and vice versa. This understanding of **dialectic**, importantly shaped by **Gestalt theory**, foreshadows the paradoxical structures of **expression** that shape all of Merleau-Ponty's work. Introducing the distinction between the objective and the **phenomenal body,** Merleau-Ponty describes how the phenomenal body is a "center of **actions** which radiate over a 'milieu'" (157). Alluding to the work of **Uexküll,** the organism is thus characterized as a living melody (159).

With the introduction of the "Human Order," Merleau-Ponty stresses the dialectical relations between the levels, and introduces the structure of **motivation** as an alternative to causal thinking. A stimulus, for example, is not a simple cause of a reaction; rather, it motivates a response in such a way that **action** must be a dialectical relation between the milieu and the organism's capabilities. This "embodied dialectic" is already a form of consciousness, emerging within the world through the dialectic between the animal's orientation toward the milieu and the milieu's solicitation of the animal. Such a structure must be understood as **expression**: "The phenomenon of life appeared therefore at the moment when a piece of extension, by the disposition of its movements and by the allusion that each one makes to all the others, turned back upon itself and began to express something, to manifest an interior being externally" (162). Moreover, the human order introduces the dialectic of culture (or "work") whereby real or potential **action** gives rise to tools and other cultural objects that reshape the organism in ways that cannot be explained according to its previous "vital" interests.

Nevertheless, even this level does not require the structures of a pure consciousness, since all of this unfolds *within* the world. I recognize a face without in fact knowing the particular color of the eyes because recognition is not an intellectual activity of **judgment,** but one of lived perception. Embodied with the vital and cultural milieus, I am oriented toward the world according to my style of responding to its solicitation, and thus I exist as a network of "involvements" and meanings. Language, above all else, has the power to reshape and reorient all of our experience, and thus nature becomes "that minimum of stage setting [...] necessary for the performance of a human drama" without thereby ever being transcended (168). Consider an example of a soccer player caught up in the action of the game. None of the objects of the situation are known "in themselves," but rather through their significance in relation to the situation of the match, as "lines of force" and solicitations for action (169). The location of the opposing goal, or the out of bounds lines, are never known thetically, but are sensed as urgencies and constraints upon the action. Moreover, "[e]ach maneuver undertaken by the player modifies the character of the field and establishes in it new lines of force in which the action in turn unfolds and is accomplished, again altering **the phenomenal field**" (169). The notion of **consciousness** thus needs to be brought back from the extreme of an all encompassing transcendental ego in order to account for the lived and multiple ways of inhabiting the world *intentionally*. That is, consciousness is not simply **reflection** or **judgment**: "Rather, consciousness is a network of significative intentions which are sometimes clear to themselves and sometimes, on the contrary, lived rather than known" (173). And as a result, human **action** is not first a representation of a goal added to some bodily mechanism through an external relation; it is a "directed melody," an "expression" in the rich sense whereby expression and the expressed cannot be distinguished.

Human action is not limited to the vital milieu; it is oriented "in relation to the possible, to the mediate" (175–6). This ability is an expression of the **categorial attitude** and is characterized by a certain **ambiguity** between expression and sedimentation by which each action creates and yet each creation calls for further expressions. Such a structure implies that what is sedimented cannot simply be the *cause* of future expressions, invoking his criticism of **Freud**'s causal descriptions of the relationship between the **unconsciousness** and consciousness. For Merleau-Ponty, there is a dialectical relationship between the orders, and the difference between pathological and normal behavior involves a different level of successful integration. The traumatic experience is not present as a thing in my past or memory, but as a structure that haunts the possibilities of my present experience, and what is essential is how I take up this past toward my future. As such, the human order is not a body plus a mind; rather, it is the appearance in the world of a "new form of unity"—neither the "human" body nor the mind exists apart from their concrete embodiment.

Perceptual Consciousness and the Relations of the Soul and the Body

Through the notion of *Gestalt* and the structure of dialectic, consciousness has been shown to emerge in the world not as the arrival of a "new substance," but as a restructuring of relations and orders. But might "consciousness" in the classical sense remain above this concrete dialectic in an isolated "universal milieu" of ideas (184)? That is, might not the critical idealist still remain convinced of the freedom of the mind? The final chapter attempts to sketch the philosophical consequences of the discovery of **perceptual consciousness**.

To begin, Merleau-Ponty emphasizes the manner in which perception is necessarily perspectival, and yet this does not mean it is locked within a single perspective. Rather our lived experience senses other perspectives on the horizon of our current one. The thing we perceive is grasped as an "in-itself" that is present "for-me." When I see a cube, this rich perceptual experience cannot be accounted for by empiricism (which is limited to the three sides actually appearing on the retina) or by intellectualism (which is limited to the "judgment" of "cube" as an added intellectual component of the experience). Our direct experience is already rich with the horizons that make this a "cube," and through a perspectival appearance I nevertheless grasp "the thing itself which transcends it" (187). Moreover, my own body is not present as a simple object in itself, but as a structuring of my experience, the "living envelope of our actions" (188). As a result, human experience is a dialectical relationship between things, body, mind, and world. All of the parts contribute to the *sense* of the experience, and if any is changed, this must represent an *existential* change in the structure. Since the mind, body, and world are dialectically intertwined rather than causally related, classical philosophy was predestined to fall short of its goal by the very inadequacies of its categories. And indeed, even **Gestalt psychology** falls victim to *causal* thinking. Since perception is the ambiguous presence of a thing in itself from a perspective, our experience cannot be explained according to causal structures. Finally, even a Kantian or "critical" attempt fails because it privileges the categories of consciousness and overlooks the role of the body in structuring our experience.

Nevertheless, the Kantian discussion of consciousness justifies a "transcendental attitude," if not a "transcendental philosophy" (201). This attitude is necessary to *understand* lived experience, so long as we do not thereby attempt to replace that experience by the **constituting consciousness** of classical intellectualism.

Consciousness emerges *in* the world, it is not *signified* in the world as a sign of a separate realm of intellectual or rational activity. Whereas critical thought errs when it posits external relations between pure opposites, the dialectical integration of experience shows that the body is nowhere a "pure thing" and the mind nowhere a "pure idea" (207). Merleau-Ponty develops his own position through an initial study of language, and in particular of the relationship between a word and a concept. He argues that we must develop a conception of this relationship by which speech is not the external accompaniment of thought, and in this manner the structure of living language provides an adequate analogy for the relation between the soul and the body (210). This analysis foreshadows the more explicit study of speech and **expression** in his later works.

In the final pages of this book, Merleau-Ponty alerts the reader to the need for a new study of perceptual consciousness, beginning this time through a phenomenological description of lived perception, the awareness of **one's own body** [*le corps propre*], and the perception of **others**. These are, of course, the main themes of *Phenomenology of Perception*. This project involves nothing short of a redefinition of transcendental philosophy itself (224).

Symbolic forms of behavior

The third level of **behavior** identified in *The Structure of Behavior*, consisting in the possibility of meaningful or creative responses to the *sense* of the situation. This makes language behavior possible and is reserved for the highest forms of behavior. Nevertheless, this level remains **dialectically** related to the lower levels (**syncretic** and **amovable**), never wholly transcending them (*SB*, 120–4).

Syncretic forms of behavior

The most basic form of **behavior** identified by Merleau-Ponty in *The Structure of Behavior*, consisting in forms of behavior closely tied to situational content that, as a meaningful whole rather than as a sum of parts, motivates an instinctual response, which is itself a meaningful form of behavior (*SB*, 104–5).

Synesthesia

A condition in which a subject experiences sensations associated with one sense through the stimulation of other sensory organs, such as when a person "hears" a color. Some studies suggest that nearly one in twenty people experiences some form of synesthesia. For Merleau-Ponty, the question of it being statistically common is irrelevant, since he argues that there is a fundamental synesthetic quality to all lived experience. On a classical account of perception that rigidly identifies one sensation with one sense, synesthesia appears paradoxical. On a phenomenological account, however, the description of lived experience quickly undermines this position, and suggests that lived gestures themselves constitute an "inter-sensory" world in which these sense worlds invade each other and are always more than a mere sum of their parts. The presence of music reshapes visual space, and the modification of one sense reconfigures them all. Sensing, then, is an existential structure, and "[s]ynesthetic perception is the rule," not the exception. The objects of our experience do not reduce to discrete properties, and "[t]he form of a fold in a fabric of linen or of cotton shows us the softness or the dryness of the fiber, and the coolness or the warmth of the fabric" (*PhP*, 238). I hear a certain hollowness or harness, I see the resistance of a branch that I bend with my hands. This is a synthesis that is *accomplished* by the body, and this perceptual and lived synthesis is never complete, as the ongoing construction of an inter-sensory experience.

Touching/touched; tangibility

In *Phenomenology of Perception*, Merleau-Ponty adopts and furthers a description of two hands touching that he finds in **Husserl**. I can touch my right hand with my left hand while my right hand is touching an object, and yet the right hand *as* *touching* is not the same as the right hand *as touched*. The first is a certain exploratory power of an operative intentionality; the second is a simple collection of bones and other materials, an object *partes extra partes*. As such, the body has two sides that cannot be collapsed, "[i]t is neither tangible nor visible insofar as it is what sees and touches," and this means that the body is never "completely constituted" (*PhP*, 94). This strange reversibility is what distinguishes my body from objects (98). In *Phenomenology of Perception*, this form of **ambiguity** can be tolerated only within the **phenomenal field**.

Although this image is arguably a secondary example in *Phenomenology of Perception*, the experience of touching/touched is carried forward and placed at the center of Merleau-Ponty's ontological reflections, becoming a particularly important image in his 1958 essay **"The Philosopher and His Shadow"** returning to Husserl. He writes, "I touch myself touching; my body accomplishes a 'sort of reflection'" (*S*, 166). Upon this reading, Merleau-Ponty recognizes the ontological implications as exploding the categories of classical ontology. In touching/touched, my body and the world are intertwined, they are of the same fabric or **flesh**, and the folding back of this "sort of reflection" opens up the spacing [*écart*] that allows Being itself to *appear*. As he writes in **"Eye and Mind"**: a "human body is present when, between the see-er and the visible, between touching and touched, between one eye and the other, between hand and hand a kind of crossover occurs, when the spark of the sensing/sensible is lit" (*MPAR*, 125). This "flesh of the world" is emphasized again in his *Preface* to **Signs**, where he recognizes that the ontology of bodies itself depends upon this reversibility of perception, on the presence of a power for touching that is itself *tangible* (*S*, 16).

The image returns as a fundamental moment in the ontological reflections of *The Visible and the Invisible*. Touching/touched is an unquestionably *worldly* activity, which insulates this ontological reflection from the threat of any philosophy of **consciousness**. Moreover, characterized as **reversibility, chiasm,** and **encroachment,** this initial *spacing* is what allows for other reversibilities as well (*VI*, 133–5). The touching/touched moment reveals a *Tangibility* that takes place *between* a passive event and an active constitution, and traditional philosophy has no name for this flesh (139).

Transcendental idealism

Kantian or Kantian-inspired philosophy geared toward the **constituting consciousness** or transcendental ego. See **intellectualism**.

Transcendental phenomenology

Across his texts, Merleau-Ponty critiques **Husserl**'s early works as remaining caught in a *transcendental phenomenology* that seeks to reach a pure or transcendental consciousness. Most explicitly, he criticizes the emphasis that Husserl puts on reaching "an eidetic of language and a universal knowledge" (*S*, 84). Merleau-Ponty embraced Husserl's development toward a **genetic phenomenology** as expressed in the late works.

Transition synthesis

See **passive synthesis/transition synthesis**

Uexküll, Jakob von (1864–1944)

German biologist and naturalist. Uexküll is famous for his development of the structure of the *Umwelt* or milieu in relation to the organism (*SB*, 159).

Ultra-things

Concept developed by **Wallon** as a description of childhood experience of certain things that would not count as "things" in an adult's "objective" experience of the world because they do not adhere to spatial or temporal laws. Merleau-Ponty believes that it is wrong to classify such components of childhood experience as "errors" that are later corrected at a more mature stage (**Piaget**), and rather suggests that in a sense the ultra-things remain on the horizon of adult experience, in objects such as one's birth or an absent friend (*CPP*, 192–3; *MPAR*, 86).

Umwelt

German term meaning "environment" or "milieu," often invoked in the context of **Gestalt psychology**'s study of **behavior**, and also developed at length in the work of Uexküll.

Unconscious

The first extended discussion of **Freud**'s notion of the unconscious is in *The Structure of Behavior*, where Merleau-Ponty critiques Freud's description of the relationship between **consciousness** and the unconscious as a *causal* one. For Merleau-Ponty, the past does not exist in our unconsciousness as a thing or determinate force, but rather sediments in such a way as to structure our present experience and thereby the very appearance of our milieu (*SB*, 176ff.). The critique is repeated in *Phenomenology of Perception*, where Merleau-Ponty argues against the unconscious being understood as a repository of unconscious representations causally influencing consciousness. Rather, the unconscious is present in our experience in the manner of an atmosphere, a meaningful haze that can privilege aspects of my experience without ever being explicitly conscious. This is our experience of the ambiguous atmosphere of our past and of our **sexuality**, without being reduced to those **dimensions** (*PhP*, 171–2).

"An Unpublished Text by Maurice Merleau-Ponty: *A Prospectus of His Work*" (1952) [*PrP*]

Written by Merleau-Ponty at the time of his nomination to the *Collège de France*, this amounts to a summary of his accomplishments and a prospectus of his future research. In addition to explicitly relating *The Structure of Behavior* and *Phenomenology of Perception*, Merleau-Ponty also sketches two future books, *The Prose of the World* and *The Origin of Truth*. The first would be abandoned around this time, later published posthumously. The second would evolve into the project from the late 1950s, also published posthumously, *The Visible and the Invisible*. "My first two works," writes Merleau-Ponty, "sought to restore the world of perception. My works in preparation aim to show how communication with others, and thought, take up and go beyond the realm of perception which initiated us to the truth" (*PrP*, 3).

In his early works, Merleau-Ponty argued that perception cannot be reduced to "external" causal relations (**empiricism**) or to the function of a **constituting consciousness** (**intellectualism**), but rather had to be understood through a phenomenological description of lived and embodied experience. The first phase involved demonstrating how the relations between the behaving organism and its milieu were not reductively mechanical. And indeed, **behavior** is oriented according to a certain "*a priori* for the organism" that is taken up without an explicit intellectual contribution. Shifting from this **outside spectator** perspective to the alternative, Merleau-Ponty's second step involved installing ourselves within meaningful behavior in order to explore the **ambiguity** in the relation between the subject, its body, and its world (4–5). The lived body, then, becomes our *perspective* on the world, rather than an object in the world. This study reconceives our oriented existence and how this simultaneously reshapes the perceived world as the "universal style" of perceiving. The "subject" of this phenomenological approach will be an embodied subject, engaged with the world, and never fully grasped in transparency. This involves establishing in general what he calls "**expression**," and here is precisely where he perceives the shift from his completed works toward his future ones (6).

This foundational work, then, establishes a particular notion of truth. In perception, existence comes before questions of truth, and truth only becomes an issue when thought shifts from the world to its own established realm. Classical thought takes this as evidence that the phenomenal world is one of mere appearance, and **transcendental phenomenology** seems to take this route as well. To avoid this temptation, two components are necessary: a *theory of truth* and a *theory of **intersubjectivity***, each represented by one of Merleau-Ponty's proposed books, and the solution must emerge from our body because "as an active body capable of gestures, of expression, and finally of language, it turns back on the world to signify it" (7). The key becomes establishing that language is not a mere instrument or accompaniment of thought, and that "communication supposes in the listener a creative re-enactment of what is heard" (8). The "origin of truth" then would be in perception, gestures, and communication, but this origin is only to open up a trajectory of expression oriented toward "truth." Hence the essential connection to the second project on **expression**, which is the process of taking up the past toward an open future, the birth of *sense* in contingency, and Merleau-Ponty here suggests that the same logic is to be found in other areas of culture and history. The study of language as living communication is thus the central model for understanding all human interrelations. Since this involves linguistics, aesthetics, sociology, political theory, and history, Merleau-Ponty identifies himself as an *interdisciplinary* thinker through the fundamental structure of the paradoxical logic of expression (10).

Merleau-Ponty concludes with a famous distinction between the **"bad ambiguity"** that haunts the study of perception, and the "good ambiguity" that can be found in the phenomenon of expression. Beyond the mere "mixture of finitude and universality, of interiority and exteriority" found in perception, expression unveils "a spontaneity which gathers together the plurality of monads, the past and the present, nature and culture into a single whole" (11). The task of philosophy, and of his late work, would be to "establish this wonder" which "would be metaphysics itself and would at the same time give us the principle of an ethics" (11). Neither promise was completed upon Merleau-Ponty's death.

Unquestioned belief in the world [*le préjugé du monde*]

Since **consciousness** is oriented toward its objects and its projects, it is necessarily directed away from itself. This fundamental structure of *intentionality* is particularly clear in the everyday or **natural attitude** that characterizes our experience. Experience forgets its perspectival contribution to its experience, and it proceeds with a generally unquestioned belief in the world (in itself) as the cause and content of its experience. In the opening chapters of *Phenomenology of Perception*, Merleau-Ponty argues that both **empiricism** and **intellectualism** share the worldview that includes this unquestioned belief. As a result, classical thinkers attempt to build perception out of the parts of the world we know about, rather than attending to phenomena, and this leads to important errors in understanding our experience (i.e., the **constancy hypothesis**). Despite their advances, even **Gestalt psychologists** succumb to this natural error that stems from the very structure of consciousness. **Phenomenological reduction**, however, offers a shift in attitude that can embrace the positive indeterminacy of the **phenomenal field** and the perceptual nature of all consciousness as **being-in-the-world**.

Ursprung

German word meaning "origin." *Ursprung* figures prominently in the title of **Husserl**'s late fragment **"The Origin of Geometry."** In *Phenomenology of Perception*, Merleau-Ponty adds a hyphen to emphasize the component words, drawing out the literal meaning "*springing-forth*" when describing the world that springs forth as that which we constitute and yet also as that which transcends us in all of our experience.

"The U.S.S.R. and the Camps" (1950) [S]

This essay is an important moment in Merleau-Ponty's public relationship with Communist politics and in his personal relationship with **Sartre**, who co-signed the essay. The essay reexamines the policies of the Soviet regime, and concludes that "there is no socialism when one out of every twenty citizens is in a camp" (*S*, 264). The editorial goes on to reassert the neutrality of *Les Temps modernes* in terms of Party or ideology, at once resisting the mystifications of Soviet politics and the naivety of American writers who declare that there is no class struggle in America. Merleau-Ponty remains committed to Marxist analysis. Despite having signed this essay, Sartre subsequently moved much closer to the Communist Party. His publication of his *The Communists and Peace* just two years later led to a series of events and personal conflicts with Merleau-Ponty, culminating in Merleau-Ponty's resignation from the journal.

Valéry, Paul (1871–1945)

French poet, writer, and critic. Although he rarely engages in direct discussion of Valéry, Merleau-Ponty's allusions suggest that he was an important influence. In addition to being mentioned in **Phenomenology of Perception**, Valéry's reading of Leonardo da Vinci is analyzed in **"Cézanne's Doubt"** and his literary practice figures in the 1953 course from *The Collège de France Lectures*. In **"Eye and Mind"** Merleau-Ponty cites Valéry's idea that "[t]he painter 'takes his body with him'" (*MPAR*, 123).

The Visible and the Invisible (1964) [VI]

When Merleau-Ponty died in 1961, his notes contained the first part of a manuscript alongside a significant set of related working notes. This project was originally conceived in the early 1950s under the working title *The Origin of Truth*, and the title evolved to *Being and Sense* prior to settling in 1959 on *The Visible and the Invisible*. After setting aside *The Prose of the World* to focus more on the ontological foundations of his emerging philosophy of expression, Merleau-Ponty was drawn toward developing a new mode of philosophical methodology (**interrogation**) through a new concept of ontology and of *sense*.

The manuscript, which is only sparsely dated, indicates that much was written in spring 1959 (primarily Chapters One and Two), with a shorter writing period in late 1960 (primarily Chapters Three and Four). The first period of writing, then, corresponds to a reduction in Merleau-Ponty's teaching load at the *Collège de France*, and would have been concurrent with his single course that year on "philosophical interrogation," an influence clearly reflected in the chapter titles. The second period of writing would have corresponded with the later essays in *Signs* (particularly the Preface and "The Philosopher and His Shadow"), "Eye and Mind" and the final years of his *Collège de France Lectures*. The notes and other textual indications suggest that what remains of this manuscript was considered by Merleau-Ponty to be the first part of a larger work, with the first part focused on philosophical method and the status of the visible and Nature, while the second and unwritten part would have shifted to a new ontology of the invisible, Nature, and *Logos*. The most suggestive pages are found in Chapter Four of the manuscript, "The Intertwining—The Chiasm," and **Lefort** suggests this final chapter could indeed be considered a first chapter or introduction to the unwritten Part Two.

Chapter One: Reflection and Interrogation

The manuscript begins by inviting us to return to the most basic experience we have: we open our eyes, and things are what we see. Nevertheless, this reveals a **perceptual faith** of the **natural attitude** by which we believe in the world and in our direct access to it. And yet, when questioned, this faith fails to justify itself. The philosopher must feign ignorance of the world in order to learn just what *seeing* is, and this requires an open and responsive form of interrogation that gears into the **evidentness** of the world without draining it of its paradoxical structures. This questioning is not a **Pyrrhonian** or skeptical doubt, but rather an interrogation of "what the being of the world means" (6). The thing in itself is what we see, what solicits our gaze, and what appears as structured according to my possible actions that give it meaning (7). Yet this embodied mediation is also what allows one to step back to the level of reflection, and the philosophy of reflection is the attempt to understand the things from this outside perspective.

Reflection, however, runs into trouble when it asks the question of the **other**. Offering the beginnings of a solution, Merleau-Ponty invokes the image of the **touching/touched**. When the touched hand reverses to touch the touching hand, the original relation is broken. I can *in principle* touch the touching hand, but *in practice* this coincidence is aborted. As such, perception is never fully subject to "my" control, it is always **anonymous**, between a pure intention and a mere event. Yet the *in principle* **reversibility** does allow for the other person to appear, since the experience another person is but "an amplification of the same paradox" (9). Moreover, there is a *genesis of meaning* by which our experience is generated as a trajectory or openness of the past being taken up toward a future, and this would require a very different understanding of **consciousness**.

Might one hope to remove all of these difficulties by positing a transcendental consciousness as a *kosmostheoros*, a consciousness capable of constituting the world precisely as it is in itself? Even physics has moved beyond the relation of an absolute knower surveying an indifferent universe. Only by recognizing that the observer and the observed are both implicated in any genuine understanding of the "real," could an inquiry enter into the question of the *"meaning of being"* (16). **Science** is not the handmaiden of objective philosophy; it belongs equally to philosophies of lived experience. As Merleau-Ponty stresses here, even the advance of **Gestalt psychology** must be raised to the level of a philosophy of lived experience. In the "ambiguous order of perceived being" there is no way of reducing our experience to purely objective components. Classical approaches rest upon an erroneous ontology that distinguishes absolutely between the subject (invisible) and the object (visible), and fail to capture that the "perceived world is beneath or beyond this antinomy" (22). Rather, the body must be re-conceived as "our living bond with nature" (27). The philosopher cannot (at least not any longer) presume to "soar over" the object of study; in philosophical interrogation, the philosopher is implicated, in the structure of a mystery rather than a **problem**.

Ultimately, the philosophy of reflection is to be praised insofar as it "practices" something like "philosophical interrogation," but its manner of reflection "is not the sole possible one" (32). Between my perception and my reflection upon that perception there is forever a duration, a gap, by which the former always remains at best on the horizon of the later, and the thing reflected upon is never the whole of that unreflected that motivated the reflection. Philosophy must develop, then, a sort of hyper-reflection, an approach that would "take itself and the changes it introduces into the spectacle into account" (38). This manner of hyper-reflection would have to "plunge into the world instead of surveying it" from above, remain fixed upon the actual world rather than retreating to its conditions of possibility and the fictionalized characters of the *kosmostheros* and the universe in itself. This would be an interrogation that brings the silence of the world to expression without thereby drowning out that very silence.

Chapter Two: Interrogation and Dialectic

Reflection was a natural outcome of the perceptual faith, yet it explains the thought *that one is seeing*, and never *seeing itself* in its lived accomplishment. Might one avoid this error by suggesting that prior to reflection there must be a wholly **ek-static** subject, a self wholly outside of itself? In other words, can philosophy gain access to the "pure in-itself" of Being by positing a subject that is a pure openness, an empty subject whose openness is so pure that nothing stands between it and Being: "no 'representations,' no 'thought,' no 'image,' and not even that epithet 'subject,' 'mind,' or 'Ego.'" Only such a *nothingness* could be sufficiently open to receive "the plenitude of the world" (52). Thus, this chapter is an extended reflection on **Sartre's** *Being and Nothingness.*

But can there ever be a genuine encounter between Being and Nothingness? At the outset, these two categories must be rigorously opposed: wherever there is Being, nothingness is absent, and vice versa. Nevertheless, each intuition of Being might be accompanied by a "negintuition" of nothingness as that openness to Being, "a fissure that deepens in the exact measure that it is filled" (53). This leads to Merleau-Ponty's critique of Sartre: any philosophy that thinks of negation as that which in one movement empties itself out as it fills itself (with Being), must be a philosophical dualism in the classical sense. The philosophy of absolute negation is also, necessarily and simultaneously, a philosophy of pure Being. The advance is to be found in the manner that Being is no longer founded upon an "I think," since Being *is* insofar as I am in **ec-stasy**, outside of myself in the things. Negintuition is not reflection, yet the philosophy of the negative falls into some of the same trappings as reflection. Since I am nothing, the other, who is also an opening upon the world, cannot actually appear *in* the world. They must be somehow "born *from my side*" (59). But then again, how could a nothingness be perceived, or two nothingnesses be distinguished?

Might "exposure" and "embodiment" overcome the failings of the philosophy of reflection, so long as one is resolved to "thinking through the negative rigorously" (63)? The ontological question "why is there something rather than nothing?" appears to be dissolved, since there is never either of these in isolation. But above all, does not the philosophy of the negative provide precisely that "contact with being" that was sought by reflection, without thereby freezing or constituting Being? Despite these possibilities, the relation between Being and Nothingness will always result in an "absolute negativism" that is synonymous with an "absolute positivism" (65). Moreover, in these adjustments, nothingness becomes not an ideal opposite of Being (as at the beginning), but rather spread out throughout Being. Originally defined via restrictive definitions, Being becomes a general term that *contains* nothingness. In short, this reflection assumes a perspective that encompasses Being and Nothingness, a *pensée de survol* that ultimately collapses into a philosophy of reflection. This philosophy implies a "Hyper-being which is mythical" (74).

This reproach of **ambivalence** cuts only against philosophies committed to the logic of opposites, and our lived experience is precisely what contains the **ambiguities** and contradictions that explode such a logic. In our lived contact with Being, it is never "full" Being, and I am forever a body in a situation, not a pure nothingness. My vision of the world is not an absolute nothingness, it is an "operative nothingness," a presence to the world and a distance from it. In this complicity, there is neither a pure in itself nor a pure for itself. The negations posited by the philosophy of negative must be "reintegrated" into Being. Moreover, the relation to others is more complicated than our being two absolute negations before the in-itself. A new ontology is taking shape according to which "every relation between me and Being, even vision, even speech, is [...] a carnal relation, with the **flesh** of the world" (83). A philosophy that would genuinely respond to this situation would have to "rediscover behind vision, as immediate presence to being, the flesh of being and the flesh of the seer" (88). This would be to begin philosophy from a place between the extremes of Being and Nothingness, as an openness in which "immanence and transcendence are indistinguishable" (89).

Might we, then, suggest that between these two terms there is not an absolute distinction, but rather a **dialectical** relation? At first glance, admits Merleau-Ponty, this is precisely the sort of solution his critique of Sartre seemed to have been seeking: an **ambivalence** "capable of differentiating and of integrating into one sole universe the double or even multiple meanings" (91). And yet, Merleau-Ponty is reluctant to adopt the word for his own thought, since "in the history of philosophy [the dialectic] has never been all that unadulteratedly" (92). The genuine dialectic is indeed inherently unstable, and is forever out of reach of being formulated, to the extent that even naming it "dialectic" is to freeze it and thus to *denature* it. Even in **Hegel** and in Sartre, thought "ceases to accompany or to be the dialectical movement, converts it into signification, thesis, or thing said" and presents an ambivalent relation that is no longer in movement. The dialectic's trap is that it can convince one that it is a thing, whereas it is nothing but a practice. The **bad dialectic**, then, is "that which, against its own principles, imposes an external law and framework upon the content and restores for its own uses the pre-dialectical thought" (94). In opposition, one must seek a good or "hyper-"dialectic, a dialectic open to an ever evolving ambiguity, a dialectic that never allows the inertia of its content to solidify into absolute opposites, a "dialectic without synthesis" (94–5). The dialectic holds the promise not of a philosophy that is mired in an absolute opposition of the for-itself and the in-itself, nor frozen in some synthetic in-itself-for-itself that would be mere ambivalence, but of a genuine philosophy from within the visible and the invisible. Philosophy's task is to discover this paradoxical "logic in action" (100).

Chapter Three: Interrogation and Intuition

The third chapter marks the shift to the second phase of writing for this project, and offers what might be termed a "critique" of **phenomenology**, considered broadly to include both **Husserl** and **Bergson**. The chapter gravitates around two key concepts: **essences** and **intuition**. The analyses of the first two chapters establish that *what* we are is not a separate constituting consciousness or an absolute nothingness, and thus philosophy ought to be neither reflection nor dialectic. Does *intuition* provide an adequate philosophical practice?

For classical thought, forced to introduce the fictions of naive thought, all that is concrete is cast into doubt. In this way, the Cartesian direction (reflection) only ever asks the ***an sit*** question ("does it exist?"), never interrogating the natal bond between the knower and the known, perceiver and perceived. This more primordial relation reveals that the *quid sit* question ("what is it?") is in fact primary, hence dissolving the need for methodical doubt by renouncing "the affirmation of an absolute exterior" (107). The subject becomes an absolute nothingness or pure spectator of a meaningful system of everything. As such, the *quid sit* question detaches philosophy from any questions of existence and focuses solely upon *meaning*, upon *essences* (108). But when the philosophy of intuition penetrates beneath the surface of doubt to the horizon of lived experience, does it "define it well or sufficiently by saying that it is the *essence*?" (109). For Merleau-Ponty, primordial experience is beneath the level of a pure spectator knowing an essence, and before asking the question of the essence, we are first always already **being-in-the-world**. Essences are determinations of Being that come after Being is already established, they are "its style, they are the *Sosein* [essence] and not the *Sein* [existence]" (109). Thus, the philosophy of intuition fails to reach the genuine opening upon Being itself. As such, *experience*, and not "truth" or essences, must be where the "ultimate ontological power belongs," and philosophical interrogation must attempt to open up to this "fabric of one sole Being" (110). If the function of the pure spectator is to establish the meaning of beings through essential predication, there must first be a primordial opening to **wild Being** that offers the milieu of *facticity*.

Thus, we do not *begin* from the position of the pure spectator. At the outset, our questions emerge from "a field of experience" in which there are no explicit essences, but rather a rich intertwining of styles. In order to go from this ambiguously meaningful experience to the explicit world of significations or essences, the subject must "intervene" by performing an eidetic variation and thereby actively *creating* the essence. If there is no pure subject at the outset, then there are no pure essences either. **Interrogation** reveals the need to rework the classical distinction between fact and essence. This distinction is necessitated only if we remain within the illusion that I am essentially a *kosmostheoros*, a pure spectator, but "am I this ray of knowing that would have to arise from nowhere?" (113). Certainly not—I see the world from within the world, and I know the essence of the world only insofar as it is the invisible of the visible, the depth of the flat present. I am this paradoxical structure, sensing/sensible, **seeing/seen**, such that I experience things as an opening "from the midst of Being" (114). We discover this realm prior to fact and essence "in the very sphere of our life" (115).

If the distinction between fact and essence is called into question, what use is the phenomenological method of **Wesensschau** ("intuition of essences")? Merleau-Ponty reminds us that Husserl repeatedly returned to the essences he discovered, not to correct the essence, but to "make it say what at first it had not quite said" (116). The *Wesensschau*, then, must be considered *expression*, since it attempts to articulate what always escapes the attempt. Our lived experience is a certain "dimensionality" prior to fact and existence. In order to gain some access to it, we must simply resist the attempt to view Being from above, and attend to the dehiscence or the springing forth that opens us to the world of facts through perception and the world of essences through speech. Just as the world is present as the invisible of each visible, the sense of speech is present as the depth or latent content of every spoken word. Ideas are not things to be possessed; they are "the texture of our experience, its style, first mute, then uttered. Like every style, they are elaborated within the thickness of being" (119). The philosophy of intuition discovers that interrogation requires not a positive answer, but a commitment to forever return to the question. Philosophical answers must always be "higher than the 'facts,' lower than the 'essences,' in the **wild Being** where they were, and [...] continue to be undivided" (121).

Nor can one retreat from Husserl's essences toward **Bergson**'s search for the immediate coincidence between fact and essence. Coincidence would collapse the very spacing by which Being appears. Rather, "our flesh lines and even envelops all the visible"; I am not fused with the things I see, I am intertwined with them; "there is overlapping or **encroachment**, so that we must say that the things pass into us as well as we into the things" (123). We never have the past in immediacy as pure coincidence, but as a strange distance that is simultaneously a proximity, a coinciding from a distance. Thus, Bergsonian intuition as the return to the immediate and Husserlian *Wesensschau* as the search for essences both fail to reach the originary source of Being. It will be the chiasmatic relation between proximity and distance, and between self and self, that reveals the inadequacy of either essence or coincidence (128). Interrogation, then, must be structured as the living trajectory of a language: the philosopher speaks, but this necessary act is an "absurd effort" insofar as it attempts to lay claim to a truth that might be frozen once and for all. Interrogation that is authentic must remain *expression*.

Chapter Four: The Intertwining–The Chiasm

Although many of the themes are introduced in his final courses at the *Collège de France*, and certain concepts are developed in his final essay "Eye and Mind," this chapter represents the most explicit and sustained account of Merleau-Ponty's emerging phenomenologically inspired ontology. With his critique of philosophical methodology (reflection, dialectic, intuition) in hand, he sets out to put into practice his method of interrogation as a description of **wild Being**, our experience *prior to* the divisions imposed by classical philosophical thought. In order to proceed, he proposes returning to experiences themselves, prior to their having been frozen and "worked over," to that milieu in which existence and essence, subject and object, have not yet been separated. That is, an actual return to our lived experiences of "seeing, speaking, even thinking" (130). These are precisely the kinds of experience that overflow any attempt to define them once and for all.

When we open our eyes, the visible world seems to exist in itself, as if our vision of it were somehow formed out there among the things seen. There is an "intimacy" between the visible and vision, and yet this proximity is never collapsed to a coincidence. The things are not out there *in themselves*, nor is my seeing itself a pure nothingness, a pure *for itself*. My gaze "envelops" the things and "clothes them with its own flesh," and yet leaves them their transcendence and their place, veiling them in order to unveil them (131). But what is it to *see* a color, for instance? Carrying forward his adoption of **Gestalt psychology,** Merleau-Ponty suggests that the red I see cannot be a simple punctual jolt or quality, since seeing red "requires a focusing, however brief" (131). Moreover, its particularity is internally structured according to its texture or configuration, as a modality of "wooly," or of "hot." This red is also a "punctuation in the field of red things," which gives it a meaning through its structural difference from all other reds. The same wavelength or *quale* is simply not the *same* red when it participates in the flag of the Revolution or the robes of a public prosecutor. The *sense* of this visible red is structured according to an immense invisible layering of relations that silently weighs upon it through our invisible gaze.

On the side of the seeing, my gaze envelops and palpates the thing *as a thing,* such as this face. Just as a hand anticipates the shape of the object it is about to grasp, the gaze to has a "prepossession of the visible"—an "art of interrogation" or an "inspired exegesis" (133). The kinship that allows for this solicitation is forged through the body's essential status as both **touching/touched** or **seeing/seen.** As he stresses in this return to the Husserlian image, there is more at stake than a shift of attention. When a touching subject "descends into the rank of things," touching is revealed as an undeniably *worldly* activity accomplished by a bodily consciousness. The **reversibility** of touching and touched is the spacing or an **encroachment** [*empiétement*] through which experience is possible, a spacing prior to existence and essence. Another encroachment occurs between vision and touch, the visible and the tangible, and the body is the place of this fold, *écart,* or **chiasm.** This leads to the necessary conclusion that the seer "cannot possess the visible unless he is possessed by it, unless he *is of it*" (134–5). Indeed, the thing can only appear because the seer is *not* nothing, and only thanks to the "thickness of flesh between the seer and the thing." The body is not just a connection between the in itself and the for itself, but is a "*sensible for itself*" or an "*exemplar sensible*" (135). All bodily being involves depths and latencies, and the human body—as both sensible and sensing—is but a "remarkable variant." Thus, the reversibility of bodily being reveals "a paradox of Being, not a paradox of man" (136). Against the classical ontology of a pure in itself and a pure for itself, the body can be understood as a node in the fabric of the world that is simultaneously subject and object, as a structure of "**Visibility**"—between the world and my body there is a "reciprocal insertion and intertwining of one in the other" (138).

This interrogation of experience leads to a decisive ontology in the concept of the **flesh**. Through the strange event of tangible or visible reversibility, there is a dehiscence of Being, a "Visibility" or a "Tangibility" takes place that is not actively constituted, and yet not passively suffered. The Sensible is the flesh as the place of folding, a concept for which traditional philosophy has no name (139). The flesh is akin to an elemental principle. The flesh is not a primordial condition that is overcome through the institution of subjects and objects, but is the principle of every moment of visibility. And as a general thing, the flesh is reversible in other ways: insofar as other bodies are sites of coiling back upon the visible, insofar as they too are sensible/sensing, there is a reversibility between our experience which guarantees an "**intercorporeality**"—"[t]he handshake too is reversible" (142). There is no contradiction in saying that two bodies genuinely communicate. Since my seeing is not accomplished by an active constituting "I," the **anonymity** of visibility in fact inhabits both of us through the primordial structure of the flesh as reversibility, yet without negating our individual perspectives from within the flesh. Visibility and Tangibility reveal nothing less than an ontology of intertwining, and this bodily communication with the other begins the "paradox of expression" (144).

From this initial structure, the layers and folds thus proliferate into further reversibilities that "pass definitively beyond the circle of the visible" (144). Between my sonorous body and my hearing of my own voice there emerges a flesh as **expression** that is nothing less than "the point of insertion of speaking and thinking in the world of silence" (144–5). The elusive coincidence or incessant eclipsing that appears in *every* experience is what ensures the spacing or *écart*. And this reveals "the most difficult point, that is, the bond between the flesh and the idea, between the visible and the interior armature which it manifests and which it conceals" (149). An "idea" is not the opposite of the visible, it is the depth or lining of a visible surface that announces it and without which it would be nothing. This is an important continuation of Merleau-Ponty's notion of **expression**. Thought is not separate from expression; one does not need to translate from speech into the purity of thought, for the thought is already present as the invisible depth of the visible expression. To know a thought, one must speak or speak again; lending one's body to the voice of the other is to welcome the invisible of the sonorous phrase through a new fold in the flesh. What traditional philosophy has called ideality or essences are not "alien to the flesh," but precisely "its axes, its depths, its dimensions" (152). There are no "pure" idealities outside of all flesh and free of any horizons, since even the idealities of geometry are born in history. The reversible between speech and what it signifies is, just as with vision, a reversibility that never resolves into a coincidence. The invisible of every speech is the sensed richness of its sense, and the act of reversing it the act of defining or determining what the speech meant, exactly. This definition never exhausts the richness of the originary speaking, and always waits to be taken up again in a new reading or a new speaking. Promising to further elaborate this movement from the "mute world to the speaking world," Merleau-Ponty here is content to establish that silence is neither destroyed nor conserved, but rather enters into a new reversibility between perception and speech in the carnal presence of the invisible ideas. Although he never completed the ontological descriptions of this rich and enticing text, we catch sight in this final moment of a non-dialectical reversibility that is, for Merleau-Ponty, "the ultimate truth" (155).

Appendix of Working Notes

Merleau-Ponty would jot down brief notes or longer arguments to be incorporated in his writing, and many of these notes are titled and dated. **Lefort** set about the difficult task of identifying a set of these notes worth including in the volume, using the criteria of completeness and relevance to the matters at hand, and published a large set of these notes (*VI*, 165–275). Although they are elusive and difficult, close reading on particular topics can indeed be rewarding. For instance, Merleau-Ponty occasionally engages in self-critique, suggesting that the results of ***Phenomenology of Perception*** need to be brought to "ontological explicitation" and that his own earlier thought had perhaps remained mired in a **philosophy of consciousness** (183, 200).

Wahrnehmung

German word meaning "perception." In equating perceptual experience with a sort of primordial truth, Merleau-Ponty writes *Wahr-Nehmung*, emphasizing the components of the word, which might be translated literally as "truth-taking" (*PhP*, 311).

Wait-and-see-Marxism

Between 1945 and 1947 (particularly in *Humanism and Terror*) Merleau-Ponty optimistically believed that history may have been unfolding toward a genuine **Marxist humanism** through a progressive Soviet Union and an emerging American class-consciousness. This optimism was shaken with news of the Soviet Camps and of the anti-communist Red Scare in the USA. With the Korean War and the revelation of the Imperial aspirations of the USSR, Merleau-Ponty renounced this optimistic position, eventually leading him to promote a **new liberalism** as proposed in his final political text *The Adventures of the Dialectic*.

Wallon, Henri (1879–1962)

Philosopher, psychologist, and medical doctor famous for his work on the stages of childhood development (See, primarily, *CPP*).

"The War Has Taken Place" (1945) [*SNS*]

Merleau-Ponty's first political essay appeared in the inaugural issue of *Les Temps modernes*. Through a personal and phenomenological reflection on the experience of the Occupation, this article enacts an indictment of any *pensée de survol* that attempts to view **history** from outside of the concrete and lived reality of historical experience. As the title makes explicit, the war has happened, and one must struggle to come to terms with this concrete reality. Given the violence and complexity of historical reality, one must seek an account of **historical responsibility**, a non-pure morality capable of responding to the paradoxical structures of lived experience.

Prior to the war, France was blinded by an "optimistic philosophy" that was unable to understand concrete and lived experience. Taking society to be a "sum of consciousnesses always ready for peace and happiness" meant assuming that history unfolds in a universal milieu of reason according to Enlightenment ideals (*SNS*, 139). The signs of an emerging threat were present, even in the conduct of German students in Paris, yet they could not be recognized as announcing the emerging *Gestalt* of fascism. Given that each member (unconsciously) perpetuated this collective blindness, Merleau-Ponty concludes that "we find culprits nowhere but accomplices everywhere" (141). The actual movement of history demands that we recognize a complex historical responsibility, where neither guilt nor innocence are ever pure, since "we all played a part in the events of 1939" (141). Anti-Semitism, for example, emerges first as an historical possibility in the imaginary of a culture and a language, and this makes possible real actions against real bodies by mystified actors who believe they are striking "*the* Jew" and no real human being. The gesture intends to do violence to "dream figures" (143). This recognition is not to remove responsibility for the racist and violent action of the individual SS officer, for instance. Rather, it is to reveal how *potential* violence is cultivated and sustained in our language and culture, and that collectively we must share in the responsibility when it is actualized. Historical responsibility is the recognition that the categories of guilt and innocence are woefully simplistic in the face of historical reality. We are all responsible for the possibilities sustained in our culture and language, and we are each responsible for our intentions *and* the consequences of our actions. Until this is recognized, "the life of society will remain a dialogue and a battle between phantoms—in which real tears and real blood suddenly start to flow" (144).

Thus, politics leads to violence through its dogmatic belief in the pure and transparent subject as the bearer of a pure responsibility. This naively optimistic "Cartesian" politics fails to recognize the ambiguous reality of political action as the **intersubjective** taking up of the past in response to the present toward a future. Since every action is necessarily *public*, I must recognize that I bear a responsibility for my intentions and the consequences of my actions, even when these consequences seem beyond my control. A Cartesian may declare such a responsibility logically impossible, but Merleau-Ponty embraces this exigent position as the fundamental tenant of an existential politics (146). Every action (including inaction) unfolds within concrete historical reality, and thus each of us bears some responsibility for the course of empirical history.

Such a position does not lead to a simple rejection of Cartesian politics in favor of a Marxist historical materialism, since a Marxism too is threatened by the interpretation that **History** has a pre-determined direction and thus our individual role is not one for which we are, properly speaking, responsible. Marxism, too, must be "taken up anew, for it threatened to confirm our prewar prejudices" (148). Existential politics must become a **Marxist humanism** where economic forces are motivations for free action, and responsibility exists though it is never pure. In short, one must be Marxist without being doctrinaire.

Weber, Max (1864–1920)

German philosopher and social theorist. Merleau-Ponty offers a positive reading of Weber's liberalism that recognizes that it must be *accomplished* through historical struggle rather than established through ahistorical ideals (*AD*, Chapter One).

Wertheimer, Max (1880–1943)

Czech-born psychologist and co-founder of the school of **Gestalt psychology**. His work influenced Merleau-Ponty's early studies of perception and behavior.

Wesensschau

Often considered the primary "method" of **phenomenology**, this German word refers to the "intuition of **essences**" or of the essential structures of intentional objects as developed in Husserl's work. Merleau-Ponty is drawn to Husserl's formulations precisely because the *Wesensschau* does not mean gaining access to a mystical realm beyond empirical facts, but rather the concrete (though universal) essences of our experience (*PrP*, 53–4). Yet he calls Husserl's conception into question when Husserl applies the same method in domains (such as language) in which the concrete experience or perception might seem to be wholly transcended by the *Wesensschau*. For Merleau-Ponty, we cannot transcend all empirical language to consider the pure essence of language in general (79). In *The Visible and the Invisible*, Merleau-Ponty attempts to offer a form of philosophical "**interrogation**" that would avoid the method of "intuition" (see, in particular, VI, 116–17).

Wild Being/brute Being

In developing his final ontology and his method of philosophical **interrogation**, Merleau-Ponty begins to call the unreflected world of experience brute Being or wild Being, as that which can never fully be articulated (*VI*, 102). The answers that a properly formulated philosophical questioning will seek are neither in the "facts" nor in "**essences**," but in the region between these two, "in the wild Being where they were, and—behind or beneath the cleavages of our acquired culture—continue to be, undivided" (121). In order to gain some access to brute Being, philosophy must remain an open trajectory of expression in the manner of **painting** ("**Eye and Mind**") or literature ("Preface" to *Signs*). For Merleau-Ponty, the "wild being" of lived experience is what the philosopher aims at and yet never expresses, it is the philosopher's shadow that haunts his or her every philosophical move with the threat of non-philosophy, and the "philosopher must bear his [or her] shadow" (*S*, 178).

The World of Perception (1948) [WP]

This book is a transcript of seven lectures delivered on a French national radio program ("The French Culture Hour") in Autumn 1948. In these lectures, Merleau-Ponty is a young and energetic thinker, exploring the insights and consequences of his philosophy in areas as diverse as perception, **painting**, and politics. He takes the opportunity as one of offering the non-academic public a guide to reaching phenomenological reflection, and the text remains an excellent introduction to his thought.

I. The first lecture begins with a return to our lived experience: the world of perception "seems at first sight to be the one we know best of all" (*WP*, 31). Yet, so long as we remain within the practical or **natural attitude**, we fail to fully grasp this experience due to our fascination with the objects or our current projects. The great achievement of modern art and thought is to have revealed, once again, our forgotten lived experience (31–2). This requires resisting the Cartesian temptation to reject experience *of* the world in favor of a science *about* the world. Art, philosophy, and **science** reveal the limitations of reductive approaches to knowledge, and even physics recognizes the importance of perspective. All three of these modern endeavors, thus, have been preparing for a return to the world of perception.

II. Leaving science aside, lecture two focuses on common sense. Art and philosophy are sometimes dismissed for running counter to "the clear and straightforward notions which common sense cherishes because they bring peace of mind" (37). Consider the concept of "**space**," which both common sense and classical science understand to be a homogeneous medium indifferent to its content. Modern science and lived experience, however, blur the boundaries between form and content, suggesting a certain priority for the perceptual over the epistemic. The example is Cézanne's painting: his attempt to capture lived perception is a rejection of the calculations and apparatuses of classical painting. His distortions of perspective are not errors; they are the attempt to capture a temporally thick experience. The painter is not a pure mind, but an embodied subject with a past and a perspective upon the world. Phenomenology reveals that any attempt to separate the intellect from the body in understanding painting or expression necessarily falsifies our experience, and this holds true in psychology and philosophy as well.

III. The third lecture offers a study of the unity we experience in perceived objects, which is richer than a mere juxtaposition of qualities. Each quality of this lemon announces others, and already solicits the other sensory pathways of my body. Things are not neutral objects; they speak to our body and appear always already "clothed in human characteristics" (49). Writers such as **Sartre** and Bachelard have begun to rethink the Cartesian notions of "distance and mastery" through the description of our lived proximity to and even intertwining with objects (51).

IV. The modern worldview, then, is distinguished from the classical one through its orientation toward our embodied and lived experience. As a result, the relationship between humans and things is, for modern thought, an **ambiguous** one. We perceive the things of the world as independent of us, and yet we only know them through the human face they receive according to our embodied intentionality. But our world is also shared with animals (and children, primitive peoples, and madmen) (55). Modern philosophy and psychology must recognize that even "normal" adult consciousness does not reach the ideal of classical intellectualism. Rather, all life unfolds as a giving of "shape" to an indifferent world.

V. This is even more obvious in our perception of **others**. Since others *appear* in the world of perception, "this other is a body animated by all manner of intentions" and the presence of a whole host of "possibilities" according to the style that is grasped "from the outside" without the aid of reflection (62). The anger, for instance, discussed between me and an interlocutor, haunts all of the aspects of our interaction and is not reducible to any one of them. There is no distinction to be repaired between the mind and the body, and even **Descartes** recognized that we *live* the union of the soul and the body. Thus, humanity in each person and as a group is *ambiguous* and relational, and the tasks of establishing an ethics and a politics, then, are endless and open. Such a theory calls for a **Marxist humanism** that focuses not on the purity of individual minds, but on the "real relationships between people" (67).

VI. The sixth lecture discusses **painting**. Rather than presenting objects according to our familiar beliefs *about* objects, painters such as Cézanne and Picasso offer an interrogation of the secret style and rich presence of objects in our lived experience. The modern painter's goal is not a perfect representation, but rather a genuine *expression*. The same could be true in film, although Merleau-Ponty believes that the art has not yet been realized. Nevertheless, in both painting and film one discovers that art is essentially *to be perceived*. Music and literature are also discussed, and since in both cases content and form cannot be separated, perception again becomes the key to understanding any work of art. Even a novel "must be perceived in its temporal progression by embracing its particular rhythm" (76). The paradoxes of the world of perception extend to all experience.

VII. The final lecture offers a broad set of conclusions through some (admittedly vague) categories. The "classical worldview" is committed to knowing nature "objectively" and purging itself of all mystery; the "modern worldview" embraces the lacunae and fissures of experience and rejects any assumption that it will reach a universal Truth. Considering the work of **Proust**, Merleau-Ponty concludes that modern art reflects a world that is never finished and a commitment in the face of an impossible task to nevertheless bring this incomplete and evolving world to expression. Human knowledge is forever embodied and situated, and can never embark upon a *pensée de survol* that could gain access to the "naked truth" (80). This also holds in politics where "we find modern man coming to grips with ambiguities which are perhaps more striking still" (80). In short, the modern worldview is a commitment to thinking through **ambiguity** and finding a path to be followed "truthfully and in all conscience" (81).

Zeigen und Greifen

German terms for "pointing and grasping." The distinction is important in **Gelb** and **Goldstein**'s study of **abstract movement versus concrete movement**. Certain patients are capable of grasping an object in a concrete movement, yet incapable of indicating or pointing to an object in an abstract movement. The impossibility of reducing these distinctions to the distinction between the body and consciousness reveals the need for an **existential** theory of the body.

SUGGESTED BOOKS AND EDITED VOLUMES IN ENGLISH

Baldwin, Thomas, ed. *Reading Merleau-Ponty: On Phenomenology of Perception*. London: Routledge, 2007.
Barbaras, Renaud. *The Being of the Phenomenon: Merleau-Ponty's Ontology*. Translated by Ted Toadvine and Leonard Lawlor. Bloomington: Indiana University Press, 2004.
Busch, Thomas W. and Shaun Gallagher, (eds) *Merleau-Ponty, Hermeneutics and Postmodernism*. Albany: SUNY Press, 1992.
Carmen, Taylor. *Merleau-Ponty*. London and New York: Routledge, 2008.
Carmen, Taylor, and Mark B. N. Hansen, (eds) *The Cambridge Companion to Merleau-Ponty*. Cambridge: Cambridge University Press, 2005.
Chiasmi International: Trilingual Studies Concerning the Thought of Merleau-Ponty. [Journal devoted to Merleau-Ponty Studies.]
Coole, Diana. *Merleau-Ponty and Modern Politics after Anti-Humanism*. Lanham, MD: Rowman & Littlefield Publishers, 2007.
Cooper, Barry. *Merleau-Ponty and Marxism: From Terror to Reform*. Toronto: University of Toronto Press, 1979.
Dillon, M. C. *Merleau-Ponty's Ontology*. 2nd edn. Evanston, IL: Northwestern University Press, 1997.
—, ed. *Merleau-Ponty Vivant*. Albany: SUNY Press, 1991.
Diprose, Rosalyn and Jack Reynolds, (eds) *Merleau-Ponty: Key Concepts*. Stocksfield, UK: Acumen, 2008.
Edie, James M. *Merleau-Ponty's Philosophy of Language: Structuralism and Dialectics*. Washington, DC: University Press of America, 1987.
Evans, Fred and Leonard Lawlor, (eds) *Chiasms: Merleau-Ponty's Notion of Flesh*. Albany: SUNY Press, 2000.

Flynn, Bernard, Wayne J. Froman, and Robert Vallier, (eds) *Merleau-Ponty and the Possibilities of Philosophy: Transforming the Tradition*. Albany: SUNY Press, 2009.
Froman, Wayne J. *Merleau-Ponty: Language and the Act of Speech*. London: Associated University Presses, 1982.
Hass, Lawrence. *Merleau-Ponty's Philosophy*. Bloomington: Indiana University Press, 2008.
Hass, Lawrence and Dorothea Olkowski, (eds) *Rereading Merleau-Ponty: Essays beyond the Continental–Analytic Divide*. Amherst, NY: Humanity Books, 2000.
Hatley, James, Janice McLane, and Christian Diehm, (eds) *Interrogating Ethics: Embodying the Good in Merleau-Ponty*. Pittsburgh: Duquesne University Press, 2006.
Johnson, Galen A. *The Retrieval of the Beautiful: Thinking Through Merleau-Ponty's Aesthetics*. Evanston, IL: Northwestern University Press, 2010.
—, ed. *The Merleau-Ponty Aesthetics Reader: Philosophy and Painting*. Translations edited by Michael B. Smith. Evanston, IL: Northwestern University Press, 1993.
Johnson, Galen A., and Michael B. Smith, (eds) *Ontology and Alterity in Merleau-Ponty*. Evanston, IL: Northwestern University Press, 1990.
Kruks, Sonia. *The Political Philosophy of Merleau-Ponty*. Atlantic Highlands, NJ: Humanities Press, 1981.
Landes, Donald A. *Merleau-Ponty and the Paradoxes of Expression*. New York: Bloomsbury, 2013.
Low, Douglas. *Merleau-Ponty's Last Vision: A Proposal for the Completion of the* Visible and the Invisible. Evanston, IL: Northwestern University Press, 2000.
—*Merleau-Ponty in Contemporary Context: Philosophy and Politics in the 21st Century*. New Brunswick, NJ: Transaction Publishers, 2012.
Mallin, Samuel B. *Merleau-Ponty's Philosophy*. New Haven: Yale University Press, 1979.
Madison, Gary Brent. *The Phenomenology of Merleau-Ponty: A Search for the Limits of Consciousness*. Athens, OH: Ohio University Press, 1989.
Marratto, Scott L. *The Intercorporeal Self: Merleau-Ponty on Subjectivity*. Albany: SUNY Press, 2012.
Matthews, Eric. *The Philosophy of Merleau-Ponty*. Montreal and Kingston: McGill-Queens University Press, 2002.
Olkowski, Dorothea and Gail Weiss, (eds) *Feminist Interpretations of Maurice Merleau-Ponty*. University Park, PA: Pennsylvania State University Press, 2006.

Romdenh-Romluc, Komarine. *Routledge Philosophy Guidebook to Merleau-Ponty and* Phenomenology of Perception. London: Routledge, 2011.
Stewart, Jon, ed. *The Debate between Sartre and Merleau-Ponty.* Evanston, IL: Northwestern University Press, 1998.
Toadvine, Ted. *Merleau-Ponty's Philosophy of Nature.* Evanston, IL: Northwestern University Press, 2009.
—, ed. *Merleau-Ponty: Critical Assessments of Leading Philosophers.* 4 vols. London: Routledge, 2006.
Toadvine, Ted, and Lester Embree, (eds) *Merleau-Ponty's Reading of Husserl.* Dordrecht and Boston: Kluwer, 2002.
Toadvine, Ted, and Leonard Lawlor, (eds) *The Merleau-Ponty Reader.* Evanston, IL: Northwestern University Press, 2007.
Weiss, Gail, ed. *Intertwinings: Interdisciplinary Encounters with Merleau-Ponty.* Albany: SUNY Press, 2008.
Whiteside, Kerry H. *Merleau-Ponty and the Foundation of an Existential Politics.* Princeton: Princeton University Press, 1998.

NOTES

1. In addition to common knowledge and the invaluable and well-known insights by Claude Lefort, this "Life and Works" section has drawn from two primary reference sources: Emmanuelle Garcia, "Vie et Œuvre: 1908–1961," in *Œuvres*, by Maurice Merleau-Ponty, ed. Claude Lefort (Paris: Gallimard, 2010), 29–99; Stephen A. Noble, "Maurice Merleau-Ponty, or the Pathway of Philosophy: Desiderata for an Intellectual Biography," *Chiasmi* XIII (2011): 63–112. In addition, I have also consulted: Théodore F. Geraets, *Vers une nouvelle philosophie transcendantale: La genèse de la philosophie de Maurice Merleau-Ponty jusqu'à la* Phénoménologie de la perception (The Hague: Martinus Nijhoff, 1971); Emmanuel de Saint Aubert, *Du lien des êtres aux éléments de l'être: Merleau-Ponty au tournant des années 1945–1951* (Paris: J. Vrin, 2004); Jon Stewart, "Introduction," in *The Debate between Sartre and Merleau-Ponty*, ed. Jon Stewart (Evanston: Northwestern University Press, 1998), xiii–xl.
2. Simone de Beauvoir, *Cahiers de jeunesse (1926–1930)*, ed. Sylvie Le Bon de Beauvoir (Paris: Gallimard, 2008), 370.
3. Merleau-Ponty is presented through the character of "Jean Pradelle" in Simone de Beauvoir, *Memoirs of a Dutiful Daughter*, trans. J. Kirkup (Harmondsworth: Penguin, 1987). See also Jon Stewart, "Introduction," xv.
4. Simone de Beauvoir, "A review of *The Phenomenology of Perception* by Maurice Merleau-Ponty," in *Merleau-Ponty: Critical Assessments of Leading Philosophers*, vol. 1, ed. Ted Toadvine (Routledge: London, 2006), 15–20.
5. Jean-Paul Sartre, *Being and Nothingness: An Essay in Phenomenological Ontology*, trans. Hazel E. Barnes, rev. Arlette Elkaïm-Sartre (New York: Routledge, 2003).
6. There are some differences between the two English versions of this course. In this discussion, I draw upon both versions. See *PrP* and *CPP*.

7   This is the only course to span two academic years. As with the previous course, differences exist between the two versions. See *PrP* and *CPP*.
8   His election was not without controversy. The *Collège* traditionally submits its top candidate for ceremonial approval by the *Académie des sciences morales et politiques*, prior to final approval by the Minister of Education. But despite his having been nominated by the assembly of professors at the *Collège*, Merleau-Ponty's name was struck from the list by the *Académie* in a shocking and unexplained move. After some vehement protests, and a reasoned critique of the process by Merleau-Ponty himself, the Minister of Education reinstated Merleau-Ponty's name and approved him as the Chair in Philosophy. This very public scandal sheds light on the context of Merleau-Ponty's Inaugural Address (see *IPP*).
9   Merleau-Ponty's lecture notes and working notes for this course are only available in French: *Le Monde sensible et le monde de l'expression: Cours au Collège de France, Notes, 1953*, (eds) Emmanuel de Saint Aubert and Stefan Kristensen (Geneva: MētisPresses, 2011).
10 Geraets, *Vers une nouvelle philosophie*, 24–6.
11 Aron Gurwitsch, "Some Aspects and Developments in Gestalt Psychology," trans. Richard M. Zaner, in *Studies in Phenomenology and Psychology* (Evanston: Northwestern University Press, 1966), 3–55.
12 Alexandre Kojève, *Introduction to the Reading of Hegel: Lectures on the* Phenomenology of Spirit, trans. James H. Nichols, Jr. (Ithaca, NY: Cornell University Press, 1980).
13 Noble, "Maurice Merleau-Ponty, or The Pathway of Philosophy," 79.
14 Simone de Beauvoir, "Merleau-Ponty and Pseudo-Sartreanism," in *The Debate between Sartre and Merleau-Ponty*, ed. Jon Stewart, 448–91 (Evanston: Northwestern University Press, 1998), 448.
15 Noble, "Maurice Merleau-Ponty, Or the Pathway of Philosophy," 75–7.
16 Jean-Paul Sartre, "Merleau-Ponty Vivant," in *The Debate between Sartre and Merleau-Ponty*, ed. Jon Stewart, 565–625 (Evanston: Northwestern University Press, 1998), 565.
17 See de Beauvoir's *Memoirs of a Dutiful Daughter* (1958). Also, Stewart, "Introduction," xv.
18 Sartre, "Merleau-Ponty Vivant," 565–625.

INDEX

In this thematic and nominal index, the numbers that appear in **bold** refer to specific entries for the term or person in question, even if the term or person does not appear on each page of the range indicated. A non-bold range of pages indicates a discussion of a term or person that spans more than one page, but within a single entry. Sequential pages indicate that the term is discussed in separate entries on adjacent pages.

a priori (versus *a posteriori*) **9–10**, 101, 138, 147, 160, 220, 229
abstract movements versus concrete movements **10**, 134, 250
action **10–11**, 12–17, 25, 54, 73–4, 91, 94, 97–9, 103–4, 110–11, 124, 127, 131, 132, 147, 155, 157, 161, 165, 167, 172, 173, 184, 193, 207, 210, 212, 214, 220–3, 245–6
activity versus passivity **11**, 39, 53–4, 63, 71, 113, 147, 159, 204
advent **11–12**, 110–11
Adventures of the Dialectic (1956) **12–17**, 19, 25, 27, 49, 52, 84, 122, 124, 128, 135, 200, 244
adversity **18**, 78, 123–5, 203
affectivity **18**, 42, 53, 154, 156, 194, 201
agrégation **18–19**, 67, 102
Alain (Émile-Auguste Chartier) 12, **19**, 119, 197
alexia **19**, 202
allochiria **20**
Alter Ego **20**, 91, 142
Althusser, Louis 118
ambiguity 16, **20–1**, 22, 25–30, 35, 42, 66, 67, 69, 73, 81, 83, 84, 96–8, 100, 111, 124, 138, 145, 146, 154, 160, 164, 166, 179, 182, 183, 188, 196, 198, 204, 207, 213, 220, 222–3, 226, 228, 229, 230, 234, 236–8, 245, 249–50
ambivalence **21**, 40, 42, 236–7
amovable forms of behavior **21**, 219, 224
an sit versus *quid sit* **21–2**, 238
anarthria **22**, 157
animality/animal behavior 9–10, 21, 28, 53, 57–8, 221, 249
anonymity/anonymous 13, 18, **22**, 60, 86–7, 115, 125, 159, 165, 174, 192, 234, 242
anosognosia **22**, 146
anti-Semitism 245
aphasia 19, **22–3**, 39, 157
aphonia **23**

apraxia **23**
Aristotle 23–4, 158, 181
Aristotle's illusion **23–4**, 158
art 12, 32, 35–6, 45, 51, 62, 75, 82, 108, 110, 156, 193, 207, 248–50
association **24**
attention **24–5**, 51, 153
  to life 25, 29, 116, 196

Bachelard, Gaston 120, 249
bad ambiguity versus good ambiguity **25**, 230
bad dialectic versus good dialectic (or hyper-dialectic) 17, **25–6**, 28, 55, 67, 135, 237
Balzac, Honoré de 35, 131, 215
"The Battle over Existentialism" (1945) **25**
Beaufret, Jean 120, 186
Beauvoir, Simone de 12, **26–7**, 73, 121, 128, 130–1, 199–200
behavior 9, 10, 11, 21, 27, 28, 34, 40, 46, 57–8, 64, 69, 88, 90, 118, 129, 133, 143, 159, 176, 194, 197, 205, 217–25, 228–9, 246
behaviorism **27–8**, 118
Being 22, 28, 29, 30, 47, 52, 54, 56–7, 59, 61–2, 72, 74, 77–80, 83, 87, 115–16, 130–1, 142, 159, 170–2, 176–7, 179, 180, 192, 198, 203, 204, 212, 226, 233–42, 247 *see also* being-in-the-world, wild Being
"Being and Having" (1936) **28**, 126
Being and Nothingness (1943) 26, **28**, 73, 77, 131, 200–1, 204, 235–6
Being and Sense 232

being-in-itself/being-for-itself **28–9**, 166
being-in-the-world (*être au monde*) 20, 22, **29**, 32, 45, 47, 64, 66, 69, 80, 81–2, 91, 93, 133, 134, 146, 147, 150, 152, 154, 165–7, 172, 196, 198, 202, 231, 238
Bergson, Henri 25, **29–31**, 50, 56, 68, 102–4, 116, 120, 138, 145, 170, 179–81, 196, 237, 239, 240
"Bergson in the Making" (1959) **30–1**, 145
Binswanger, Ludwig **31**, 43
Biran, Maine de 103
body 31, **32**, 54, 60, 67, 74–6, 153–61, 192, 204, 226, 234
  embodiment/embodied experience 20, 28, 32, 42, 45, 50, 73, 74, 86, 83, 89, 91, 93, 103, 111, 114, 124, 139–41, 147, 155–6, 165, 168, 172–3, 184, 186, 189–92, 204, 211–13, 221–2, 229, 236, 248–50
  and expression 74, 79, 90, 93, 108, 110, 125, 232, 243, 248–9
  and flesh/reversibility 70, 75–6, 83, 115, 175–6, 192, 198, 204, 226, 241–2
  habitual *see* habit
  human 61–2, 76, 222, 226, 241–2
  lived 66, 70, 90–1, 93, 126, 133–4, 141, 155, 157, 159, 193, 211, 229
  objective 25, 29, 75, 91, 124, **137**, 146, 147, 163, 218
  one's own 24, 29, 32, 65, 68, 75–6, 90, 117, 134, 135,

141, 149, 154–61, 171, 208, 225
phenomenal 137, **147**, 161, 163, 221
schema (image) **32–3**, 50, 61, 90, 92, 121, 155, 202
soul and 30, 56, 58, 66, 74, 102–4, 124, 165, 185, 195, 196, 211, 222–4, 249
Bréhier, Émile **33**, 186
Brunschvicg, Léon 19, **33**, 103, 119
Bukharin, Nicolai 96–9, 118, 132

Camus, Albert 62
Cassirer, Ernst **33–4**
categorial attitude **34**, 39, 157, 222
Cézanne, Paul **34–5**, 36, 78, 82, 107, 109, 143–4, 163, 207–8, 248–9
"Cézanne's Doubt" (1945) **35–7**, 143, 232
chiasm 21, **37–8**, 70, 74, 86, 198, 205, 212, 226, 233, 23, 240–1
child drawing 40–1, 193
Child Psychology and Pedagogy: The Sorbonne Lectures (1949–52) 21, **38–46**, 64, 119, 142, 151
"Christianity and Ressentiment" (1935) **46**, 201
classic 151, 210
classical philosophy/objective thought 19, 24, 28, 35–6, 47, 54–5, 58–9, 61, 64, 73, 86, 88, 107, 113, 134, 141, 143, 152–7, 158–61, 167, 172, 197, 202, 205–6, 212, 218, 223, 225, 229, 234, 238, 240–1, 248–9
Claudel, Paul **47**, 62, 169

cogito 16, **47**, 65, 103–4, 141, 158, 162, 166–9, 178, 186
spoken vs. tacit 47, 168–9
coherent deformation 12, 18, **47–8**, 53, 60, 65, 106, 110–11, 113, 116, 123–4, 140, 175, 190, 203, 212, 215
coincidence 30, 55, 60, 83, 179–80, 198, 233, 239–40, 242–3
Collège de France **48**, 120, 129, 142, 178, 187, 214, 228, 233, 240
The Collège de France Lectures (1952–61) 25, **48–63**, 93, 102, 113, 120, 194, 232, 233
color 9, 34, 36, 65, 76–8, 86, 106, 156, 159, 163, 168, 211, 225, 240
communication 36, 40–1, 48, 60, 63, 74, 76, 89, 105, 140, 147, 153–4, 157, 160, 165–6, 188–93, 195, 211–12, 229–30, 242
communion 41, **63**
Communism/Communist Party 12–17, 81, 96–9, 118, 128–9, 135, 137, 199–200, 207, 210, 213, 215, 231–2, 244
"Concerning Marxism" (1946) **63**
consciousness 9, 16–17, 18, 24, 25, 29, 39, 40–4, 51, 54, **64**, 68, 70, 114, 129, 136, 150, 167, 171, 174, 184, 193, 203, 222
and behavior 69, 217
and body 23, 165, 218, 241, 250
constituting 18, 65, 69, 87, 99, 104, 113, 132, 163, 171,

173, 175–7, 197, 211, 223, 227, 229, 233, 237
non-thetic/thetic 23, 27, 73, 87, 136, 141, 152, 162, 169, 234
perceptual 49, 64, 93, 143, 145, **146**, 153, 167–8, 222–4
philosophy of 47, 52, 64, 65, 113, 226, 243
Consciousness and the Acquisition of Language **64**
constancy hypothesis 24, **64–5**, 82, 88, 90, 117, 118, 152–3, 187, 205, 231
constituted language/constituting language 48, 50, **65**, 168, 215
constituting consciousness *see* consciousness
contingency **9–10**, 24, 101, 137, 139, 141, 177, 183, 191, 193, 230
of history 13–15, 18, 98, 125–6, 190
crisis 13, 43, 58–9, 68, 101

Darwinism 48, 62
Dasein 59, 93, 150, 169
Deleuze, Gilles 120
depth 77–8, 132, 145, 161, 211–12, 241–3
Descartes, René 33, 47, 55, 56, 63, **65–6**, 71, 77, 103, 117, 144, 166–8, 249
Deutsch, Hélène 44
diachronic 139
dialectic/dialectical reasoning 12–17, 21, 25–6, 28, 54–5, 63, **66–7**, 72, 92, 104, 111, 116, 135, 146, 160, 188, 209–10, 219–24, 235–7, 243

hyper- 25–6, 74, 237
Diderot 46
dimension 9, 17, 18, 20, 32, 64, 66, **67**, 72–4, 78–80, 85, 100, 103, 114, 115, 127, 130, 134, 156, 160, 166, 170, 194, 198, 208, 228, 239, 243
double sensations 23, **67**, 154
duration (*durée*) 30–1, 79, 179–80, 234

earth 56, 60, 101, 196
écart (gap, divergence, spacing) 54, 83, 198, 204, 226, 241–2
École normale supérieure (ENS) 19, 27, 33, **67**, 102, 122, 199
eidetic reduction 43, **68**, 70, 127, 227, 238
"Einstein and the Crisis of Reason" (1955) **68**
ek-stase/ecstasy **68**, 93, 170–1, 235
embodiment *see* body
empiricism (or mechanism) 34, 45, **68–9** 124, 126, 187, 223
versus intellectualism 12, 24, 28, 39, 47, 57, 66, **69**, 75, 88, 113, 117, 123–4, 143, 144, 147, 149–50, 152–3, 167, 171, 195 218–22, 229, 231
encroachment (*empiétement*) 59, **69–70**, 80, 115, 176, 192, 198, 204, 211, 226, 239, 241
ENS *see* École normale supérieure
enveloping/enveloped 31, 39, **70**, 78, 83, 112, 142, 162, 198, 239–41

epochē see phenomenological reduction
essences 21, 30, 34, **70**, 71, 73, 127, 135, 150, 152, 237–43, 247
ethics 25, 26–7, 94, 96, 97, 98, 100, 206, 210, 230, 249
"Everywhere and Nowhere" (1956) **71–2**, 121
evidentness 72, 162, 168, 233
existential analysis 10, 18, 23, 66, 67, **72–3**, 84, 94, 114, 127, 146, 156, 158, 161, 194, 208
existentialism 16, 26, 28, 72, 73, 92–3, 101, 116, 126–7, 177–8, 207
expression 11–13, 16–17, 18, 25, 30, 35–7, 39, 46, 47–8, 49–54, 65, 67, 71–2, 73–4, 75–80, 86, 89–90, 104, 105–12, 113, 115–16, 123–6, 130–1, 138–41, 142, 156–8, 161, 168, 175–6, 180, 181, 187–93, 203, 205–8, 210, 212–13, 215, 220–4, 229–30, 232, 235, 239–40, 242–3, 247–8, 250
"Eye and Mind" (1960) 49, **74–80**, 115, 143, 198, 204, 209, 226, 232–3, 240, 247

facticity 68, 70, **80**, 150, 238
faith 80–1, 175, 177, 181, 183, 188
"Faith and Good Faith" (1946) **80–1**
field 9, 18, 20, 22, 24, **81–2**, 88, 109–13, 158–61, 169, 170, 172, 187, 192, 195, 220
  existential 17, 54

perceptual/visual 30–1, 57, 75, 82, 153, 164
phenomenal 20, 66, 81, 88, 115, 132–3, 143, **147–8**, 153, 155, 161, 192, 195, 222, 226, 231, 238, 241
  of presence 170, 177
figure/ground structure **82**, 88, 153, 217, 219
"The Film and the New Psychology" (1945) **82–3**
Fink, Eugen **83**, 101, 149
flesh 21, 38, 61, 70, 74, 76–8, **83**, 112, 115, 124, 176, 187, 194, 198, 204–5, 211, 226, 236, 239–43
"For the Sake of Truth" (1946) **84**
form **84**, 87–1, 160–1, 183, 217–22
freedom 11, 13, 17, 26, 32, 35, 37, 46, 69, 70, 93, 94, 96, 108, 137, 146, 158, 172–4, 182, 200
  situated 11, 35, 94, 108, 173, **214**
Freud, Anna 42
Freud, Sigmund 35, 40, 42, 44, **84–5**, 93, 194
"From Mauss to Claude Lévi-Strauss" (1959) **85–6**, 128
Fundierung **86**, 168, 176

Gaulle, Charles de 210
gaze 70, 76–7, 153, 159, 204, 233, 240–1
Gelb, Adhemar 10, 23, 34, **86**, 90, 155, 202, 219, 250
generality 22, **86–7**, 115, 159, 173–4, 192
genetic phenomenology *see* phenomenology

Gestalt psychology/Gestalt theory 36, 38–9, 41–4, 50–1, 65, 81, 82, 84, 86, **87–8**, 90, 95, 103, 118, 129, 132, 135, 146, 148, 153, 154, 163, 183–4, 186, 197, 202, 205, 207, 216–18, 220, 222–3, 231, 234, 241, 245, 246
gestural theory of meaning **89–90**, 157, 206
gesture 9, 10, 12, 24, 31, 32, 89, 90, 108–12, 133, 139–40, 156–7, 168, 189
God's eye view 12, 130, 145, 186 see *pensée de survol*
Goldstein, Kurt 10, 23, 34, 51, 86, 88, **90**, 118, 155, 202, 219, 250
Greco, El 144
Gurwitsch, Aron 88, **90**

habit 9, 32, 46, **90–1**, 133–4, 140, 161, 168
habitual body versus actual body **91**, 146
haecceity **91–2**
hallucination 39, 164
Head, Henry 32, **92**
Hegel, G. W. F. 55, 58, 63, 66, 71, **92**, 102, 111, 125, 237
"Hegel's Existentialism" (1946) **92–3**
Heidegger, Martin 29, 31, 43, 59, 60–1, 68, 72, 73, **93**, 141, 150, 169, 199, 211
Herder, Johann Gottfried **93**, 160, 208
Hesnard, Angelo 85, **93**, 194
historical responsibility 11, 13, 15, 17, 70, **94**, 97–100, 111, 128, 131, 132, 137, 181, 183, 209, 213, 245

historicism 43, **94**, 173, 210
history 11, 12–17, 18, 45, 52–3, 57, 71, 80, 84, **94–5**, 98–100, 103–4, 108–12, 124–5, 126–7, 130, 137, 141, 173–4, 182–3, 189–90, 206, 209–13, 243, 244–6
history of philosophy 33, 60, 62, 69, 71, **95**, 103–4, 116, 120, 123, 151, 174, 237
horizon/horizonal structure 15, 25, 36, 39, 41, 44–6, 53–4, 60–1, 81, **95–6**, 110, 131, 154, 159–64, 166–7, 170–1, 176, 178, 184–5, 191, 204, 223, 228, 234, 243
humanism *see* Marxist humanism
Humanism and Terror (1947) 15, **96–101**, 118, 131, 132, 137, 200, 244
Husserl, Edmund 19, 39, 43, 45, 56, 59–61, 70, 72, 86, 87, 95, **101**, 102, 109, 112, 113, 114, 115, 133, 134–5, 136, 138, 140, 141, 142, 144, 148–50, 152, 169–71, 174–7, 193, 196, 225–6, 227, 231, 237–41, 247
Husserl Archives at Louvain 83, **101–2**, 150
Hyppolite, Jean 92, **102**, 186

the "I can" 56, 75, **102**, 133–4, 140, 155, 175, 202
in-itself/for-itself 28, 32, 52, 56, 59, 79, 111, 159, 223, 235–7, 241
The Incarnate Subject: Malebranche, Biran, and Bergson on the Union of Body and Soul **102–4**
"Indirect Language and the Voices

of Silence" (1952) 11, 48, 95, **104–12**, 121, 123, 143, 187, 190, 201, 215
Ineinander (intertwining) 59, 61, 70, **112**, 198
institution (*Stiftung*) 17, 52–4, 56, 58, 60, 109–11, **112–13**, 140, 191
intellectualism (or idealism) **113–14**
versus empiricism *see* empiricism
intentional arc 76, 102, **114**, 155, 157
intentionality 46, 49, 68, **114**, 134, 148, 150–1, 154, 172, 176, 185, 230
lived/operative 114, 139, **141**, 145, 151–2, 155–6, 164–5, 249
motor 11, 23, 91, 102, **133**, 154–5, 197, 202
non-thetic/thetic 114, 136–7, 151, 226
intercorporeality/intersubjectivity 17, 20, 52, 59, 70, 75, 87, 89, 92, **115**, 124, 126, 130, 131, 136, 138, 140, 142, 176, 177, 178, 198, 204, 213, 230, 242, 245
interrogation 26, 28, 52, 53, 58–9, 67, 69, 74, 80, 113, **115–16**, 145, 175, 203, 209, 212–13, 232–5, 237–42, 247
intersubjectivity *see* intercorporeality
intertwining *see* chiasm, *Ineinander*
introspection 134, 152 *see also* reflective analysis
intuition 29–31, 70, 135, 149, 180, 235, 237–40, 247

Jakobson, Roman 39, 51
Janet, Pierre **116**, 196
Jaspers, Karl 43, 73, **116**, 118, 178
judgment 24, 36, 51, **117**, 138, 153, 161–4, 184, 221, 223

Kant, Immanuel 9, 33, 55, 56, 92 113, 114, 119, 144, 151, 185, 196, 223, 227
kinesthetic sensations **117**, 154
Klee, Paul 107, 144
Klein, Melanie 21, 42
Koestler, Arthur 96–101, **117–18**, 132
Koffka, Kurt 87, 88, **118**, 220
Köhler, Wolfgang 87, **118**, 129
Kojève, Alexandre **118–19**
kosmotheoros 234–5, 239

Lacan, Jacques 40, 42, 118, **119**, 216
Lachelier, Jules **119**
Lachièze-Rey, Pierre **119**
Lagneau, Jules 19, **119**, 197
language 38–9, 48, 49–51, 53–4, 57, 61, 65, 73–4, 89, 104–7, 111–12, 113, 124–5, 129–30, 138–40, 142, 143, 157, 165, 167–8, 170, 174, 187–92, 203, 205–6, 207, 212, 215, 216–17, 221, 230, 240, 245, 247
Lavelle, Louis **120**, 179
Le Roy, Edouard 179
Lebenswelt see life-world/lived world
Lefort, Claude 15, **120**, 187, 200, 233, 243
Lenin/Leninism 14
Leonardo (da Vinci) 35, 37, 232

Les Philosophes célèbres (1956) 71, **120–1**
Les Temps modernes 15, 27, 38, 96, 120, **121**, 129, 187, 200, 214, 215, 231, 244
level 161, 163
Lévi-Strauss, Claude 41, 85–6, 119, **121**, 128, 216
Lhermitte, (Jacques) Jean 32, 33, **121**
life-world/lived world (*Lebenswelt*) 17, 36, 54, 59, 67, 75, 78, 103, 152, 140, 177, 183, 203
lived body *see* body
lived experience 17, 20, 27, 28, 32, 35–6, 41, 44, 47, 64, 67, 72, 73–4, 85, 105–6, 141, 145, 147, 153, 156, 160–4, 171, 189, 192, 203, 211, 223, 225, 234, 238–9, 245, 248–50
lived space *see* space
logicism 43, **122**, 195
logos 61, 62, 79, 171, 233
Lukàcs, Georg 14, 52, **122**
lycée 18–19, 120, **122**, 178

Madame Merleau-Ponty (Suzanne Berthe Jolibois) **122**
Malebranche 71, 103
Malraux, André 47, 104, 107, 109–10, **123**, 190
"Man, the Hero" (1948) **125–6**
"Man and Adversity" (1951) 18, **123–5**
Marcel, Gabriel 28, 32, 72, 90, **126**, 178, 186
Marx/Marxism 12–17, 19, 40, 41, 58, 63, 92, 96–101, 126–7, 128, 129, 182, 207, 209–10, 246

Marxist analysis 96, **127**, 194, 232
Marxist humanism 12, 14, 84, 94, 97–101, 124, **127–8**, 136, 137, 200, 244, 246, 249
wait-and-see-Marxism 12, 84, 96, 135, 209, **244**
"Marxism and Philosophy" (1946) **126–7**
Matisse, Henri 106, 144
Mauss, Marcel 41, 85, **128**
"Merleau-Ponty and Pseudo-Sartreanism" 12, 27, **128**, 200
Mésaventures de l'anti-Marxism: Les malheurs de M. Merleau-Ponty (1956) 12, **128–9**
"The Metaphysical in Man" (1947) **129–30**
"Metaphysics and the Novel" (1947) 27, **130–2**
milieu 34, 40–1, 57, 66, 76, 114, 175, 156, 161, 172, 197, 211, 218, 220–3, 228, 229, 238, 245
Minkowski, Eugène 39, 43, **132**
Montaigne 55, 196
The Moscow Trials 15, 118, **132**
motivation 37, 85, **132–3**, 148, 153, 161–2, 221, 246
motor intentionality *see* intentionality
motor signification 90, **133**, 155
motricity [*motricité, Motorik*] 10, 50, **133–4**, 155

natural attitude 130, **134–5**, 146, 148, 150, 175, 231, 233, 248
natural world 69, 95–6, 163–4, 166

nature 29, 32, 48, 55–62, 64, 79, 107, 127, 158, 176, 203, 218, 221, 230, 233–4
"The Nature of Perception: Two Proposals" (1933/1934) 88, **135**
necessity (vs. contingency) **9–10**, 127 *see also* contingency
negintuition 235
new liberalism 12, 17, 84, 128, 129, **135–6**, 209, 244
Nietzsche 19, 46, 58, 73, 92, 126
Nizan, Paul 213
noesis/noema 70, 87, **136**, 148–9, 177
non-thetic/pre-thetic/thetic consciousness or act 23, 27, 35, 64, 89, 114, 133–4, **136–7**, 141, 143, 145, 151–2, 155–6, 162, 169, 172, 174, 176, 192, 205, 218
nothingness 16, 31, 52, 54, 56, 77, 131, 159, 174, 204, 212, 235–7, 238, 240
"A Note on Machiavelli" (1949) **137**

objective body *see* body
"On Sartre's Imagination" (1936) **138**, 199
"On the Phenomenology of Language" (1951) **138–41**
one's own body (*le corps propre*) *see* body
operative intentionality *see* intentionality
"The Origin of Geometry" (1936) 59–60, 138, 141, **142**, 150, 231
"The Origin of Truth" (or *"The Genealogy of Truth,"* or *"Being and the World"*) **142**, 187, 229–30, 232
other(s) [*autrui*] 17, 20, 31, 38–9, 42, 44, 45–6, 51, 52, 59–60, 69–70, 77, 89, 99, 101, 111, 115, 126, 131, 140, **142**, 157, 162–6, 171, 173–4, 176, 178, 181, 185, 189, 192–3, 204, 211–13, 223–4, 233–4, 235, 236, 242–3, 249
outside spectator 64, 69, 103, **143**, 218, 229

painting 11, 35, 45–6, 74–80, 109–12, 113, 116, **143–4**, 198, 203, 204, 207, 247, 248–50
paradoxical logic of expression 39, 51, 53, 74, 79, 86, 109, 113, 131, 176, 207–8, 230, 242
paraphasia **144**
partes extra partes 56, 68, 137, **144**, 154, 226
passive synthesis/transition synthesis/bodily or lived synthesis 24, 45, **144–5**, 160–1, 164, 167, 170–1, 184–5, 225
Pavlov, Ivan 27, 219
Péguy, Charles 31, **145**
pensée de survol 12, 14, 35, 39, 49, 61, 75, 77, 80, 109, 143, **145**, 153, 158, 174, 180, 184, 186, 191, 211–12, 236, 244, 250
perceptual consciousness *see* consciousness
perceptual faith **146**, 233–4, 235
phantom limb syndrome 20, 22, 39, 91, 121, **146**, 154, 197
phenomenal body *see* body

phenomenal field *see* field
phenomenological description 11, 35, 63, 76, 103, 118, 129, **148**, 149–50, 169, 170, 212, 218, 224, 229
phenomenological reduction (*epochē*) 43, 83, 88, 90, 134, 135, **148–9**, 150, 152, 175, 207, 217, 231
phenomenology 20, 31, 35–6, 38, 43–4, 53, 59, 65, 68, 69, 70, 72, 78, 85, 87, 88, 92, 93, 95, 101, 108, 114, 127, 134–5, 137, 138–40, 147, 148, **149–51**, 152, 154, 162, 166, 174–7, 184, 186, 188, 199, 203, 227, 237, 247, 248
    genetic 43, **87**, 101, 114, 127, 145, 149–50, 227
    transcendental 43, 59, 68, 87, 101, 113, 136, 138, 147, 150, 174–5, **227**, 229
"Phenomenology and the Sciences of Man" **151**
Phenomenology of Perception (1945) 9, 11, 20, 22, 25, 27, 32, 47, 63, 64, 69, 74, 86, 89, 90, 101, 133, 136, 141, 145, 146, 147, 150, **151–74**, 183, 200, 203, 204, 206, 214, 215, 226, 229, 231, 243
"The Philosopher and His Shadow" (1958) 60, **174–7**, 226, 233
"The Philosopher and Sociology" (1951) 85, **177**
"The Philosophy of Existence" (1960) 73, **177–8**
Piaget, Jean 39–41, **178**, 227
Plato 51, 55, 70, 119
Pos, H. 43

In Praise of Philosophy (1953) 48, 120, **178–83**
"The Primacy of Perception and Its Philosophical Consequences" (1946 [1947]) 33, 102, 151, **183–6**
primordial faith 175
problems and mysteries (Marcel) 28, 31, 126, 178, **186**, 190–1, 234
project of the world 47, 169, 173, **186–7**, 226, 241
projection of memories 153, **187**
The Prose of the World (~1952/1968) 49, 104, 120, 142, **187–93**, 201, 229, 232
protention (and retention) 95, 154, 170, **193**
Proust, Marcel 35, 51, 53, 62, 131, **194**, 207
psychoanalysis 18, 38, 40, 41, 42, 44, 59, 84, 92, 93, 109, 124, 127, **194–5**, 207, 208, 216
psychologism 43, 94, 103, 109, 122, 162, **195**, 210, 215
Pyrrhonism **195**, 233

quale (pl. *qualia*) **195**, 241
quasi-object 56, 60–1, 177, **196**
Queneau, Raymond 118
quid sit see *an sit* versus *quid sit*

"Reading Montaigne" (1947) **196**
"reality function" (Janet) 116, **196**
reflective analysis 19, 33, 65, 91, 113, 117, 119, 152, 158, **196–7**, 208
reflex 25, 28, 154, **197**, 218
repression 23, 41, **197–8**
retention *see* protention

reversibility; sensing/sensed; sensibility 21, 29, 32, 38, 61, 69–70, 74, 76–8, 83, 115, **198**, 204–5, 211, 226, 234, 239, 241–3
Rodin, Auguste 79
Ryle, Gilbert 120

Saint-Exupéry, Antoine de 126, 174, **198–9**
Sartre, Jean-Paul 12, 15–17, 26–7, 28, 50, 56, 62, 73, 104, 120, 121, 128, 138, 159, 177, **199–201**, 213, 214–15, 231–2, 235–7
Saussure, Ferdinand de 38, 39, 51, 105, 190, **201**, 216–17
"A Scandalous Author" (1947) **201**
Scheler, Max 39, 43, 46, 178, **201**
Schilder, Paul 32–3, **201–2**
Schneider case 10, 23, 33, 86, 90, 133, 155–7, **202**, 219
science 36, 43, 57, 61–2, 68, 75, 148, 188, 191, **202–3**, 234, 248
sedimentation 18, 53–4, 89, 105, 108, 113, 123, 125, 139–41, 154, 165, 167, 172, 189–90, 191, 192–3, **203**, 206, 210, 215, 222, 228
seeing/seen; visibility 61, 76–7, 83, 172 198, **204–5**, 212, 239, 241–2
sensation 11, 23, 24, 25, 36, 50, 63, 67, 68, 78, 82, 117, 118, 152–3, 154, 159, 195, **205**, 225
sense (*sens*) 11, 17, 24, 34, 36–7, 45–6, 53, 60, 67, 74, 78, 80, 81, 82, 89–90, 91, 93, 94, 97, 106, 108, 110–11, 113, 114, 116, 134, 139, 140–1, 152, 156, 157–8, 163, 171, 189, 191, **205–6**, 208, 209, 214, 215, 218–19, 223, 224, 230, 232, 239, 241
 of history 13, 80, 94, 99, 123, 125, 141, 172–3, 190, 213, 246
 vs. non-sense 171, 207
Sense and Non-Sense (1948) 35, 84, **206–8**
sensing 63, 76, 159–69, 147, 198, 225, 239, 241–2
sensorium commune 93, **208**
sexuality 18, 32, 40, 67, 72–3, 84–5, 156, 158, 194, **208**
shadow 177, 247
Signs (1960) 71, 121, 128, 200, **208–14**, 226, 233, 247
Sinngebung 134, 172, **214**
Sinngenesis 114, 151, **214**
situated freedom *see* freedom
Skinner, B. F. 27
sleep 11, 53–4, 63, 169
"Socialism and Liberty" 17, 27, 84, 199, **214–15**
sociologism 43, **215**
Socrates 181
solipsism 59, 166
space/spatiality 11, 72, 75, 79, 154–7, 160–2, 167, 170, 193, 248
speaking speech versus spoken speech 65, 188–9, **215**
Stalin 99, 120
Stendhal (Henri Beyle) 50–1, 131, **215**
Stiftung see institution
Stratton, George Malcolm 158, 161, **216**
structuralism 18, 38, 39, 43, 53, 85, 105, 121, 124, 138,

139, 182, 201, 209, 215, **216–17**
structure 9–10, 11, 40, 82, 84, 85, 87–8, 95, 105, 111, 118, 153–8, 178, 184, 191, 203, 216, **217**, 218–24
The Structure of Behavior (1938/1942) 10, 21, 28, 32, 34, 64, 66, 69, 84, 135, 143, 146, 152, 154, **217–24**, 228, 229
style 37, 46, 82, 89, 92, 105, 107–11, 140, 150, 157, 163–4, 170, 180, 185, 210–11, 220–1, 229, 238–9, 249–50
symbolic forms of behavior 219, **224**
synchronic 139
syncretic forms of behavior 219, **224–5**
synesthesia 160, **225**

time/temporality 30, 41, 43, 50, 53, 59, 66, 68, 79, 81, 82, 86, 93, 95, 104, 145, 154, 155, 160–2, 164–71, 174, 176, 179, 193
touching/touched; tangibility 20, 21, 32, 38, 61, 67, 76, 83, 174–6, 198, 204, 211, **225–6**, 233, 241–2
transcendental ego 113, 135, 149, 156, 166–7, 222, 227
transcendental idealism 33, 87, 130, 192, **227**
transcendental phenomenology *see* phenomenology
transgression *see* encroachment (*empiétement*)
transition synthesis *see* passive synthesis/transition synthesis

Trotsky, Leon 15, 98–9
truth 9–10, 22, 36, 43, 50, 60, 71–2, 73, 84, 89, 108, 112, 122, 141, 142, 146, 152, 162–3, 167–8, 181, 187–9, 191, 196, 198, 203, 213, 229–30, 232, 238, 240, 243, 244, 250

Uexküll, Jakob von 57, 221, **227**, **228**
ultra-things 41, **227–8**
Umwelt 57–8, 218, 227, **228**
unconsciousness 40, 52, 53–4, 124, 197, 222, **228**, 245
"An Unpublished Text by Maurice Merleau-Ponty: *A Prospectus of His Work*" (1952) 25, 188, **228–30**
unquestioned belief in the world (*le prejugé du monde*) 64, 117, 129, 134, 148, 152, 154, 156, 205, **230–1**
unthought 60, 175–6
Urdoxa 175
Ursprung 166, **231**
"The U.S.S.R. and the Camps" (1950) 200, **231–2**

Valéry, Paul 35, 37, 50, 75, 215, **232**
Van Breda, H. L. 101
Van Gogh, Vincent 211
The Visible and the Invisible (1964) 21, 26, 49, 58, 64, 115–16, 120, 142, 187, 198, 204, 209, 226, 229, **232–43**, 247

Wahrnehmung 244
wait-and-see-Marxism *see* Marxism

Wallon, Henri 41, 42, 44, 227, **244**
"The War Has Taken Place" (1945) **244–6**
Weber, Max 13–14, 52, **246**
Wertheimer, Max 87, **246**
Wesen 150
Wesenschau 70, 149, 239–40, **247**
Whitehead, Alfred North 57

wild Being/brute Being 47, 74, 115–16, 176, 238–40, **247**
The World of Perception (1948) **248–50**
writing 50–1, 60, 89, 106, 112, 142, 207

Zeigen und Greifen (pointing and grasping) 10, **250**
Zeno 55, 105, 162

www.ingramcontent.com/pod-product-compliance
Lightning Source LLC
Chambersburg PA
CBHW050136240426
43673CB00043B/1686